The 78th **Art Directors Annual**

Executive Director
Myrna Davis

Editor
Laetitia Wolff

Design
Vertigo Design, NYC

Copy Editor
Beth Sutinis

Editorial Assistant
Gwendolyn Leung

Contributing Editors
Chris Sekin, Edward Sorel
Judith Wilde, Jeff Newelt

Jacket, divider pages, and endpaper design
Stacy Drummond

Jacket illustration
Stacy Drummond, Tracy Boychuk, Jordan Nogee
(MTV Off-Air Creative)

Photographers
Jack Louth for the Advertising and
Graphic Design judges,
Brian Carson for the New Media judges

Published and distributed by
RotoVision SA
7 Rue du Bugnon
1299 Crans
Switzerland

RotoVision SA Sales Office
Sheridan House
112/116A Western Road
Hove, West Sussex BN3 1DD
England
Tel: (44) 1273 72 72 68
Fax: (44) 1273 72 72 69

Production and color separation by
Provision Pte Ltd., Singapore
Tel: (65) 334 77 20
Fax: (65) 334 77 21

The Art Directors Club
104 West 29th Street
New York, NY 10001
United States of America

RotoVision SA
ISBN: 2-88046-471-4

Printed in Hong Kong

Table of Contents

Convergence. Fusion. Cross-over. The buzzwords of the day.

The lines between creative disciplines are blurring more and more. Advertising art directors are doing editorial design. Illustrators are doing photography. Painters are designing Web sites. Musicians are directing films. Copywriters are designing clothing. Furniture designers are illustrating CD covers.

Today's creative people don't want business cards. They don't want offices. They don't want payroll jobs. They do have cell phones and e-mail. They are on the move.

Today's creative people are seeking and finding the hottest opportunities across many different businesses, diving in headfirst for three months, then moving on to the next, whatever or wherever that might be.

Today's creative people don't want business cards. They don't want offices. They don't want payroll jobs. They do have cell phones and e-mail. They are on the move.

At a glance, it appears everything is out of control. It appears that everything is all over the place.

Actually, all of this cross-over creativity is represented in one place—the Art Directors Club. For almost a century, the Art Directors Club has been recognizing, supporting, and celebrating multi-disciplined creative work and the people who make it.

This year's *Art Directors Annual* is the best compilation of this unique body of work. John Hegarty (Bartle Bogle Hegarty), Neil Powell (Duffy Design), and Charles Altschul chaired the categories of advertising, design, and new media, respectively, and figured out what was the absolute finest of all this fused creativity. Special thanks to them. Congratulations to the winners. To everyone else, enjoy the convergence.

—Bill Oberlander,
PRESIDENT OF THE
ART DIRECTORS CLUB

I t is a great pleasure to present the 78th *Art Directors Annual* in this handsome new format. The design and format were developed by Vertigo Design in collaboration with editor Laetitia Wolff, who worked thoughtfully and diligently to improve it in many respects, including creating a flexible system of credits to allow as much space as possible for visuals, and as many complete scripts for TV as possible. The *Annual* also includes a lively CD-ROM designed by Funny Garbage that features all the New Media winners.

The *Art Directors Annual*, which includes the competition, the traveling exhibition, and, ultimately, this invaluable reference book, covers the best work of the year in visual communications from around the world.

Outstanding student work is included for the first time. Students were invited to submit work in any category, and the judges were asked to bring the same high standards to their entries as to the professional work. The only allowance made was that the work could be unpublished.

The *Art Directors Annual*, which includes the competition, the traveling exhibition, and, ultimately, this invaluable reference book, covers the best work of the year in visual communications from around the world. Last spring three separate juries sifted through 15,265 entries from twenty-one countries to choose the winners featured in this book.

The *Annual* also makes possible most of the ADC's many educational programs, including Saturday High School Workshops for talented high school juniors; scholarships for college-level art school students; our annual Speaker Series; the Hall of Fame; varied panel discussions, exhibitions, and other projects. Special thanks to the board of directors, the membership, the ADC staff, the ADC Publications Committee, and the corporate members and sponsors who support our programs during the year.

This book is visual fuel. If you aspire, may it inspire. If you are in it, congratulations.

—Myrna Davis,
EXECUTIVE DIRECTOR OF THE ART DIRECTORS CLUB

hall of

fame

The Art Directors Hall of Fame was established in 1971 to recognize and honor those innovators whose lifetime achievements represent the highest standards of creative excellence.

Eligible for this coveted award, in addition to art directors, are designers, typographers, illustrators, and photographers who have made significant contributions to art direction and visual communications.

The Hall of Fame Committee, from time to time, also presents a Hall of Fame Educators Award to those educators, editors, and writers whose lifetime achievements have significantly shaped the future of these fields.

1972
M. F. Agha
Lester Beall
Alexey Brodovitch
A. M. Cassandre
René Clark
Robert Gage
William Golden
Paul Rand

1973
Charles Coiner
Paul Smith
Jack Tinker

1974
Will Burtin
Leo Lionni

1975
Gordon Aymar
Herbert Bayer
Cipes Pineles Burtin
Heyworth Campbell
Alexander Liberman
L. Moholy-Nagy

1976
E. McKnight Kauffer
Herbert Matter

1977
Saul Bass
Herb Lubalin
Bradbury Thompson

1978
Thomas M. Cleland
Lou Dorfsman
Allen Hurlburt
George Lois

1979
W. A. Dwiggins
George Giusti
Milton Glaser
Helmut Krone
Willem Sandberg
Ladislav Sutnar
Jan Tschichold

1980
Gene Federico
Otto Storch
Henry Wolf

1981
Lucian Bernhard
Ivan Chermayeff
Gyorgy Kepes
George Krikorian
William Taubin

1982
Richard Avedon
Amil Gargano
Jerome Snyder
Massimo Vignelli

1983
Aaron Burns
Seymour Chwast
Steve Frankfurt

1984
Charles Eames
Wallace Elton
Sam Scali
Louis Silverstein

1985
Art Kane
Len Sirowitz
Charles Tudor

1986
Walt Disney
Roy Grace
Alvin Lustig
Arthur Paul

1987
Willy Fleckhaus
Shigeo Fukuda
Steve Horn
Tony Palladino

1988
Ben Shahn
Bert Steinhauser
Mike Tesch

1989
Rudolph deHarak
Raymond Loewy

1990
Lee Clow
Reba Sochis
Frank Zachary

1991
Bea Feitler
Bob Gill
Bob Giraldi
Richard Hess

1992
Eiko Ishioka
Rick Levine
Onofrio Paccione
Gordon Parks

1993
Leo Burnett
Yusaku Kamekura
Robert Wilvers
Howard Zieff

1994
Alan Fletcher
Norman Rockwell
Ikko Tanaka
Rochelle Udell
Andy Warhol

1995
Robert Brownjohn
Paul Davis
Roy Kuhlman
Jay Maisel

1996
William McCaffery
Erik Nitsche
Arnold Varga
Fred Woodward

1997
Allan Beaver
Sheila Metzner
B. Martin Pedersen
George Tscherny

1998
Tom Geismar
Chuck Jones
Paula Scher
Alex Steinweiss

HALL OF FAME EDUCATOR'S AWARD

1983
Bill Bernbach

1987
Leon Friend

1988
Silas Rhodes

1989
Hershel Levit

1990
Robert Weaver

1991
Jim Henson

1996
Steven Heller

1998
Red Burns

I n a world of followers and emulation, it is rare that we experience visual or aural stimulation that makes us stop and say: That's unique or Why didn't I think of that? It's obvious, so easy.

The Art Directors Club Hall of Fame is where innovation and excellence of thought separate the good from the great. The 1999 laureates deserve more than their share of praise, for rousingly they prove that the assumption everything has been done before is not true.

The Art Directors Club Hall of Fame is where innovation and excellence of thought separate the good from the great.

To the best and brightest of the coming millennium, this year's laureates show us that there always is a new approach. My warmest congratulations to the Hall of Fame laureates R.O. Blechman, Annie Leibovitz, Stan Richards, and to Richard Wilde for the Hall of Fame Educator's Award.

—Rick Levine,
CHAIRPERSON,
1999 HALL OF FAME
SELECTION COMMITTEE

**1999 HALL OF FAME
SELECTION COMMITTEE**

Paul Davis
Lou Dorfsman
Carl Fischer
Steve Frankfurt
Milton Glaser
Eileen Hedy Schultz
Peter Hirsch
Ruth Lubell
Bill Oberlander
Rochell Udell

One assumes that when R.O. Blechman came into the world in 1930, he came quietly. It is difficult to imagine him being loud or obstreperous even in the trauma of birth. His speaking voice never quite reaches that of a stage whisper, but it fits perfectly his persona of determined understatement. And his drawings reflect the man: seemingly tremulous and uncertain, but, in fact, boldly original.

Bob was born in Brooklyn. His mother, determined to have an artistic son, obliged him to take the entrance exam for the High School of Music and Art. He was accepted. The die was cast. By the time he entered Oberlin College, he thought of himself as a cartoonist and began drawing for *The Oberlin Review*. It is these drawings that constituted much of his portfolio when he returned to Manhattan and sought assignments in illustration in the early 1950s. An editor at Henry Holt liked one of his hand-sewn books and asked him to produce a similar one with a Christmas theme. The result was *The Juggler of Our Lady*, which proved a critical and commercial success.

At this pinnacle of his young career, he was drafted into the U.S. Army. He was not, however,

1

R.O.**Blechman**

2

entirely unlucky. While others of his age were serving in the still-active war in Korea, he was assigned to Asbury Park, New Jersey. It was less exotic, but a lot safer. After his discharge, he accepted an invitation from John Hubley to join Storyboard Inc., a studio that specialized in animated films for advertising agencies. Although Blechman describes his time there in gloomy terms, it was nonetheless where he learned animation, and animation was the art form in which he would produce his most imaginative work.

During the '60s, commissions were forthcoming, his checkbook stabilized, and his name became known. Before long his unique drawing style could be seen in a variety of magazines, notably, *Harper's Bazaar, Trump, Punch, Esquire, Humbug, Theater Arts*, and *Show*. Most of these features were sequential drawings, a form of comic strip that reflected his strong social concerns in a humorous way. Humor was also the basis of his memorable print campaign for Capezio shoes, as well as drawings for Irving Trust, the New School, Kaufman Carpets, and

3

4

5

7

MUSEUM MILE FESTIVAL ON FIFTH AVENUE, JUNE 12TH

8

6

9

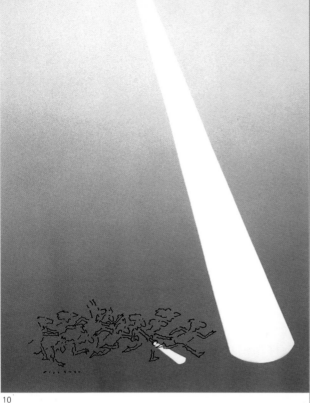

10

11

12

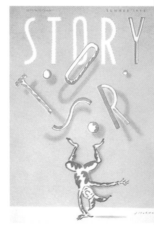

13

15

D'Orsay perfumes. In 1967, he created the storyboard and drawings for an animated commercial for Alka-Seltzer which remains a classic of American advertising.

In the early 1970s, he started his own animation studio, The Ink Tank, which was devoted largely to producing commercials.

Forays into the editorial world were less rewarding. The lack of interest in his first book, *Onion Soup* (1964), so discouraged him that he did not produce another for nearly a decade. Readers of the *Village Voice* were likewise unenthusiastic about his Vietnam cartoons. By the early 1970s, however, his projects were attracting more interest. *Tutto Esaurito* (No Vacancies), a small book published in Italy, was an ironic observation on the birth of the Christ child to an unwelcoming world. With the agonies of the Vietnam War still playing out in the national consciousness, Blechman turned to the Old Testament as the source for a metaphorical retelling of Abraham and Issac, that near-tragic story in which the father– that is, the state–offers the life of his son–the next generation–in ful-fillment of an old belief. Arnold Black was the composer for this film, as well as for the next, a more technically accomplished one called *Exercise* for the Children's Television Workshop.

In 1967, he created the storyboard and drawings for an animated commercial for Alka-Seltzer which remains a classic of American advertising.

Late in that decade, the Public Broadcasting Company offered Blechman the opportunity to create a Christmas special. *Simple Gifts* was an ambitious undertaking incorporating separate segments by Maurice Sendak, James McMullan, Seymour Chwast, Charles B. Slackman, and Blechman. It was a great success, and is still repeated at Christmastime.

In an entirely different vein, he later created an Emmy award-winning sixty-minute animated film, *L' Histoire du Soldat* (*The Soldier's Tale*). Inspired by the music Stravinsky wrote for this fable, Blechman provided visual effects that make this one of the most inventive animated films ever made.

The last two decades have more than fulfilled the promise of those earlier times. His stunning habitat on West 47th street with its arched ceiling and stained glass windows thrives as an animation studio. From there have come animated commercials for clients including Barney's, Perrier, Hershey's, and MTV. Bob also turns out covers for a variety of magazines–some twenty for the *New Yorker*, but also for the *Atlantic Monthly* and his special interest, the quarterly, *Story*. With the exception of two very early issues, he has drawn every cover of *Story* for the past ten years.

Bob and his lovely wife Moisha Kubinyi have two abodes–one on Central Park West and the other up in Columbia County–both of which reflect their favored life style, their perfect taste, and attention to detail. Their sons are grown now–Nicholas is currently the art editor of *The New York Times* Op-Ed page, and Max is a candidate for a doctorate of Philosophy from the Sorbonne. Causes for pride.

Oh, yes, about those initials, R.O. They are taken from a transposition of Blechman's given name, Oscar Robert. —EDWARD SOREL

1 ALKA-SELTZER. **Illustrator:** R.O. Blechman, **Agency:** Jack Tinker & Partners, Inc., **Art Director:** John Danza, **Client:** Alka-Seltzer, 1967

2 THE NEW YORK TIMES BOOK REVIEW cover. **Illustrator:** R.O. Blechman, **Art Director:** Steven Heller, **Client:** *The New York Times*, 1997

3 RODINTIUS RODENTIUS. **Client:** *The Nation*, 1997

4 MOTHER'S DAY–THE NEW YORKER magazine cover. **Illustrator:** R.O. Blechman, **Art Director:** Lee Lorenz, **Client:** *The New Yorker*, 1990

5 THE NEW YORKER magazine cover. **Illustrator:** R.O. Blechman, **Art Director:** Françoise Mouly, **Client:** *The New Yorker*, 1996

6 THE NEW YORKER Poster. **Illustrator:** R.O. Blechman, **Art Director:** Lee Lorenz, **Client:** *The New Yorker*, 1980

7 BALANCING ACT (Serigraph). **Illustrator:** R.O. Blechman, personal project, 1990

8 MUSEUM MILE FESTIVAL ON FIFTH AVENUE, June 12th poster. **Art Director and Illustrator:** R.O. Blechman, **Client:** Museum Mile Festival, 1981

9 THE BOTTOM LINE. **Illustrator:** R.O. Blechman, **Art Director:** Jack Hough, **Design:** Jack Hough Associates, Inc., **Client:** Potlach Corp., 1981

10 ENDPAPER. **Illustrator:** R.O. Blechman, **Art Director:** Fred Woodward, **Client:** *Rolling Stone*, 1992

11 STORY magazine cover. **Art Director and Illustrator:** R.O. Blechman, **Client:** *Story* magazine Autumn, 1998

12 STORY magazine cover. **Art Director and Illustrator:** R.O. Blechman, **Client:** *Story* magazine Spring, 1998

13 STORY magazine cover. **Art Director and Illustrator:** R.O. Blechman, **Client:** *Story* magazine Summer, 1994

Annie Leibovitz's witty, powerful portraits have been appearing on magazine covers for more than twenty-five years. In that time she has become one of the world's most celebrated photographers. Beginning with her legendary work for *Rolling Stone*, and continuing through her long affiliation with *Vanity Fair* and *Vogue*, she has established herself as an astute observer of American popular culture. In addition to her magazine work, Leibovitz was commissioned to be the official portrait photographer for the World Cup Games in Mexico in 1985, and created prize-winning advertising campaigns for American Express and The Gap. In 1990, Leibovitz documented the creation of the White Oak Dance Project for Mikhail Baryshnikov. She has worked with many other artistic organizations, including American Ballet Theatre and the Mark Morris Dance Group.

Annie**Leibovitz**

1

During the siege of Sarajevo, Leibovitz traveled to Yugoslavia and created a series of portraits that were exhibited in 1993 at the Art Gallery of Bosnia and Herzegovina. In 1995, she was commissioned to create the official portfolio for the twenty-sixth Olympic Games in Atlanta, Georgia.

Leibovitz's groundbreaking museum exhibition, Annie Leibovitz Photographs 1970–1990, organized by the International Center of Photography in conjunction with the Smithsonian Institution's National Portrait Gallery, has been traveling the world to great acclaim since its debut in 1992.

This Fall, Random House will publish *Women*, a book of Leibovitz's portraits, with an essay by Susan Sontag. An accompanying exhibition of Leibovitz's portraits of women will open at the Corcoran Gallery in Washington, D.C., in October 1999.

1 WHOOPI GOLDBERG, Actress, Berkeley, California, 1984

2 LIL' KIM, Rap Artist, New York City, 1999

3 DAN AYKROYD AND JOHN BELUSHI, Actors, Hollywood, 1979

4 FAMILY VISITING TIME ON CHRISTMAS DAY AT SOLEDAD PRISON, Soledad, California, 1971

5 APOLLO 17, Cape Kennedy, Florida, 1973

6 WILLIAM S. BURROUGHS, Writer, Lawrence, Kansas, 1995

7 JOHN LENNON AND YOKO ONO, Musicians, New York City, 1980

3

2

4

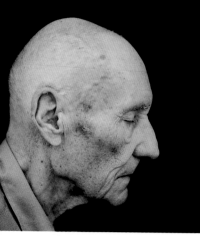

5

6

7

8

9

10

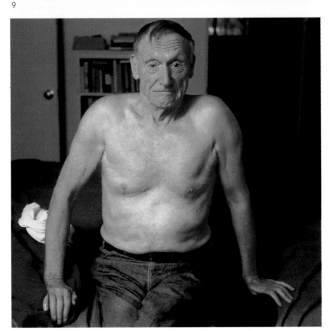

11

12

8 THE ROLLING STONES, Philadelphia, 1975

9 MARILYN LEIBOVITZ, Photographer's Mother, Clifton Point, Rhinebeck, New York, 1997

10 FALLEN BICYCLE OF TEENAGE BOY JUST KILLED BY A SNIPER, Sarajevo, 1994

11 ROBERT PENN WARREN, Novelist, Poet, Fairfield, Connecticut, 1980

12 KEITH HARING, Artist, New York City, 1986

"Stan has to
be intensely
involved in
every creative
moment.
That's what
drives him.**"**

—Steve Horn

Stan Richards, like the advertising and design he's created over the last four decades, has never been tied to any preconceived notions of how things should be done.

This became obvious the moment he graduated from New York's Pratt Institute in 1953. With a newly minted portfolio, Stan headed for Los Angeles. But a funny thing happened on the way to his new career: he stopped in Dallas. The city was barely a speck on the design world map, but Stan thought it looked, well, interesting. So he stuck.

He freelanced at first, won a bunch of awards, and accepted a creative director position at what is now Publicis-Bloom at the ripe old age of 22. In a year he was back to

Stan**Richards**

freelancing because "he couldn't do the kind of work he liked in an agency." So, from his corporate headquarters/garage apartment, Stan began designing like nobody in Dallas had ever seen. His work was fresh, sophisticated, contemporary. He used bold images and unexpected typography. And designers everywhere began to sit up and take notice.

Suddenly, there was this place that was winning awards out the wazoo in a city where you could afford both food and shelter. By the late '60s, The Richards Group had become the preeminent creative resource in the Southwest—and a top training ground for young talent. Talent that Stan had a sixth sense for spotting, claims designer Jack Summerford. "He had an infallible ability to recognize potential in people and give them ample opportunity to grow."

Over the next 20 years, they produced a staggering amount of great work. Ideas born not only out of solid design, but also strong conceptual and strategic thinking. In 1976, a major Texas bank asked Stan to compete for their entire account. Translation: make The Richards Group a full-service agency. Not an easy decision, considering he'd have to go up against the very agencies who'd been buttering his bread.

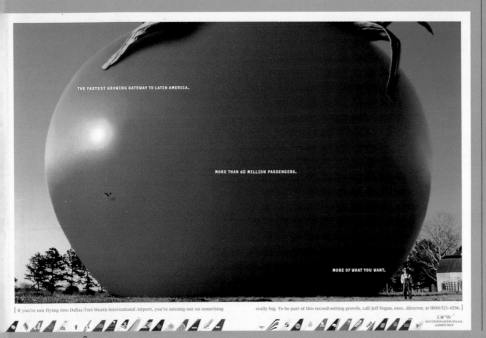

THE FASTEST GROWING GATEWAY TO LATIN AMERICA.

MORE THAN 60 MILLION PASSENGERS.

MORE OF WHAT YOU WANT.

[If you're not flying into Dallas/Fort Worth International Airport, you're missing out on something   really big. To be part of this record-setting growth, call Jeff Fegan, exec. director, at (800) 521-4296.]

DFW INTERNATIONAL AIRPORT

2

3

4

5

8

6

For reservations, call
1-800-4-MOTEL 6

MOTEL 6 SCRIPT

Open on black.
SUPER: Copyright Motel 6.

V.O.:
Hi. Tom Bodett for Motel 6 with some insight for the traveler. Well, this is what one of our rooms looks like when you're sleeping. And you know, it looks just like those big fancy hotels. Only difference is ours won't cost you nearly as much money. In fact, Motel 6 always has the lowest prices of any national chain on a clean, comfortable room. Makes you sleepy just looking at it.

SUPER: Phone number.
SUPER: Logo

V.O.:
Well. I'm Tom Bodett for Motel 6 and we'll leave the light on for you.

7

individuality. One all about you. Experience this remarkable season at Neiman Marcus. Where you'll find the collection — and the expertise — to help you choose your own direction.

Neiman Marcus
How to look.

9

WARNING: Keep Tongue Off Billboard.

10

1 CHICK-FIL-A "EAT MORE CHICKEN" Outdoor Board. **Creative Director:** Stan Richards **Writer, Art Director:** David Ring, **Client:** Chick-Fil-A, 1993

2 DFW INTERNATIONAL AIRPORT "TOMATO" Spread Ad. **Art Director, Designer:** Jeff Hopfer, **Writer:** Ron Henderson, **Creative Director:** Stan Richards, **Photographer:** Joe Baraban, **Client:** DFW International Airport, 1998

3 CONTINENTAL AIRLINES "WOODSTOCK" Sponsorship Ad. **Art Director, Designer:** Margaret Johnson, **Writer:** Vinnie Chieco, **Creative Director:** Stan Richards, **Client:** Continental Airlines, 1995

4 CHILI'S Annual Report. **Creative Director:** Stan Richards, **Art Director, Designer:** Brian Boyd, **Writer:** Kevin Johnson, **Illustrator:** Regan Dunnick, **Photographer:** Robert Latorre, **Client:** Chili's, Inc., 1988

5 LOMAS AND NETTLETON Annual Report. **Art Directors:** Steve Miller, Stan Richards, **Creative Director:** Stan Richards, **Writer:** Steve Stone, **Photographer:** Greg Booth, **Client:** Lomas and Nettleton Financial Corp., 1979

6 Q & A PERGO Spread Ad. **Art Director, Designer:** Dennis Walker, **Writer:** David Culp, **Creative Director:** Stan Richards, **Photographer:** Bruce Wolfe, **Client:** Perstorp, 1997

7 DANGEROUS IDEAS Poster. **Creative Director:** Stan Richards, **Art Director, Designer, Illustrator:** Brian Boyd, **Client:** AIGA, 1989

8 BLANK SCREEN Television Spot, 30 seconds. **Creative Director:** Stan Richards, **Art Director:** Brian Nadurak, **Writer:** Thomas Hripko, **Client:** Motel 6, 1988

9 NEIMAN MARCUS "WINDSOCK" Newspaper Ad. **Art Director, Designer:** Dennis Walker, **Writer:** Kevin Swisher, **Creative Director:** Stan Richards, **Photographer:** Kent Barker, **Client:** Neiman Marcus, 1993

10 RAINIER BEER Outdoor Board. **Creative Director:** Stan Richards, **Art Director, Designer:** Jeff Hopfer, **Writer:** Ron Henderson, **Photographer:** Tom Ryan, **Client:** G. Heilman Brewing Co., 1993

They won the account, so Stan maintained the design firm as a separate shop called RBM&M, and The Richards Group became an agency. Within six years it was named by *Adweek* as one of the eight most creative agencies in the country.

As expected, Stan didn't build his agency as expected. While others were engaging in dog and pony shows to lure new business, he was engaging in honest, endearing, brilliant advertising. His creative philosophy: do terrific work and great clients will find you. Today, Stan leads one of the nation's largest privately-held agencies, with more than 450 employees and $435 million in billings.

It's an advertising success story with some of the most memorable chapters ever written. From the familiar Motel 6 campaign where folksy Alaskan Tom Bodett waxes philosophical and always offers to "leave the light on for you" to the more recent Chick-fil-A spokes-animals: cows whose best interest lies in getting you to "eat more chicken." The Richards Group story is highlighted with virtually every major award given, as the sea of Cubes, Pencils, Lions, and Clios on the shelves in his lobby indicates.

> **"Stan's like that person who can tell you to go to hell and make you look forward to the trip."**
>
> —Woody Pirtle

Even the team-oriented agency structure Stan pioneered goes against the industry grain. At his place, art directors sit with media planners, writers with account planners, and production managers with account executives to foster creativity in every discipline. "Stan has to be intensely involved in every creative moment. That's what drives him," says Steve Horn, Stan's college roommate (and Hall of Fame member himself).

Of course, you don't have to tell that to anyone who's worked for Stan. He sets the bar at a very high level and refuses to lower it. He has this way of critiquing your work, while making you feel good about it. Says designer Woody Pirtle, "Stan's like that person who can tell you to go to hell and make you look forward to the trip."

Clearly, Stan's passion for his craft is contagious. Just drop by The Richards Group during one of his famous agency stairwell meetings and you'll see a veritable who's who list of creatives. Many who've been upholding his exacting standards for ten, fifteen, twenty years or more. Like Creative Group Head Glenn Dady who says, "I would hate to think what the design and advertising landscape in the Southwest would look like without Stan. Pretty barren is my guess."

Hershel Levit, one of Stan's earliest influences from Pratt, believed that great design is what's left after all the trite, graceless, superfluous elements have been ruthlessly pruned. From where many of us sit, the same can be said of a great designer and art director named Stan Richards. —CHRIS SEKIN

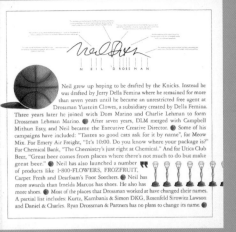

1

Richard Wilde is a man who wears many hats, but for over a quarter of a century, the most important hat he's worn has been that of educator.

Wilde's philosophy of teaching is that it is in questioning that development is molded. His emphatic belief is that everyone is born creative but that unfortunately, through early education and social constraints, this innate quality is often buried. The teacher's role is to help recover creativity by creating conditions that foster a personal investigation in finding one's own signature. Richard believes in putting students into the realm of the unknown where they develop problem-solving capabilities that go beyond their initial understanding. With great results he has implemented his philosophy— a combination of converging ideas that begins with a search for one's uniqueness using the tool of questioning, and a grounding in formalism supported by experimentation, all of which occurs in a climate where risk-taking is made possible. This is why *Critique* magazine calls Richard "The guru of graphic design thinking."

Richard**Wilde**

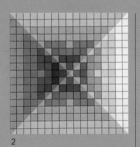

2

Richard Wilde was born in Brooklyn in 1944. He grew up in the Sea Gate, Coney Island area where he attended Lincoln High School and met his first important teacher, Leon Friend, also a recipient of the Hall of Fame Educator's Award.

Richard received his BFA in graphic design and advertising at Pratt Institute where his mentor, Jeffrey Metzner, taught him the fundamentals of conceptual thinking and trusting his instincts. This led Richard to connect to his work in a meaningful and personal way. He received his MFA in fine arts from Pratt Institute while working as the design director of their publications department. He was Pratt's youngest instructor. And so began a uniquely multifaceted career.

In 1966, Wilde married Judith Landau, his high school sweetheart, with whom he's worked on educational and design projects resulting in the creation of their studio, Wilde Design, and their two children, Brandon and Trilby.

After spending a year as assistant professor at the University of Texas at Austin, Richard honed

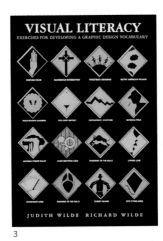

VISUAL LITERACY
EXERCISES FOR DEVELOPING A GRAPHIC DESIGN VOCABULARY

JUDITH WILDE   RICHARD WILDE

3

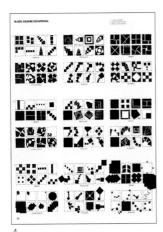

4

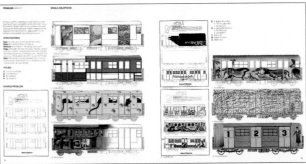

PROBLEMS:SOLUTIONS
Visual Thinking for Graphic Communicators

PROBLEM:
Make a visual statement about the USA

SOLUTION:

6

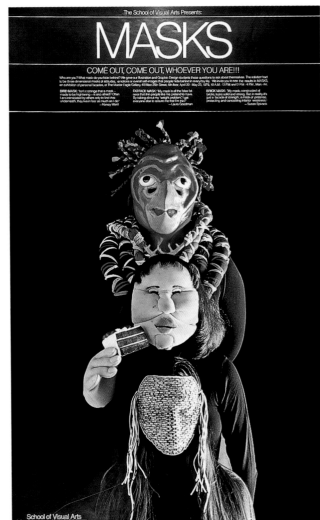

7

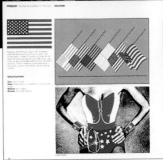

5

8

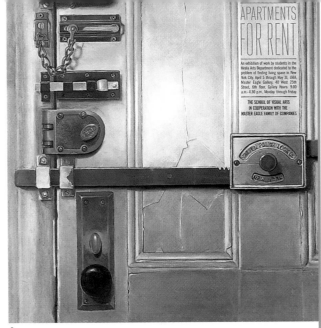

9

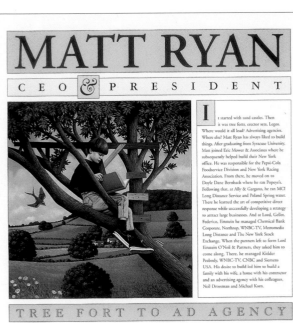

10

1 NEIL DROSSMANN promotional poster. **Art Director:** Richard Wilde, **Designers:** Roswitha Rodrigues, Richard Wilde, **Copywriter:** Neil Drossmann, **Client:** Ryan, Drossman & Partners, 1998

2 LOGO FOR RYAN, DROSSMAN & PARTNERS AGENCY. **Art Director:** Richard Wilde, **Designers:** Roswitha Rodrigues, Richard Wilde, **Client:** Ryan, Drossman & Partners, 1998

3 VISUAL LITERACY book jacket. **Art Director and Designer:** Richard Wilde, **Copywriter:** Judith Wilde, **Illustration:** various students from the School of Visual Arts, **Publisher:** Watson-Guptill, 1999

4 VISUAL LITERACY single page and spread. **Art Director, Designer:** Richard Wilde, **Copywriter:** Judith Wilde, **Art:** various students from the School of Visual Arts, **Publisher:** Watson-Guptill, 1991

5 *PROBLEMS: SOLUTIONS, VISUAL THINKING FOR GRAPHIC COMMUNICATORS* book jacket (front) and spreads. **Art Director, Designer:** Richard Wilde, **Copywriter:** Judith Wilde, **Illustrator (cover):** Chris Bobbin, **Art:** various students from the School of Visual Arts, **Publisher:** Van Nostrand Reinhold, 1986

6 EXTINCTION poster. **Art Director, Designer:** Richard Wilde, **Copywriter:** Judith Wilde, **Illustrator:** Joseph Ianelli, **Client:** School of Visual Arts, 1973

7 MASKS poster. **Art Director, Designer:** Richard Wilde, **Copywriter:** Judith Wilde, **Photographer:** Ken Ambrose, **Client:** School of Visual Arts, 1978

8 THE SIDE SHOW poster. **Art Director, Designer:** Richard Wilde, **Copywriter:** Judith Wilde, **Illustration:** various students from the School of Visual Arts, **Client:** School of Visual Arts, 1972

9 APARTMENT FOR RENT poster. **Art Director, Designer:** Richard Wilde, **Copywriter:** Judith Wilde, **Illustrator:** Kam Mak, **Client:** School of Visual Arts, 1984

10 MATT RYAN promotional poster. **Art Director:** Richard Wilde, **Designers:** Roswitha Rodrigues, Richard Wilde, **Copywriter:** Neil Drossmann, **Client:** Ryan, Drossman & Partners, 1998

his teaching skills by being verbally challenged in a place where no one spoke or understood "Brooklynese."

Returning to New York in time for Woodstock, Richard was hired by Jeffrey Metzner at Daniel and Charles advertising agency, and by Bob Giraldi to teach at the School of Visual Arts.

In 1971, Silas H. Rhodes, Hall of Fame laureate, founder and chairman of the board at the School of Visual Arts, invited Richard to chair the advertising department and to be art director of the school's publications department.

This proved to be an ideal arrangement. In 1973, acting as the creative director, Richard facilitated the Public Advertising System, a not-for-profit advertising agency staffed with SVA faculty members. This agency enabled students to use their diverse talents to create ads for human rights and health and safety issues, and to interact directly with the industry, a situation that resulted in numerous professional awards.

In 1974, Richard founded the graphic design department at the School of Visual Arts. Within ten years, the department boasted an enrollment of more than 700 students. Over the years, the graphic design and advertising departments at SVA have offered new and innovative courses that have expanded the definition of visual communications.

Richard's unparalleled ability in hiring instructors has been central to the creation of a dynamic, cutting edge department. Tom Monahan, president of Before & After Creative Thinking Center says, "Richard has an uncanny sense for finding other teachers, or better, facilitators, to leverage his position and insure a more rewarding education for more people than he could possibly touch personally."

Richard authored *Problems: Solutions*, published by Van Nostrand Reinhold in 1986, and co-authored *Visual Literacy* with Judith Wilde, published by Watson-Guptill in 1991. These two books illucidate Richard's teaching philosophy and are used worldwide as texts at many colleges. He also co-authored *101 Ways to Stay Young* with Judith Wilde, published by Warner Books in 1996.

Currently, Richard is a senior vice president at Ryan Drossman Marc USA advertising agency, a board member of the Art Directors Club since 1984, and a board member of the Type Directors Club and the American Institute of Graphic Arts. He has won over 150 professional awards. Richard is the New York editor of *HOW* magazine. He has conducted creativity workshops on five continents. Through teaching, lecturing, and workshops, he has impacted thousands of graphic design and advertising students and professionals.

Richard Wilde is a gentle man. He is kind, generous, and frequently late for dinner or meetings, often because he is detained by the urgent requests, needs, and pleas of students. He speaks haltingly yet quickly, unable to communicate his thoughts as fast as they occur. And he touches people where they live and breathe. His focus is always on creativity, which is why he is a sought-after lecturer. He is always approachable and available. He is a "natural born" educator. —JUDITH WILDE

ad

vertising

Advertising is a fantastic bellwether of an economy. It measures it in a multitude of interesting ways, turning dry facts into fascinating observations.

For me, the most interesting observation is in seeing which industries are now dominating advertising.

In the *Art Directors Annual* you will see very little work from the traditional advertisers: food, consumer durables, and cars. Instead, the people making the "running" are media brands, computer and Internet companies, and sportswear brands.

What this means is that new industries, with new ways of talking, are making for new ways of advertising. The *Annual* is a unique way of seeing where our business is going.

For me, the most interesting observation is in seeing which industries are now dominating advertising.

The question everyone always asks is: Was it a vintage year? I did not think it was. But that's my opinion. Perhaps a better question is: Are we making advertising interesting enough?

As you flip through these pages, you will make up your own mind. Whatever conclusion you reach, you'll be the richer for it.

JOHN HEGARTY, creative director and chairman of Bartle Bogle Hegarty, started as a junior art director at Benton and Bowles in 1965. He then joined a small Soho (then Camden) agency, John Collings & Partners. In 1967, he joined the Cramer Saatchi consultancy which, in 1970, became Saatchi & Saatchi, where he was a founding shareholder. One year later he was appointed deputy creative director. He left in 1973 to co-found TBWA as creative director. In 1982, he left to form BBH.

—John Hegarty,
BARTLE BOGLE HEGARTY
ADVERTISING CHAIR

MARCELLO SERPA is partner/creative director of Almap/BBDO in São Paulo, Brazil. He studied visual and graphic design in Germany where he lived for seven years, working at the GGK and R.G. Wiesmeir agencies. Back in Brazil, he worked at DPZ Rio, DPZ São Paulo, and DM9.

LARRY BARKER is creative director of BMP DDB where his career began with work on campaigns for Channel 4, Foster's, and Alliance and Leicester, including the "Fry and Laurie" campaign that ran for eight years. He has worked for AMV, BBH, and WCRS, as creative director at the latter, before returning to BMP DDB.

LIONEL HUNT co-founded Australia's The Campaign Palace. In June 1998, he left after twenty-six years as copywriter, chairman, and group creative director. In November 1998, Hunt and Lowe & Partners Worldwide launched the creation of a new Australian agency, Lowe Hunt & Partners.

ADAM GOLDSTEIN is creative director at Ammirati Puris Lintas. He joined the agency in 1992 to work on BMW, MasterCard, Compaq, and Burger King, and went from there to Ogilvy & Mather Paris. He returned to Ammirati in 1996, where he is a creative director responsible for GMC, RCA, UPS, and Labatt USA's Rolling Rock, Labatt Blue, and Dos Equis beer brands.

CHRIS LANDI began as an art director at Korey Kay & Partners working on Comedy Central and Virgin Airlines. He then switched to copywriter and partnered with Ty Montague at Montague &, working for a variety of agencies and clients. He has freelanced for Fallon McElligott Berlin, McKinney Silver, Chiat/Day, Spike DDB, Devito Verdi, and others. He's now working full-time at Fallon McElligott.

DAVID BALDWIN is senior vice president/executive creative director of McKinney Silver in Raleigh, North Carolina, overseeing accounts including Audi, Aetna/US Healthcare, and Ben and Jerry's. He began his career at Deutsch and Della Femina/Travisano, then became a senior copywriter at Hal Riney & Partners, SF, and Cole & Weber, Portland, where he created the first brand image campaign for Dr. Martens.

KERRY CASEY is executive creative director/writer at Carmichael Lynch, Minneapolis, overseeing clients including American Standard, Harley Davidson, Honeybaked Ham, Northwest Airlines, and Volvo Trucks. He was hired by Ron Anderson at Bozell in 1984, and after two years, came to Carmichael Lynch as a writer.

IZZY DEBELLIS became a partner and creative director of Berlin Cameron and Partners when they opened in 1997. Current clients include Coca-Cola, Ralston Purina, General Motors, *The Washington Post*, Condé Nast Publications, Reebok, Beth Israel Hospital, The National Basketball Association, and Creative Artists Agency. He has worked for Wolf Advertising, Saatchi & Saatchi Compton Hayhurst, Chiat/Day Toronto, Chiat/Day New York, and Wieden & Kennedy Philadelphia.

TY MONTAGUE, creative director of Bartle Bogle Hegarty US, began his career in 1986 at Scali McCabe Sloves where he worked on Continental Airlines, Ralston Purina, and Volvo. He then moved to Chiat/Day NY to work primarily on Reebok. In 1994, he started his own consultancy, Montague &, whose clients include Wieden & Kennedy Portland, Fallon McElligott Minneapolis, and Ogilvy & Mather NY.

JEAN REMY VON MATT is a founder and partner of Jung von Matt Hamburg. Clients include Audi, Axel Springer, Minolta, and Daimler. His career began in 1975 as a copywriter for BMZ Düsseldorf and then, in 1977, for Ogilvy & Mather Frankfurt. In 1979, he became creative director of Eiler & Remel/BBDO Munich, and from 1986 to 1991 he was partner and manager at Springer & Jacoby in Hamburg.

BERTRAND SUCHET is creative director of Louis XIV, Agence de Publicité, Paris. Clients include Rossignol, Yamaha, Audi A3 and A4, and Regina Rubens. He directs television commercials and creates award-winning print campaigns.

LYLE OWERKO is creative director of Compound, NYC. His work ranges from the creation of the logo for ESPN2 and the broadcast launch identity for the Sundance Channel, to directing commercials for companies such as Casio and videos for recording artists including Rufus Wainwright. He has also photographed and designed numerous CD packages. Compound produces all the work relating to a client's image, sound, and packaging.

SCOTT CARLSON was a creative director at TBWA Chiat/Day where he worked on America Online, Absolut, and ABC Television. He art directed and directed the recent award-winning broadcast identity for ABC which included "Bug Zapper," "Jello," and "Cow." Carlson is now a full-time freelance director.

ARTHUR BIJUR is president/executive creative director and a founding partner of Cliff Freeman and Partners. He oversees accounts including Staples, Coca-Cola, Ameritech Cellular, and Hollywood Video. His Little Caesars work has been called some of advertising's best ever.

JOHN BUTLER is the co-creative director and a founding partner of Butler, Shine & Stern. Current clients include Seagram Wines, Jamba Juice, 989 Studios, Millers Outpost, Comedy Central, and e-greetings. Butler was a senior art director at Goodby, Berlin, and Silverstein, where he worked on the Sega and Isuzu accounts.

CHARLES HALL is senior vice president/creative director of Spike DDB. Current clients include L'Oréal's Soft Sheen Products, New Era Cap Company, and The Miami Heat. Prior to Spike DDB, Hall worked as creative director on Infiniti for TBWA Chiat/Day Los Angeles and on Pepsi International at BBDO. He is best known for his work on Reebok/Above The Rim ("You Got the Love") and for Partnership for a Drug-Free America.

Multiple Awards

GOLD

**TV: 30 SECONDS OR LESS,
CAMPAIGN**
Band • Cannon • Forehead

and DISTINCTIVE MERIT

TV: 30 SECONDS OR LESS
Band

Art Director Roger Camp
Creative Director Eric Silver
Copywriter Eric Silver
Producer Nick Felder
Director John O' Hagan
Editor Gavin Cutler
Studio hungry man
Agency Cliff Freeman and Partners
Client Outpost.com
Country United States

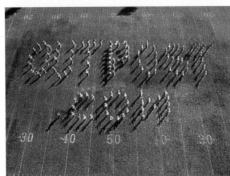

The place to buy computer stuff online.

BAND

We open on an older gentleman talking to the camera. He sits in a leather chair in a makeshift living room (like Masterpiece Theater).

NARRATOR:
In an effort to get people to remember our name, Outpost.com, we contacted the local high school marching band and asked them to help us out.

Cut to footage of high school kids marching. They are dressed up in their band outfits and playing their instruments. They spell Outpost.com (like you see at football games). Cut back to narrator.

NARRATOR:
And to help make this memorable, next we decided to release a pack of ravenous wolves.

Cut back to footage of marching band playing their instruments in their assigned positions. Then we see a pack of wolves leave their cage and enter field. The band members immediately drop their instruments and run off screaming as the wolves attack. Cut back to narrator.

NARRATOR (proud):
That's good stuff.

We cut to a screen that flashes:

SUPER: Send complaints to Outpost.com.

LOGO: Outpost.com. The place to buy computer stuff online.

CANNON

We open on an older gentleman talking to the camera. He sits in a leather chair in a makeshift living room (like Masterpiece Theater).

Camera reveals the "set" where we see an Outpost.com sign hanging from the ceiling. The "o" in Outpost looks like a target. A (fake) gerbil shoots out of the cannon and flies through the air hitting the brick wall.

This time a gerbil shoots out of the cannon and goes over the whole structure.

Cut to series of shots showing gerbils hitting the sign. Narrator shoots us a cocky look.

A gerbil then goes through the "o." A siren goes off.

SUPER: Send complaints to Outpost.com.

LOGO: Outpost.com. The place to buy computer stuff online.

NARRATOR:
Hello. We want you to remember our name, Outpost.com. That's why we've decided to fire gerbils out of this cannon through the "o" in Outpost.

NARRATOR:
Cute little guy... Fire!

NARRATOR:
And again.

NARRATOR:
So close.

FOREHEAD

We open on an older gentleman talking to the camera. He sits in a leather chair in a makeshift living room (like Masterpiece Theater).

We see footage of cute six-year-old kids running around day care center laughing.

Cut to footage of tattoo artist and kids with huge Outpost.com tattoos on their head. The kids are now crying. Cut back to narrator.

We cut to a screen that flashes:

SUPER: Send complaints to outpost.com

LOGO: Outpost.com. The place to buy computer stuff online.

NARRATOR:
We want people to remember our name, Outpost.com. That's why we went to day care centers all across this great country of ours and met with the youngsters.

NARRATOR:
Then we permanently tattooed their foreheads with our name.

NARRATOR:
Excessive? Maybe. But we're on a mission.

Multiple Awards

GOLD

TV: 30 SECONDS OR LESS
Rope

and SILVER

**TV: 30 SECONDS OR LESS,
CAMPAIGN**
Rope • Horse • Pick-up

Art Directors Roger Camp,
Taras Wayner
Creative Directors Cliff Freeman,
Eric Silver
Copywriter Kevin Roddy
Producer Liz Graves
Director Noam Murro
Editor Ian MacKenzie
Agency Cliff Freeman and Partners
Studio HKM
Client FOX Sports
Country United States

ROPE

Open on two guys standing near a tall ladder next to the side of a barn. One of the guys grabs a rope attached to a tree and climbs to the top of the ladder. Once at the top, he takes a big jump and swings down, crashing face first into the side of the barn and falling to the ground.

SFX:
Thud

The other guy, who's been watching this whole event, looks at the guy lying on the ground.

MAN:
That sounded like Anderson.

Cut to actual game footage of Brady Anderson making a catch by crashing into the outfield wall. We hear the thud via sounds of the game.

ANNOUNCER:
Brady Anderson at the wall... leaps and makes a spectacular catch. Wow, now you have to hope he's alright...

Cut to Major League Baseball logo and title treatment.

SUPER: FOX sounds of the game. Don't try it at home.

SUPER: FOX Saturday game of the week

FOX CATCHER CAM
DON'T TRY IT AT HOME

FOX CATCHER CAM
DON'T TRY IT AT HOME

HORSE

Open on a guy standing next to a horse. Another guy, dressed in catcher's gear, steps into frame and crouches down behind the horse.

GUY 1:
Ready?

GUY 2:
Yep.

Cut to the first guy slapping the horse on the rear end. The horse reacts by kicking the other guy crouched behind him in the catcher's mask. Cut to a close-up of the guy on the ground. The other guy walks over and stands over him.

GUY 1:
That, uh, look like the foul tip into Rodriguez?

Cut to actual catcher cam game footage of Rodriguez getting hit by a foul tip.

ANNOUNCER:
Rodriguez really gets nailed on this one. Even off his mask that's gotta hurt. Makes you wonder why anyone wants to be a catcher. Tools of ignorance or not, that's gotta hurt.

Cut to Major League Baseball logo and title treatment.

SUPER: FOX catcher cam. Don't try it at home.

SUPER: FOX Saturday game of the week

PICK-UP

Open on a guy, dressed in catcher's gear, crouched down in a squatting position on the side of a road.

SFX:
Speeding truck

Cut to a guy standing in the back of a speeding pick-up truck, leaning over to one side, holding a baseball.

Cut back to the guy on the side of the road as the truck quickly speeds toward him. Suddenly, from this P.O.V., we see the guy in the back of the truck heave the ball directly at him.

Cut to see the ball hit the guy's glove with such force, it knocks him backward. As the truck skids to a stop, the guy on the ground turns and yells back.

MAN:
Yeah, that looked like a Johnson fastball.

Cut to actual catcher cam game footage of Randy Johnson throwing a fastball.

ANNOUNCER:
Johnson is really bringing the heat today. All game long it's been grab a bat... have a look... and take a seat.

Cut to Major League Baseball logo and title treatment.

SUPER: FOX catcher cam. Don't try it at home.

SUPER: FOX Saturday game of the week

TV: SPOTS OF VARYING LENGTH, CAMPAIGN

MTV Video Music Awards–Ben Stiller

Art Directors Tim Abshire,
Tom Kuntz, Mike Maguire
Creative Directors Allan Broce,
Christina Norman
Copywriters Allan Broce, Tom Kuntz,
Mike Maguire
Directors Tim Abshire, Tom Kuntz,
Mike Maguire (Madonna spot)
Agency MTV In-House
Client MTV Video Music Awards
Country United States

WU-TANG

Open on exterior shot of a Los Angeles hotel. Cut to interior of the hotel room. Ben is getting dressed to go to rehearsal as members of the Wu-Tang Clan are splayed out on the bed. The Wu-Tang guys are all rapt by the movie on spectravision: *The First Wives Club.* Cut to TV where we see Goldie Hawn, Diane Keaton, and Bette Midler singing *You Don't Own Me.* Ben, too, watches intently as he continues to dress.

They all watch a little more.

The Wu-Tang Clan all stare at Ben then look back at the TV.

Cut back to TV, big smilin' singing Diane.

Cut to Video Music Awards logo.

Cut back to Wu-Tang antagonizing Ben on his way out.

BEN:
Ok, guys, I'll see you later... I've got to cut out to go to rehearsal.

RZA:
Hang out, B., this is the best part.

METHOD MAN:
Yo, Ben, I think they should book one of them birds on the show.

GHOSTFACE:
Yeah, Diane Keaton's banging!

BEN:
Yeah, gee, I dunno. Diane Keaton? I mean, she's great, but, you know, it's the Video Music Awards... I don't see...

RZA:
Oh, I get it. You an actor/director, she's an actor/director. Ain't no room for two. Man, that ain't right.

METHOD MAN:
You know, the show's bigger than *you.* It ain't no Ben Stiller awards.

BEN:
That's not the point, it's not like an ego thing, Killah, it's just I don't know what we'd get her to do.

RZA:
Get her ass to co-host, yo. She won a Oscar, I think she can co-host the damn Video Music Awards.

BEN (bewildered):
Yeah, well, I'm pretty sure you can put some of the wet towels in the hamper one day, that's what I'm pretty sure of.

V.O.:
It's the MTV Video Music Awards. Live from L.A. September 10th at 8. Hosted by Ben Stiller.

WU-TANG (under their breath):
Ben Gay...Zipper...

BEN:
Stop it with the zipper.

SILVER

TV: OVER 30 SECONDS
Doctor

Art Directors Cathy Carlisi, Eddie Snyder
Creative Director Eddie Snyder
Copywriter Jerry Williams
Producer Christine Sigety
Director David Shane (hungry man)
Music AcousTech
Editor Sarah Iben (FilmCore)
Agency Fitzgerald+CO
Client Television Bureau
Country United States

Open on guy talking into bullhorn in middle of street. He is shouting in general direction of an office building.

GUY:
Dr. Kessler? Um, I have kind of a … a … a growth on my buttocks. I noticed swelling, some chafing … It's oozing kind of a milky fluid. What does gangrene look like? Is it green like the name or … I haven't been able to take a (beep of car horn) in a week.

Looks at old lady watching him on street. Pulls bullhorn away from mouth.

GUY:
I'm sorry, are you Doctor Kessler?

Goes back to bullhorn

GUY:
It's flaking off in sheets, Doc.

Looks back at old lady. Pulls bullhorn away from mouth. Goes back to bullhorn.

GUY:
I don't know if you want to squeeze it or just leave it. It's spongy. When I poke it my finger springs back.

SUPER: When you want to talk to someone, why talk to everyone?

GUY:
Basically it's an oozing, gelatinous, festering mass with a crusty layer on top.

SUPER: Use local television and really connect with your audience. Local TV. A better connection.

SFX:
Police sirens in background

GUY:
I'd like to speak to my lawyer.

COP:
Yeah, downtown.

Guy bending down to bullhorn in cop's hand and talking up to same building.

GUY:
Larry, Larry Levy.

TV: 30 SECONDS OR LESS, CAMPAIGN
Boat • Mayonnaise • Router

TV: 30 SECONDS OR LESS
Boat

Art Director Jeff Williams
Creative Director Susan Hoffman
Copywriter Jeff Kling
Executive Producers Robert Fernandez, Jon Kamen, Frank Scherma
Director Errol Morris
Agency Wieden & Kennedy
Production Company @radical.media
Client Miller Brewing Company
Country United States

40

BOAT

We see the back of a man standing on his front lawn, leaning on a rake, and holding a bottle of Miller. Across the street a neighbor makes several failed attempts to back up his boat and truck in his driveway.

V.O.:
This is enough to put a High Life man off his lunch. Time was, a man knew how to command his own vehicle. Just how far are we willing to fall?

V.O.:
Better reacquaint yourself with the High Life, soldier, before someone tries to take away your Miller Time.

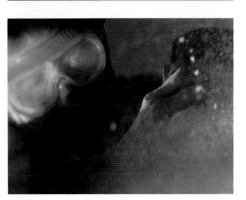

MAYONNAISE

Close up of hand using spatula to get mayo into a bowl.

V.O.:
It's hard to respect the French when you have to bail them out of two big ones in one century. But we have to hand it to them on mayonnaise. Nice job Pierre.

Shot of top of Mayo jar with spatula sticking out.

ROUTER

Through flying sawdust we see a man sawing a piece of wood with a router.

V.O.:
Ever wonder what goes on inside that miracle worker you call a tool? Watch it take that edge right off. And when your router's done its job, here's something else to take the edge off. That's right. Here's to you, router.

SILVER

TV: 30 SECONDS OR LESS, CAMPAIGN
Shopping Cart • Pole • Head

Art Directors Roger Camp,
Taras Wayner
Creative Directors Cliff Freeman,
Eric Silver
Copywriter Kevin Roddy
Producer Liz Graves
Director Noam Murro
Editor Ian MacKenzie
Agency Cliff Freeman and Partners
Studio HKM
Client FOX Sports
Country United States

SHOPPING CART

Open on a man filling a shopping cart with concrete blocks, bags of cement, etc. He then begins pushing the cart as fast as he can across a parking lot.

Cut to a man wearing catcher's gear, crouched in the middle of the lot.

Cut to the shopping cart now speeding closer to the crouching guy. Suddenly, with extreme force, the cart smashes into him, knocking him backward to the ground.

The guy who pushed the cart walks over to him.

GUY 1:
Did that look like Bernie Williams?

Cut to actual catcher cam game footage of Bernie Williams charging home plate.

ANNOUNCER:
Here comes Williams...
He's out at the plate. A major collision but Wilson was able to hang on...

Cut to Major League Baseball logo and title treatment:

SUPER: FOX catcher cam. Don't try it at home.

SUPER: FOX Saturday game of the week.

FOX SOUNDS OF THE GAME
DON'T TRY IT AT HOME

FOX SOUNDS OF THE GAME
DON'T TRY IT AT HOME

POLE

Open on two guys standing next to a flag pole.

GUY 1:
Ready?

One of the guys has his ear against the pole.

GUY 2:
Uh umm.

The other guy swings a huge sledgehammer and hits the pole as hard as he can, directly opposite the other guy's ear.

SFX:
Loud metal thud

The guy whose ear was against the pole gets knocked back by the force of the hit and the intense vibration and sound it creates. He's visibly shaken.

Cut to actual game footage of a Ken Griffey, Jr. home run hitting the foul pole. We hear it hit via sounds of the game.

ANNOUNCER:
Junior cracks it down the right field line... he hit the foul pole. A little music for his trot.

Cut to Major League Baseball logo and title treatment:

SUPER: FOX sounds of the game. Don't try it at home.

SUPER: FOX Saturday game of the week

HEAD

Open on an empty dirt field. We see a guy step into frame and lay down to put his head on the ground.

SFX:
Footsteps running, getting closer

Suddenly, we see another guy run into frame and do a stand-up slide, feet first, into the guy's head.

SFX:
Sliding through dirt

The guy who did the sliding remains standing on the other guy's head. The guy on the ground spits out a mouthful of dirt before speaking.

GUY 1:
That sounded like Lofton.

Cut to actual game footage of Kenny Lofton sliding into second. We hear the slide via sounds of the game.

ANNOUNCER:
And Lofton is safe at second. That's his third stolen base of the game. He's really hot today...

Cut to Major League Baseball logo and title treatment:

SUPER: FOX sounds of the game. Don't try it at home.

SUPER: FOX Saturday game of the week

Multiple Awards

SILVER

**TV: 30 SECONDS OR LESS,
CAMPAIGN**
Feet • Kids • Old Man

and SILVER

TV: 30 SECONDS OR LESS
Feet

and DISTINCTIVE MERIT

TV: 30 SECONDS OR LESS
Old Man

Art Director Kilpatrick Anderson
Creative Director Eric Silver
Copywriter Kevin Roddy
Producer Nick Felder
Director Rocky Morton
Editor Greg Dougherty
Agency Cliff Freeman and Partners
Studio MJZ
Client FOXsports.com
Country United States

44

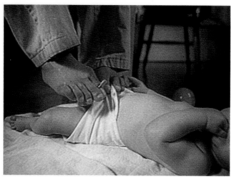

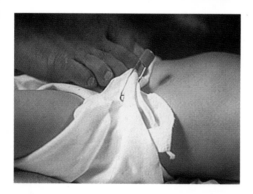

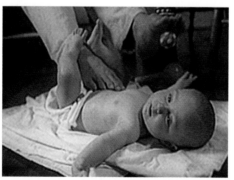

FEET

This spot is shot like a public service announcement. It's dramatic and sympathetic throughout. Open on a tight shot of a pair of men's feet adeptly changing an infant's diaper with a diaper pin. It's an amazing display of skill in that the feet act like hands.

V.O.:
These feet belong to Roger Camp, an extraordinary man who overcame a tremendous challenge. Roger is determined to lead an ordinary life, to perform the everyday tasks that you and I take for granted....

Pan up the man's legs to reveal that he is sitting at a computer. He is using his feet only because he doesn't want to take his attention off FOXsports.com.

V.O.:
...so he won't miss a second of FOXsports.com.

Cut to a series of FOXsports.com screens over his shoulder as the announcer talks about each one.

V.O.:
Whether it's daily insights from John Madden or real-time scores and stats, it's like having the NFL on FOX, on-line.

Cut to a wider shot of the man still intently watching the computer as he shakes a rattle lodged between his toes over the baby lying on a blanket on the floor.

SUPER:
FOXsports.com.
Making a difference.

KIDS

OLD MAN

This spot is shot like a public service announce-ment. It's dramatic and sympathetic throughout.

Open on an inner city play-ground with several teenage kids just hanging out. We see a man walk up to the kids.

Cut to the same teenagers now working. We see them painting; cleaning up trash and leaves; scrubbing the cement; planting a tree, etc.

Cut to an interior as one of the inner city youths is vacu-uming a rug. Camera reveals Wayne Best sitting at a computer on FOXsports.com. The kids have been doing chores around his home the whole time.

One of the kids continues vacuuming under the man's chair, accidentally knocking it, which disturbs the man's concentration.

Cut to exterior shot of his suburban home with lots of kids performing chores.

SUPER: FOXsports.com. Making a difference.

V.O.:
Meet Wayne Best. He saw the kids in his community without direction and did something about it...

V.O.:
...He got them off the street and put them to work, teaching impor-tant lessons in community service, responsibility, and helping others...

V.O.:
...so he can spend all his time on FOXsports.com where he enters his zip code to get the latest on his favorite home teams. It's like FOXSports Net, on-line.

This spot is shot like a public service announce-ment. It's dramatic and sympathetic throughout.

Open on the interior of a kitchen. We see an elderly man with a walker trying to reach up for a jar of peaches on a shelf, but not quite able to get at it.

The old man finally reaches the jar and begins to pull it down, but he drops it. The jar crashes to the floor.

Pan down to a younger man in the foreground, sitting at a table. We can see the old man behind him, but the younger man ignores him.

We see a series of FOXsports.com screens over the man's shoulder.

We see the old man pathetically looking down at the peaches, unable to clean them up. And the younger man is still staring at the computer screen.

SUPER: FOXsports.com. Making a difference.

V.O.:
This man is ninety-eight years old. Life's not so easy for him any-more. But everyday he learns the importance of being independent...

V.O.:
...and self reliant, thanks to this man...

V.O.:
Meet Nick Felder. Nick ignores him and spends all day on FOXsports.com.

V.O.:
With breaking news and inside scoop from the pros, it's like FOXsports, on-line.

OLD MAN:
Nick?

SILVER

TV: LOW BUDGET (UNDER $50,000)
President's Message

Art Directors Lori Campbell,
Stephen Pearson, Scott Vitrone
Creative Director Lori Campbell
Copywriters Lori Campbell,
Stephen Pearson, Scott Vitrone
Directors Mark Foster, Hank Perlman
Production Company hungry man
Agency Dweck & Campbell
Client Comedy Central
Country United States

Open on Larry Shanet,
president of Comedy
Central, sitting behind
a desk dressed as a
clown.

LARRY:
Hi, I'm Larry Shanet, president
of Comedy Central. I'd like to
remind you that Comedy
Central has quality comedy
programming while other
networks don't. CNN, not
funny. VH1, not funny. C-Span,
not funny. The Discovery
Channel, well, those baboons
with the red asses, they're kind
of funny. But how often do you
see those things? Comedy
Central, that's your best bet.

GOLD

ANIMATION

Hete-Roy

Designer J.J. Sedelmaier
Copywriter Robert Smigel
Animators Don McGrath,
J.J. Sedelmaier, Mike Wetterhahn
Composer Steven M. Gold
Audio Post Mike Fisher
Voices Andrew Daly, Carey Prusa,
Robert Smigel
Agency NBC
Client Saturday Night Live
Country United States

Multiple Awards

SILVER

**CONSUMER NEWSPAPER:
FULL PAGE**

Words: Senna • Vietná

and DISTINCTIVE MERIT

**POSTERS AND BILLBOARDS:
PROMOTIONAL**

Words: Senna • Vietná • Hitler •
Charles Chaplin • Neil Armstrong

Art Director Tomás Lorente
Creative Directors Nizan Guanaes,
Tomás Lorente
Copywriter Carlos Domingos
Photographer Archive Image
Illustrator Monica Kornfeld
Producer Elaine Carvalho
Agency DM9 DDB Publicidade
Client Folha de São Paulo Newspaper
Country Brazil

48

Folha de S.Paulo Newspaper. Illustrating life with words for 77 years.

Folha de S.Paulo Newspaper. Illustrating life with words for 77 years.

Folha de S.Paulo Newspaper. Illustrating life with words for 77 years.

Folha de S.Paulo Newspaper. Illustrating life with words for 77 years.

Folha de S.Paulo Newspaper. Illustrating life with words for 77 years.

Multiple Awards

GOLD

**POSTERS AND BILLBOARDS:
PUBLIC SERVICE, CAMPAIGN**

Massachusetts Society for the
Prevention of Cruelty to Children
(MSPCC) campaign

and SILVER

**POSTERS AND BILLBOARDS:
PUBLIC SERVICE**

Kiss/Punch

and SILVER

**POSTERS AND BILLBOARDS:
PUBLIC SERVICE**

Comb/Pull

and DISTINCTIVE MERIT

**POSTERS AND BILLBOARDS:
PUBLIC SERVICE**

Hug/Fondle

and SILVER

**NEWSPAPER: PUBLIC SERVICE,
LESS THAN A FULL PAGE**

Change/Beat

and DISTINCTIVE MERIT

**NEWSPAPER: PUBLIC SERVICE,
LESS THAN A FULL PAGE**

Encourage/Degrade

Art Director Kevin Daley
Creative Directors Gary Greenberg,
Peter Seronick
Copywriter Craig Johnson
Photographer Russ Quackenbush
Agency Greenberg Seronick
O'Leary & Partners
Client Massachusetts Society for the
Prevention of Cruelty to Children
Country United States

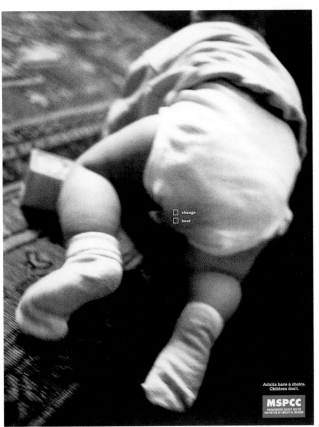

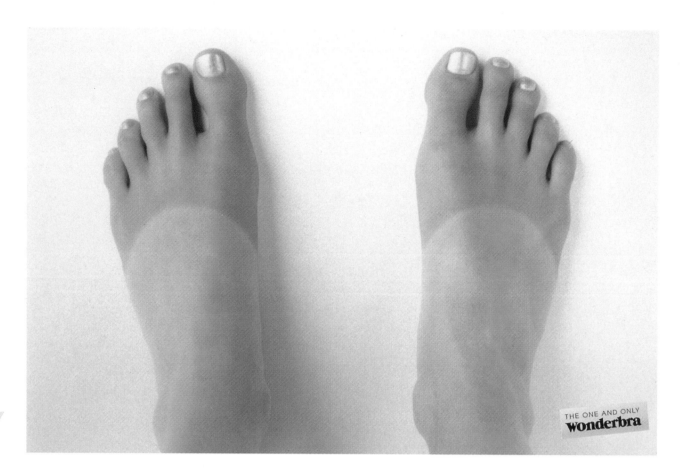

THE ONE AND ONLY
wonderbra

Multiple Awards

SILVER

**POSTERS AND BILLBOARDS:
POINT-OF-PURCHASE**

and DISTINCTIVE MERIT
CONSUMER NEWSPAPER: SPREAD

and DISTINCTIVE MERIT
CONSUMER MAGAZINE: SPREAD
Feet

Art Directors Erich Funke, Stuart Walsh
Creative Director Tony Granger
Copywriters Erich Funke, Stuart Walsh
Photographer Michael Meyersfeld
Agency TBWA Hunt Lascaris
Client Playtex/Wonderbra
Country South Africa

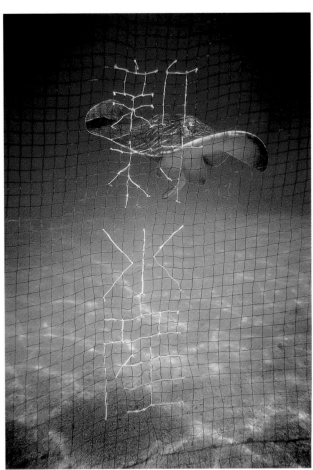

SILVER

PROMOTIONAL
Fishing Net

Art Director Norito Shinmura
Copywriter Kazutaka Sato
Designer Norito Shinmura
Photographer Kogo Inoue
Artist Masashi Shinmura
Studio Shinmura Design Office
Client Shinmura Fisheries
Country Japan

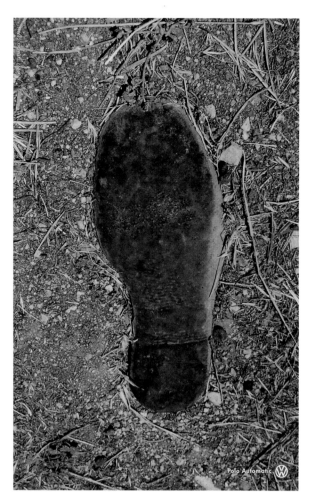

SILVER

PRODUCT

Shoe-Writtle • Shoe-Westbourne •
Shoe-Guadix • Shoe-Paddington •
Shoe-Weymouth • Shoe-Channel

Art Director Richard Flintham
Copywriter Andy McLeod
Photographer Neil Cummings
Agency BMP DDB Ltd.
Client Volkswagen
Country England

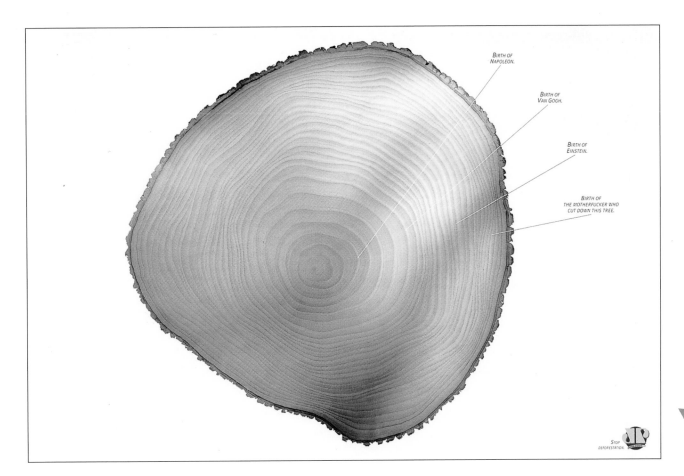

BIRTH OF
NAPOLEON.

BIRTH OF
VAN GOGH.

BIRTH OF
EINSTEIN.

BIRTH OF
THE MOTHERFUCKER WHO
CUT DOWN THIS TREE.

STOP
DEFORESTATION.

SILVER

PUBLIC SERVICE

Birth of Napoleon/Birth of van
Gogh/Birth of Einstein/Birth of the
Motherfucker Who Cut Down
This Tree

Art Director Valdir Bianchi
Creative Directors Marcello Serpa, Eugenio Mohallem
Copywriter Cassio Zanatta
Photography Archive Tony Stone (Argentina)
Producer Jose Roberto Bezerra
Agency Almap BBDO
Client Jovem Pan
Country Brazil

GOLD

RADIO: OVER 30 SECONDS

Good Will Hunting

and SILVER

**RADIO: OVER 30 SECONDS,
CAMPAIGN**

Good Will Hunting • Wag the Dog •
The Wedding Singer

Creative Director Arthur Bijur
Copywriters Adam Chasnow,
Ian Reichenthal
Producer Arlene Adoremos
Engineer Roy Kamen
Studio Kamen Entertainment Group
Agency Cliff Freeman and Partners
Client Hollywood Video
Country United States

56

GOOD WILL HUNTING

**All dialogue and SFX
extremely fast
throughout**

ANNOUNCER: Hollywood Video presents...Sixty Second Theater. Where we try (unsuccessfully) to pack all the action and drama of a two-hour Hollywood Production into sixty seconds. Today's presentation..."Good Will Hunting."

SFX: Chalk on chalkboard

PROFESSOR (Swedish accent): Class, it took me and my colleagues two years to solve this math problem.

STUDENT: It only took the janitor ten minutes.

PROFESSOR: Where is this genius-janitor?

STUDENT: In jail.

PROFESSOR: Why?

STUDENT: He's an extremely violent genius-janitor.

SFX: Jail doors opening

PROFESSOR: I'll get you out of jail, genius-janitor, if you teach me math and see a shrink.

WILL (Matt Damon sound-alike, thick Boston accent): No, thanks.

SFX: Jail doors closing

CELLMATE (deep voice): Hi cutie, I'm your cellmate.

WILL (yells): Whoaaa! Math and shrink sounds good!

SFX: Door opening

MCGUIRE (Robin Williams sound-alike): Will, I'm Dr. McGuire.

WILL: You're a shrink? You're crazier than I am!

MCGUIRE (screaming): Don't you ever call me crazy! You got that chief!? (calmly) I'll see you next Thursday at 4:30.

SFX: Door closes. Car horn

CHUCKIE (Ben Affleck sound-alike, thick Boston accent): Hey Will, let's go to a haavaahdd baahh and beat up some smaaahht kids.

WILL: Or I could humiliate them with my vast knowledge of pre-revolutionary economic modalities.

CHUCKIE: Nah, let's just beat 'em up.

SFX: Car tires screeching to stop

WILL: Hey smaaahht kid, I'm smaahtaahh than you are.

PREPPY: You don't sound smart.

WILL: No one from Boston does.

SKYLAR (Minnie Driver sound-alike, British accent): Hi, I'm Skylar.

WILL: Hi, Skylaaaah.

SKYLAR: No, Sky-LER. Wanna go back to my dorm room?

SFX: Key into door; door opens

SFX: Barry White-style music

SKYLAR: I'm not going to shag you until I meet your friends.

SFX: Needle-scratch; Barry White-style music stops

WILL: Chuckie, Billy, Maahgan this is Skylaahh—Skylaahh, Chuckie, Billy, Maahgan.

SFX: Barry White-style music

SKYLAR: I love you, Will.

WILL: I love you, Skylaaahh.

SKYLAR: It's Sky-LER! SKYLER!!

ANNOUNCER: If this doesn't satisfy your urge to see "Good Will Hunting," (and we can't say we blame you) then rent it today at Hollywood Video where "Good Will Hunting" is guaranteed to be in-stock, or next time it's free. Welcome to Hollywood. Hollywood Video. Celebrity voices impersonated.

All dialogue and SFX
extremely fast
throughout

ANNOUNCER: Hollywood Video presents..."Sixty Second Theater." Where we try (unsuccessfully) to pack all the action and drama of a two-hour Hollywood Production into sixty seconds. Today's presentation..."Wag the Dog."

AMES (Anne Heche sound-alike): The presidential election is only two weeks away and we have a crisis. Get me the spin doctor!

SFX: Footsteps

BREAN (Robert deNiro sound-alike): I'm the spin doctor. What's the crisis?

AMES: The President made a pass at a girl scout during a White House tour.

BREAN: That's terrible.

AMES: I know, the poor thing.

BREAN: No, I mean that he did it two weeks before the election.

AMES: So what are we going to do?

BREAN: Spin a story even bigger than a girl scout-groping president.

AMES: What could be bigger than a girl scout-groping president?

BREAN: A war.

AMES: With who?

BREAN: I'm working on it. (pause) Okay, I worked on it. We're going to war with Albania.

AMES: Where's Albania?

BREAN: Hollywood. Let's go.

SFX: Airplane landing

BREAN: Mr. Showbiz, we need you to produce a war.

MOTSS (Dustin Hoffman sound-alike): I produce movies. Not wars.

BREAN: What's the difference?

MOTSS (excited): Can the war have a song?

BREAN: Knock yourself out.

CHOIR (singing): We're going to blow Albania off the map...

AMES: I can't believe we're at war with Albania.

BREAN: We're not.

AMES: Oh, yeah!

MOTSS: I can't wait to tell everyone I produced a war.

BREAN: You can't do that.

MOTSS: Yes, I can.

BREAN: No, you can't.

MOTSS: Yes, I can.

SFX: Frying pan hitting head; pool splash

BREAN: No, you can't.

AMES: Well, the war we never had is over. The song was a flop. And Mr. Showbiz mysteriously died by his Hollywood pool.

BREAN: But the girl scout-groping president was reelected.

AMES: And we get to keep our jobs!

ANNOUNCER: If this doesn't satisfy your urge to see "Wag the Dog" (and we can't say we blame you) then rent it today at Hollywood Video where "Wag the Dog" is guaranteed to be in-stock, or next time it's free. Welcome to Hollywood. Hollywood Video. Celebrity voices impersonated.

All dialogue and SFX
extremely fast
throughout

Open on wedding
singer finishing
singing an '80s-style
love song

ANNOUNCER: Hollywood Video presents... "Sixty Second Theater." Where we try (unsuccessfully) to pack all the humor and romance of a two-hour Hollywood production into sixty seconds. Today's presentation..."The Wedding Singer."

ROBBIE (Adam Sandler sound-alike): "...'cause you're in love....

ROBBIE (over P.A. system): We're going to take a short break while you try to chew your rubber chicken entree.

SFX: Mic feedback/click

ROBBIE: Hi, I'm the wedding singer.

JULIA (Drew Barrymore sound-alike): Hi, I'm the new banquet hall waitress.

ROBBIE: You're cute.

JULIA: You're cuter!

ROBBIE: I'm engaged.

JULIA: So am I!

ROBBIE: My fiancee's a witch.

JULIA: My fiancee's a jerk!

ROBBIE: I'm getting married next week.

JULIA (excited): Oh, you're so lucky!

SFX: Church organ playing wedding march

ROBBIE: Umm...Has anyone seen my fiancee?

SFX: Church doors open

WOMAN (yells): She's not coming!

ROBBIE: Why not?

WOMAN: Because you're a wedding singer!

ROBBIE (crying): I'll never love anyone again.

JULIA: Hi, Wedding Singer.

ROBBIE (stops crying): I love you. I mean, (crying) waaahh!!!

JULIA: Would it cheer you up to sing at my wedding?

ROBBIE: I can't sing weddings anymore. They're too painful.

JULIA: Then I'll have a Bar Mitzvah.

ROBBIE: But you're not Jewish.

SFX: Robbie sings "Hava-Nagila" with his wedding band

JULIA: I love you, Bar Mitzvah singer, good thing I didn't get married.

ROBBIE (Stops singing; wedding band continues playing Hava-Nagila): I love you, Banquet Hall Waitress, good thing I was left at the altar!

Continues singing
Hava-Nagila.

ANNOUNCER: If this doesn't satisfy your urge to see "The Wedding Singer," (and we can't say we blame you) then rent it today at Hollywood Video where "The Wedding Singer" is guaranteed to be in-stock, or next time it's free. Welcome to Hollywood. Hollywood Video. Celebrity voices impersonated.

Multiple Awards

DISTINCTIVE MERIT

**TV: 30 SECONDS OR LESS,
CAMPAIGN**
Duct Tape • Donut • Deviled Egg

---

and DISTINCTIVE MERIT

TV: 30 SECONDS OR LESS
Duct Tape

---

and MERIT

TV: 30 SECONDS OR LESS
Deviled Egg

Art Director Jeff Williams
Creative Director Susan Hoffman
Copywriter Jeff Kling
Executive Producers Robert
Fernandez, Jon Kamen,
Frank Scherma
Director Errol Morris
Production Company @radical.media
Agency Wieden & Kennedy
Client Miller Brewing Company
Country United States

58

DUCT TAPE

We watch a man tape
up his refrigerator
with duct tape.

In slow motion we see
a hand opening the
fridge which contains
only Miller bottles and
cans, a box of baking
soda, and a jar
of pickles.

V.O.:
Even when a man has his tool
box handy, isn't it nice to turn
to this all-purpose helper?
The High Life Man knows that
if the pharaohs had duct tape,
the Sphinx would still have a
nose. We salute you duct
tape. You help a man get to
Miller Time.

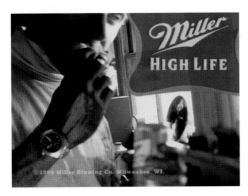

DONUT

We open on a table covered with some tools, a powdered donut, and a can of Miller High Life. We see a pair of greasy hands working with one of the tools. One of the hands picks up a piece of the powdered donut.

We then see the man eating the donut while holding his Miller High Life can.

V.O.:
Sometimes a man gets too hungry to clean his hands properly. The powdered sugar on this donut puts a semi-protective barrier between your fingerprint and your nutrition. But even if some grease does get on that donut, well, that's just flavor to a High Life Man.

DEVILED EGG

Through a kitchen door we see a heavy man standing in a kitchen staring at a plate of food.

We see the lone deviled egg.

He looks at his Miller Lite.

He ponders as he looks at the last deviled egg.

He picks up the deviled egg and devours it whole.

V.O.:
Hmm. That last egg's looking real good.

You had quite a few though. Maybe you shouldn't.

But...if you make a light choice here, maybe you will have room for just one more.

See there? When you live the High Life you can have it both ways.

Multiple Awards

DISTINCTIVE MERIT

**TV: 30 SECONDS OR LESS,
CAMPAIGN**
Wrestler • Enticing Bottle • Bobsled

and MERIT

TV: 30 SECONDS OR LESS

and MERIT

TV: OVER 30 SECONDS
Wrestler

Art Directors Kevin Amter,
Scott Davis
Creative Director Bill Westbrook
Copywriters Stephanie Crippen,
William Gelner
Producers Julie Hampel,
Jack Nelson, Clair Grupp
Directors Tarsem, Enda McCollion,
Geraldde Thame
Music Asche & Spencer, RTG
Production Companies
@radical.media, HSI, Mars Media
Agency Fallon McElligott
Client Miller Brewing Company
Country United States

WRESTLER

Open on Miller
Time logo.

MUSIC:
Miller Time music

ANNOUNCER:
This place is bananas...

Cut to several shots of
two wrestlers hitting
and kicking one
another, but clearly
missing every time.
Yet they react like
they've been hurt.

The chiropractor with a
clothesline...

Low blow, what is this?

This continues
throughout.

It's over.

Cut to wrestlers in
a bar.

WRESTLER:
Miller Lite.

They open Miller
Lite cans without
touching them.

They pour the beer
but miss their
glasses.

They high-five each
other but miss. When
they go to drink, they
miss their mouths.

LOGO: Miller Time

ENTICING BOTTLE

BOBSLED

Open on Miller Time logo.

MUSIC:
Miller Time music

A man enters a peepshow booth. He puts a coin into a slot and the window slides up.

Through the window we see a woman. She pulls a bottle of Miller Lite from behind her back and seductively peels the top label off.

MUSIC:
Old tango music

She starts to peel the bottom label, but the window starts to close. The man searches for more change, but it falls to the floor. He tries to stop the window, but it closes on his fingers.

LOGO: Miller Time

Open on Miller Time logo.

MUSIC:
Miller Time music

Everything that occurs in the spot happens in fours and in unison.

Four men grab Miller Lites and turn toward a pretty woman.

Four men pass by on crutches.

A woman passes. Her shirt reads "4U."

Four men shoot pool. They turn toward the woman.

Four men throw darts. The darts hit number four.

Four figures on bathroom sign.

A woman passes four moose heads. Their eyes follow her.

Four records drop onto four turntables.

Four men dance with the woman.

Four men walk out. One has his arm around the woman, the others imitate.

Neon sign:
"Bob's Bobsled Bar"

LOGO: Cut to Miller Time bobsled

DISTINCTIVE MERIT

TV: 30 SECONDS OR LESS, CAMPAIGN

Cornermen • Locker Room/Good Clean Writing • Perfect Show

Creative Director Stacy Wall
Copywriter Ernest Lupinacci
Director of Photography Joe DeSalvo
Producer John Towse
Executive Producers Peter Cline, Stephen Orent
Director Paul Norling
Editor Gordon Carey (FilmCore)
Agency Wieden & Kennedy
Production Company hungry man
Client ESPN Sportscenter
Country United States

ON SET COMMERCIAL BREAK
6:23 a.m., August 18, 1998

CORNERMEN

RICH EISEN:
Stuart and I get the playoff picture back from the darkroom when we come back.

X-TRA:
We're cleared.

RICH EISEN:
The prompt is going too fast, I can't keep up.

LOU (trainer):
C'mon, it's not the teleprompter, it's you. Now stop the b*lls**t.

RICH EISEN:
My throat. I can hardly talk.

LOU:
Give him some tea. Give him some tea.

RICH EISEN:
Ah, I can't go back out there. I don't want to go back out there. Cut me. Cut me Lou.

LOU:
C'mon baby, c'mon. Snap out of it. Don't be a lollipop. Get out there. Tonight's your night.

RICH EISEN:
Well, without question these days, the word on everybody's list...

LOCKER ROOM/GOOD CLEAN WRITING

PERFECT SHOW

GARY MILLER:
Doing a show is emotionally
and physically exhausting.
Afterwards the last thing you
want to do is talk to the media.

DAN PATRICK:
Well, I mean, it felt good. The
tie, the tie went with the suit.
Segues were good. Good,
good clean writing. It was a
good show.

KENNY MAYNE:
Well, I mean you saw it. You
know. We had some problems
in the third segment. But, ah,
we move on, we don't dwell on
it. Well, I'm working the crowd
in the room; if they like it, I
assume the people out there in
television land like it. But, you
know, I get paid every two
weeks.

DAN PATRICK:
It's starting to wear on me,
that's all. It's starting to wear
on me. I mean (mumble), yeah,
it is the greatest job in the
world. That's what I tell you
guys.

STUART SELIG:
Yeah, you know. Every once
in a while it all just comes
together and you do have that
perfect show.

Clip of Bob Lee   Bob Lee had one back in '89.

Clip of Charley Steiner   Steiner had his in '91.

Dan had one working last
season. It got crazy out there.
During the commercial breaks
the crew, they wouldn't talk to
him. Kenny wouldn't even look
at him. It was intense.

DAN PATRICK:
And that, of course, is the
sort of thing that can't never
happen in a playoff race.

X-TRA:
What did he just say?

X-TRA (referee):
That's a double negative.

STUART SELIG:
At the end, he just let it get
away from him.

Multiple Awards

DISTINCTIVE MERIT
TV: 30 SECONDS OR LESS
UFO

and DISTINCTIVE MERIT
TV: 30 SECONDS OR LESS
Soul

and MERIT
**TV: 30 SECONDS OR LESS,
CAMPAIGN**
UFO • Soul • Dream • Flower

and MERIT
TV: 30 SECONDS OR LESS
Dream

Art Director Alan Pafenbach
Creative Directors Lance Jensen,
Alan Pafenbach
Copywriters Stuart D'Rozario,
Lance Jensen
Cinematographer Salvatore Totino
Producer Bill Goodell
Director Nick Lewin
Visual Effects Bill
Lead Digital Artist Kieran
Editor Gordon Carey (FilmCore)
Production Company Manifesto
Recording Studio Photo Mag
Agency Arnold Communications, Inc.
Client Volkswagen of America
Country United States

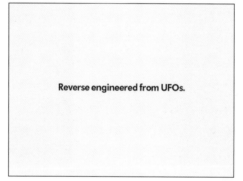

UFO

SUPER: Reverse engineered from UFOs.	MUSIC: Fluke, "Absurd"
SUPER: Drivers wanted.	CAR: Silver beetle
LOGO: Volkswagen	

SOUL

SUPER: If you sold your soul in the 80s...	MUSIC: Hurricane #1 "Step into My World"
SUPER: ...Here's your chance to buy it back.	CAR: Blue beetle
SUPER: Drivers wanted.	
LOGO: Volkswagen	

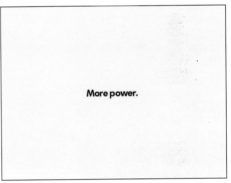

DREAM

SUPER: What color do
you dream in?

MUSIC:
The Orb, "Little Fluffy Clouds"

CAR:
Multi-color beetles

SUPER: Drivers
wanted.

LOGO: Volkswagen

FLOWER

SUPER: Less flower.

MUSIC:
Stereolab, "Parsec"

CAR:
Yellow and black beetles

SUPER: More power.

SUPER: Drivers
wanted.

LOGO: Volkswagen

DISTINCTIVE MERIT

**TV: 30 SECONDS OR LESS,
CAMPAIGN**

Action • Don • Musical

Art Director Matt Vescovo
Creative Director Arthur Bijur
Copywriter Eric Silver
Producer Nick Felder
Directors Baker Smith, Todd Philips
Editor Gavin Cutler
Composer David Horowitz
Studios Tate & Partners,
Moxie Pictures
Agency Cliff Freeman and Partners
Client Hollywood Video
Country United States

66

ACTION

Open inside Hollywood Video store.	
Woman approaches clerk in aisle.	<u>WOMAN:</u> Action adventure?
Clerk leads woman to action adventure section. There we see an older cowboy teaching two clerks how to throw a fake punch.	<u>CLERK:</u> Sure. Follow me.
	<u>COWBOY:</u> So the trick is to come as close as you can to the person and let the camera do the rest. Do it.
Clerk A rears back and hits Clerk B square in the face. Clerk B cries out in pain. Cowboy turns to Clerk A.	
	<u>COWBOY (patient):</u> That's a good start—except we don't want to actually hit the person. Do it again.
Clerk A rears back and again hits Clerk B square in the face. Clerk B again cries out in pain.	
	<u>COWBOY:</u> Okay. Let's try one more where you don't actually hit him. Do it.
Clerk A rears back and hits Clerk B. Clerk B drops to his knees, grabbing the cowboy on the way down.	
	<u>COWBOY:</u> Ooooohhh. That was so close.

DON

Open inside
Hollywood Video store.

Couple approaches
counter and woman
hands movie to clerk.

WOMAN:
Hi. Could you tell us a little
about this movie?

The clerk gestures for
couple to wait one
second and then
knocks on cabinet
underneath desk.

CLERK:
Don, we need you up here.

The door slides open
and we see a man in a
suit crammed inside
the cabinet.

The man then pops up
from behind the
counter, looks at the
movie box, and then
begins speaking. When
he talks we realize it is
the voice of virtually
every movie trailer.

DON:
From flesh to steel. From blood
to blade. From man to mutant.
Evil has a new enemy. Justice
has a new weapon. And the
world has a new hero.

Don looks at the clerk.
The clerk looks back at
Don a little emotional.

CLERK:
That was real nice, Don.

DON (dry):
Uh–huh.

Cut to couple who
look stunned by what
has just transpired.

MUSICAL

Open inside Hollywood
Video store. Clerk hands
customer her movies.

CLERK:
Okay, have these new releases
back by Monday.

Clerk 1 then begins
singing (very campy).

WOMAN:
Isn't that five days?

CLERK 1:
Five days to watch these movies.

Clerk 2 then slides across
floor (à la Fred Astaire)
and begins to sing.

CLERK 2:
Five days including new
releases.

Clerks start to sing and
dance in unison.

CLERKS:
Everything in the store is five days.

Clerks join hands and
begin spinning each
other.

CLERK 1: It can't be.

CLERK 2: It sure is.

CLERK 1: No way.

CLERKS: Five days.

Clerk 1 accidentally
throws Clerk 2 through
plate glass window. Clerk
2 lies motionless. Clerk 1
goes on with the show.

CLERK 1:
Each and every rental—five days.

SUPER: Welcome to
Hollywood.

LOGO: Hollywood Video

DISTINCTIVE MERIT

TV: 30 SECONDS OR LESS
Ball Boys

Art Directors Chris Brignola,
C. J. Waldman
Creative Directors Lee Garfinkel,
Todd Godwin, Gary Goldsmith,
C. J. Waldman
Copywriter Todd Godwin
Executive Producers Robert
Fernandez, Jon Kamen,
Frank Scherma
Agency Producer Bob Nelson
Director Frank Todaro
Production Company @radical.media
Agency Lowe & Partners/SMS
Client Heineken
Country United States

Open on a man in a
bar pouring a
Heineken into a glass.
The moment he places
the empty bottle
down on the table, it
is picked up. We see
this happening at
other tables.
We see from above
that ball boys all over
the bar are (with great
skill and precision)
picking up empty
Heinekens from the
tables and running
back to their spots.

One ball boy returns
with a newly gotten
Heineken bottle. The
other ball boy runs off.

SFX:
Sneakers running on floor

BALL BOY 1:
Good Get.

BALL BOY 2:
Thanks.

SFX:
Sneakers running on floor

DISTINCTIVE MERIT

TV: 30 SECONDS OR LESS

Got a Problem with Church?

Art Director Jeff Hopfer

Creative Directors Ron Henderson, Jeff Hopfer

Animator J.J. Sedelmaier

Copywriter Ron Henderson

Producer Justine Marengo-Rowe

Director J.J. Sedelmaier

Agency The Richards Group

Studio J.J. Sedelmaier Productions, Inc.

Client Episcopal New Church Center

Country United States

Open on cartoon father and son in yard.

FATHER:
Guess what, Timmy? Tomorrow, your mother and I are going to take you to church! Not only will you get to learn about the wages of sin and eternal damnation, but you can play fun games like Bible sword drill, and sing inspirational songs like Kumbaya and "I got joy joy joy joy down in my heart...(CLAPS) down in my heart... down in my heart..."

Boy walks into road and waits for semi to flatten him.

V.O.:
Got a problem with church? Let's fix it. The Episcopal New Church Center.

Multiple Awards

DISTINCTIVE MERIT

TV: 30 SECONDS OR LESS, CAMPAIGN
Screen Door • Hatchback • Bus

and MERIT

TV: 30 SECONDS OR LESS
Screen Door

Art Director Jim Carroll
Creative Directors Lee Garfinkel, Gary Goldsmith
Copywriters Chris Brignola (Hatchback), John Brockenbrough
Editor Tom Scherma
Executive Producer Maddi Carlton
Agency Producer Liz Hodge
Producer Jeff Arnold
Editorial House Consulate
Director Nicholas Barker
Music Marshall Grupp Sound Design
Production Company Chelsea Pictures
Agency Lowe & Partners/SMS
Client Excite, Inc.
Country United States

With Excite.com, she instantly sends photos to friends around the world.

excite.com

SCREEN DOOR

Open on young woman carrying dishes from kitchen to outdoor deck. She puts dishes down on table, then goes to sliding screen door, opens it, walks inside, closes it.

SUPER:
With Excite.com, she instantly sends photos to friends around the world.

A few moments later she comes back outside, again opening and closing screen. She takes a few steps, but then pauses and turns to go back inside to get something she forgot. Only this time she plows right through the screen.

SUPER: If she can, why can't you?

LOGO: Excite.com

With Excite.com,
he met his wife
in an online chat room.

With Excite.com,
he got a free e-mail account.

HATCHBACK

BUS

Open on guy starting
to close car hatchback
in parking lot.
He realizes his cargo
needs to be pushed in
further and moves in it
accordingly.

SUPER: With
Excite.com, he met his
wife in an online chat
room.

Finally, he checks the
clearance one more
time and then slams
the hatchback shut.
His cargo crashes
right through the
window.

SUPER: If he can do it,
why can't you?

LOGO: Excite.com

Open on a young
guy in coat and tie
sitting on bus between
other passengers. He
crosses his leg and
notices a slight bulge
in his pants leg, just
below the knee.

SUPER: With
Excite.com, he got a
free e-mail account.

Cut back to guy
surreptitiously pulling
something down out
of his pants leg,
which we realize
is yesterday's
underwear. Looking
straight ahead,
he quickly conceals
underwear in his
jacket pocket.

SUPER: If he can,
why can't you?

LOGO: Excite.com

Multiple Awards

DISTINCTIVE MERIT

TV: 30 SECONDS OR LESS
Produce

and MERIT

**TV: 30 SECONDS OR LESS,
CAMPAIGN**
Produce • Head-Butt • Wedding

and MERIT

TV: 30 SECONDS OR LESS
Head-Butt

and MERIT

TV: 30 SECONDS OR LESS
Wedding

Art Director Holland Henton
Creative Director Brian Brooker
Copywriter Brian Brooker
Executive Producers Robert
Fernandez, Jon Kamen,
Frank Scherma
Agency Producer Dottie Martin
Director Frank Todaro
Music Hum Music & Sound Design
Production Company
@radical.media
Agency GSD&M/Dallas
Client Southwest Airlines
Country United States

PRODUCE

Open on woman in
grocery store. She
picks up a melon in
the produce section.
She accidentally drops
it. Five women dive
on the melon like it's a
loose football.

SUPER: Must be
football season.

SUPER: Southwest
Airlines:
Proud Sponsor
of the National
Football League.

SFX:
Music throughout

HEAD-BUTT

Open on two businesswomen talking in a corridor.

WOMAN 1:
Do you have the flow charts?

WOMAN 2:
Yup.

WOMAN 1:
We can win this, Judy.

WOMAN 2:
Yeah. Let's get that account.

They stop outside of a door and head-butt each other football style.

SUPER: Must be football season.

SUPER: Southwest Airlines: Proud Sponsor of the National Football League.

WEDDING

Open on a bride and groom alone on the dance floor for their "first dance." They are barely moving. They are gazing into each others eyes.

Behind them we see two guys sneak up on them with a punch bowl and pour it on their heads à la football Gatorade pouring.

SUPER: Must be football season.

SUPER: Southwest Airlines: Proud Sponsor of the National Football League.

SFX:
Music throughout

Multiple Awards

DISTINCTIVE MERIT
TV: 30 SECONDS OR LESS

and DISTINCTIVE MERIT
TV: LOW BUDGET (UNDER $50,000)
Diver

and MERIT
**TV: 30 SECONDS OR LESS,
CAMPAIGN**
Diver • Saddam • Video Date

and MERIT
TV: LOW BUDGET (UNDER $50,000)
Saddam

Art Director Matt Mowat
Creative Directors Jim Nobel,
Brian O'Neill
Copywriter Chuck Meehan
Title design Fuel
Producer James Horner
Director Tom Schiller
Recording Studio
Crescendo! Studios
Editor Anthony Lucero
(Digital Gumbo)
Production Company Five Union
Square Productions
Agency Goldberg Moser O'Neill
Client Ameristar Casinos, Inc.
Country United States

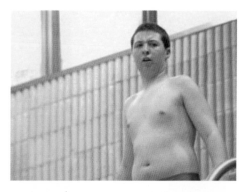

DIVER

Open with long shot of overweight boy. Camera follows him up diving board.	V.O.: Stevie Moyer will be attempting a forward three-and-one-half somersault with two-and-one-half twists.
Zoom in for medium shot.	
Music comes in.	
SUPER: No chance.	
SUPER: Ameristar Casino logo.	
SUPER: Chance.	

SADDAM

Open with close-up of Saddam at a press conference.

SUPER SUBTITLES: To show the world that I am a man of peace, I am having a big pool party at the palace for all the UN inspectors. We'll share some laughs, eat cocktail weenies, play beach volleyball, and have drinks in the hot tub. It will be the mother of all wing-dings!

Music comes in.

SUPER: No chance.

SUPER: Ameristar logo

SUPER: Chance.

SADDAM (speaking Arabic)

VIDEO DATE

Open on a portly bald man sitting in a chair.

SUPER: Meet Will, #471

SUPER: No chance.

SUPER: Ameristar Logo

SUPER: Chance.

WILL:
Oh hi, uh, I like attractive natural blondes, with long shapely legs. I'm a real leg man. I like a toned and firm body. Maybe a dancer, preferably an exotic dancer...would be good.

SFX:
Coins hitting metal tray

DISTINCTIVE MERIT

TV: 30 SECONDS OR LESS
Open Road

Art Director Adam Glickman
Creative Director Don Pogany
Copywriter Craig Feigen
Producer Greg Popp
Agency DDB Needham Chicago
Client Anheuser-Busch
Country United States

A Bud truck driver (Bob) sees a cow in the road. He swerves around it. Bob then passes two backpackers who call out for some free Bud. He continues driving. A convertible with four women pulls up beside him.

WOMAN:
Hey, Bud Man, follow us! C'mon!!!

The women turn off to a dirt road. As Bob follows them, the scene outside the window freezes; the word "FAIL" flashes on. Reveal an instructor sitting next to driver.

INSTRUCTOR:
Not so good!

Cut to a Bud Truck Simulator inside a hangar. A long line of would-be uniformed truck drivers stand in line to take the test.

SUPER: This Bud's for you.

Cut to our defeated truck driver exiting the simulator, he hands his hat to another instructor.

INSTRUCTOR (taking hat):
The convertible, huh?

DRIVER (dejected):
Yeah.

DISTINCTIVE MERIT

TV: OVER 30 SECONDS
The Unexpected

Art Director Joanna Wenley
Copywriter Jeremy Craigen
Producer Howard Spivey
Director Frank Budgen
Agency BMP DDB Ltd.
Client Sony
Production Company
Gorgeous Enterprises
Country England

Open on a man in his mid 20s. He is standing outside an American diner, filming his girlfriend with his Sony camcorder.

She sees a dog and playfully throws it a bit of food.

The camcorder's low battery sign flashes up on screen.

The screen then goes blank.

The man lowers the camcorder and unclips the battery.

At this point the dog runs into the road, in front of an on-coming pick-up truck. The truck swerves to avoid the dog, causing barrels to spill off.

One crashes through the diner's window.

TV: OVER 30 SECONDS, CAMPAIGN
Coolio/Disposable Income •
Henry/Monkey

Creative Director Allan Broce (MTV)
Copywriter Allan Broce (MTV)
Director of Photography
Douglas Cooper
Producer Lalou Dammond
Director David Shane
Editor Sarah Iben (FilmCore)
Agency MTV Networks
Executive Producer Stephen Orent
Production Company hungry man
Client MTV
Country United States

COOLIO/DISPOSABLE INCOME

MATTY GRIPER:
So, Cool, you made a beautiful dollar last year. Mazel, mazel.

COOLIO:
Thanks, homey.

MATTY GRIPER:
I love when you call me homey.

COOLIO:
Big homey.

MATTY GRIPER:
I love that. Stop it.

COOLIO:
Big man.

MATTY GRIPER:
Stop that, now listen. Now we got business here, you know, 'cause you got a lot of disposable income here, you know. You know what we say about disposable income?

COOLIO:
Yup. I know what we say, man.

MATTY GRIPER:
I know, you know what we say, but you gotta, ya know, gotta say it out loud.

COOLIO:
If you don't dispose of disposable income come April time, you'll hate the outcome.

MATTY GRIPER:
That's what we say (giving Coolio a noogie).

COOLIO:
Be cool on the hair, man.

MATTY GRIPER:
Okay.

COOLIO:
Okay.

HENRY/MONKEY

MATTY GRIPER:
All right, so Henry, brace
yourself with the dreaded
"a-word." All right, we're
talking tax audit, all right.
Now I can represent you—

HENRY ROLLINS:
Let them come. Let them
come. 'Cause it's all about
destruction at the end of the
day. At the end of the day, it's
all about confrontation and
destruction. And when they
come to destroy me, I've got
something planned for 'em.
Bang, bang, bang. The tax
weasles get nothing from me.

MATTY GRIPER:
Maybe I'll go by myself.

Multiple Awards

DISTINCTIVE MERIT

TV: OVER 30 SECONDS
Arctic Ground Squirrel

and MERIT

**TV: SPOTS OF VARYING LENGTH,
CAMPAIGN**
Arctic Ground Squirrel •
Wrestlers • Wannabe

Art Directors Lori Campbell,
Stephen Pearson, Scott Vitrone
Creative Director Lori Campbell
Copywriters Lori Campbell,
Stephen Pearson, Scott Vitrone
Director John O'Hagan (hungry man)
Producer Larry Shanet
Editors Mackenzie Cutler, Dave Koza
Agency Dweck & Campbell
Production Company hungry man
Client Dial-A-Mattress
Country United States

80

ARCTIC GROUND SQUIRREL

Open on
Dial-A-Mattress
deliverymen who are
met by an irritable
man dressed as an
Arctic Ground Squirrel.

SQUIRREL:
We're gonna put this around
back.

Mattress men stare in
disbelief.

SQUIRREL (defensively):
What are you looking at?

SQUIRREL (yelling):
You would hibernate, too, for
eight months if you had to live
with what I live with upstairs.

WIFE (voice from upstairs):
Honey, what's going on down
there?

SQUIRREL (screams):
I'm talking to the mattress
guys! Thank you. (Turns to
deliverymen) I'm sorry I'm
taking this out on you. You
know what it is...lack of sleep.
(The deliverymen hand him a
form to sign). Love to,
but...(holds up paw) ...three
fingers. Let that woman let
you out.

SUPER:
Dial-A-Mattress.
Always out there.

WRESTLERS

Open on
Dial-A-Mattress
deliverymen
delivering a mattress.
A man wearing a
wrestling singlet, a
robe, and wrestling
headgear answers
the door.

MAN:
Just drop it right there, guys.
(Taking off his robe).

The man begins to
sign for the mattress
when his wife,
wearing a similar
outfit, comes flying
into frame and
blindsides him. She
drives him into the
mattress and they
begin wrestling.

The deliverymen stare
at the spectacle in
disbelief as the
woman bites her
husband's arm and
knees him in the
crotch. The
deliverymen get the
man to sign for the
mattress while he's
being pummeled.

WIFE:
You are a wuss.

SUPER:
Dial-A-Mattress.
Always out there.

WANNABE

Open on
Dial-A-Mattress
deliverymen standing
next to a garage
door that begins to
rise, revealing an
odd-looking man. A
deliveryman wannabe.
He just motions to
come in as he
delicately strokes
their uniforms.

WANNABE:
I got the middle.

DELIVERYMAN 2:
That's O.K., sir.

WANNABE:
I know what I'm doing, I've
done this before.

SFX:
Smack (the wannabe slams into
the wall and falls to the floor)

WANNABE:
This is a really nice place you
guys have here. Can I use your
bathroom? (The deliverymen
exchange looks of confusion).

Cut to the wannabe as
he signs for the
mattress and gives the
deliveryman a hug.

SUPER:
Dial-A-Mattress.
Always out there.

DISTINCTIVE MERIT

**TV: PUBLIC SERVICE/
NON-PROFIT, CAMPAIGN**

Happily • Warning Label •
New Brand

Art Director Paul Renner
Creative Directors Pete Favat,
Rich Herstek
Copywriter Carl Loeb
Producer Amy Feenan
Director Pete Favat
Recording Studio Soundtrack
Production Company Picture Park
Productions
Agency Arnold Communications, Inc.
Client Massachusetts Department
of Public Health
Country United States

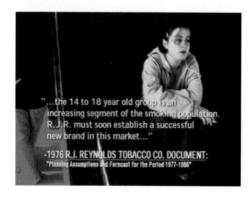

HAPPILY

Open on lockdown of
eleven-year-old girl
smoking a cigarette.

A quote from an R.J.
Reynolds memo fades
up over the image of
the girl, one phrase at
a time, until the quote
is complete.

"Happily... for the
tobacco industry...

...nicotine is both
habituating...

...and unique...

...in its variety of
physiological actions."

The quote stays on
the screen as the
document title fades
up under it.

SUPER: 1972 R.J.
Reynolds Tobacco Co.
Memo: "The Nature of
the Tobacco Business
and the Crucial Role of
Nicotine Therein."

Black screen.

SUPER: They knew.
They always knew.

SUPER: It's time we
made smoking history.
Massachusetts
Department of Public
Health. For the full
document visit
WWW.quitnet.org.
For information call
1-888-4-NO-TOBACCO.

SFX:
Children's playground

DISTINCTIVE MERIT

TV: PUBLIC SERVICE/NON-PROFIT
Funniest Home Videos–April 8, 1998

Art Director Ray Mendez
Copywriter Gregg Wasiak
Producers Miriam Buise,
Ronald Milton
Agency TBWA/Campaign Company
Client Consument en Veiligheid
(Consumer Safety)
Country The Netherlands

ADVERTISING TELEVISION AND CINEMA COMMERCIALS

83

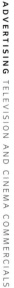

In the past few years, the rate of serious injury caused by falling accidents has increased dramatically among young children in Holland. 80% of these accidents actually happen under parental supervision.

The TV commercial starts with real home-video clips ranging from a little boy toppling off a toilet bowl to a toddler apparently breaking his neck after falling off a windowsill.

These clips are accompanied by "Funniest Home Video" SFX. After a while the funny music and sound effects are taken off and the real sounds of the falls are heard. The viewers realize with shock that the kids are getting very seriously hurt. They are embarrassed that they initially found these clips funny. The message (communicated by a series of titles) is for parents to learn faster than their kids do.

An outdoor campaign was done with the television commercial. Extremely realistic dolls, some moving and laughing, were placed in high, dangerous places around Amsterdam.

They were on lampposts, on the tops of bridges, in trees, on buildings, etc. All were placed in unstable positions, looking like they might fall at any moment. A poster was placed near each doll that read "Don't be surprised by your child. Learn to prevent falling accidents."

This outdoor campaign and TV commercial generated a number of newspaper articles, TV news stories, talkshow segments, and radio discussions. It was estimated that eight of a possible fifteen million people in the Netherlands saw and read about the TV commercial before it actually ran.

DISTINCTIVE MERIT

TV: PUBLIC SERVICE/NON-PROFIT
Surfing Monkey

Art Directors Marne Brobeck,
Greg Wells
Creative Directors Tom Cordner,
Steve Levit, Josh Miller
Copywriter Greg Collins
Producer Julie Shannon
Director Kyle Bergersen
(November Films)
Agency Team One Advertising
Client Partnership for a
Drug-Free America
Country United States

HOST (V.O.):
...Once again, folks, item J-343 is—the surfing monkey coin bank! It's great for graduations, wedding gifts, and I believe we sold out on this one last time, so please, do not let this one pass you by. Now, let's go to caller...Scott in Nashville.

SCOTT (V.O.):
Hello...

HOST (V.O.):
...Now Scott, I understand you just bought fifteen of our surfing monkey banks. Is that true?

SCOTT (V.O., trying to maintain his composure):
...Yeah...

SFX:
Pot-influenced laughter and coughing

Cut to black.

SUPER: Marijuana.
A very expensive habit.

SUPER: Partnership
For A Drug-Free
America

SCOTT (V.O.):
Chill, man...I'm on TV.

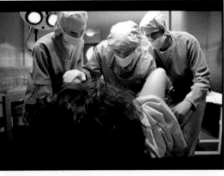

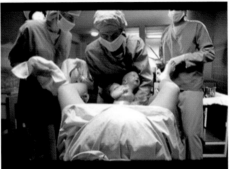

In an operating room, a woman is giving birth to her child. The scene is quite moving but typical. The woman is pushing, her husband is holding her hand, the doctor is sweating and focused. Suddenly, the baby is born. The doctor takes the baby in his hands and gives it the usual pats on its little buttocks. Upon seeing this, the father jumps up and punches the doctor in a fit of rage.

SUPER: If there´s nothing you won´t do for your child...

The father continues punching the doctor.

SUPER: ...have them take a simple routine test.

SUPER: The Argentine Foundation of the Hearing Impaired. 381-9049

Multiple Awards

Art Director Maureen Hufnagel
Creative Directors Pablo Battle,
Juan Cravero, Hernán Jáuregui
Copywriter Sebastián Castañeda
Producers José Bustos, Carlos Volpe
Director Luciano Podcaminsky
Agency Lautrec Nazca
Saatchi & Saatchi
Client The Argentine Foundation
of the Hearing Impaired
Country Argentina

DISTINCTIVE MERIT

TV: PUBLIC SERVICE/NON-PROFIT
Tree

Art Director Valdir Bianchi
Creative Directors
Eugenio Mohallem, Marcello Serpa
Copywriter Cassio Zanatta
Photographer Amon
Producer Zero Filmes
Director Amon
Music Play it Again
Agency Almap BBDO
Client Jovem Pan
Country Brazil

Open in a forest. We see the trunk of a fallen tree. A tracking shot of the rings that show the tree's age.

A SUPER points to a very old ring, almost in the center: "Birth of Napoleon." Then the SUPER goes to a more recent ring: "Birth of van Gogh." Then to an even more recent ring: "Birth of Einstein." Finally the SUPER indicates one of the most recent rings: "Birth of the mother fucker who cut down this tree."

FINAL SUPER:
Stop Deforestation.
Jovem Pan FM.

SFX:
Forest sounds

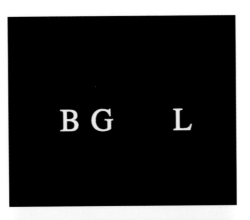

DISTINCTIVE MERIT
**SPECIAL PROMOTION
VIDEO/INFOMERCIAL**

The Fastforward Film

Art Director Arndt Dallmann
Creative Directors Arndt Dallmann,
Guido Heffels
Copywriter Guido Heffels
Designer Oliver Bock
Producer Jassna Sroka
Director Oliver Bock
Agency Springer & Jacoby
Werbung GmbH
Client Markenfilm, Wedel
Country Germany

This film—a total of
210 seconds long—
was shown in the
commercial break of
the *Shots* advertising
VHS magazine. Since
this "commercial part"
is generally seen in
rapid sequence, the
message from
Germany's biggest film
production company
was only visible in
fastforward-mode:

A BIG HELLO TO ALL
FASTFORWARD-USERS
FROM MARKENFILM,
GERMANY.

DISTINCTIVE MERIT

**CONSUMER NEWSPAPER:
FULL PAGE**
Wedding

Art Director Neil Dawson
Copywriter Clive Pickering
Photographer Paul Reas
Agency BMP DDB Ltd.
Client Volkswagen
Country England

Botero
at the São Paulo
Museum of Art.
From March 17 to May 17.

Multiple Awards

DISTINCTIVE MERIT

CONSUMER NEWSPAPER: SPREAD

and DISTINCTIVE MERIT

**POSTERS AND BILLBOARDS:
ENTERTAINMENT
OR SPECIAL EVENT**

Botero

Art Director Pedro Cappeletti
Creative Directors Nizań Guanaes, Tomás Lorente
Copywriter Jáder Rossetto
Photographer Alexandre Catan
Producer Elaine Carvalho
Agency DM9 DDB Publicidade
Client MASP–São Paulo Museum of Art
Country Brazil

DISTINCTIVE MERIT

**CONSUMER MAGAZINE:
MULTI-PAGE**
Just Married

Art Directors Rui Alves, Jan Jacobs,
Gareth Lessing
Creative Director Tony Granger
Copywriters Jonathan Davenport,
Gareth Lessing, Clare McNally
Photographers Martin Taylor,
Karl Bieker
Illustrator Rui Alves
Typographers Bibi Lotter,
Janine Wittrowski
Agency TBWA Hunt Lascaris
Client Land Rover
Country South Africa

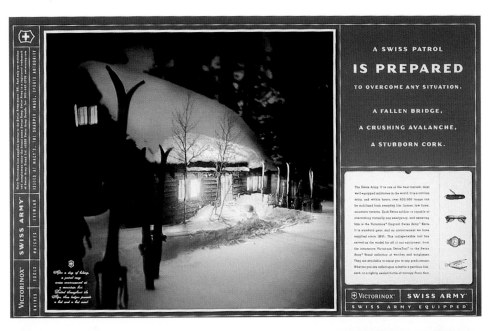

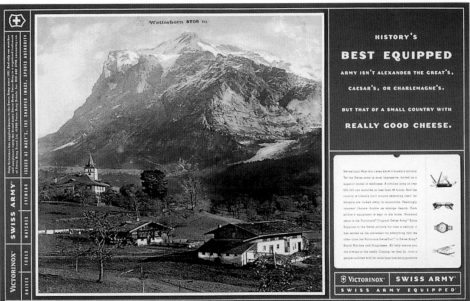

DISTINCTIVE MERIT

CONSUMER MAGAZINE: SPREAD
Stubborn Cork • Cheese •
Hardware Store

Art Director Monica Taylor
Creative Directors Greg Bokor,
Jim Garaventi
Copywriter Dylan Lee
Photography Ray Meeks,
Geoff Stein, and Stock
Typography M&H Type
Agency Mullen Advertising
Client Swiss Army Brands
Country United States

Multiple Awards

DISTINCTIVE MERIT

TRADE MAGAZINE: FULL PAGE
Traffic Jam

---

and MERIT

TRADE MAGAZINE: FULL PAGE, CAMPAIGN
Traffic Jam • Hooker • Riot

Art Director Steve Mitchell
Creative Directors Doug Adkins, Steve Mitchell
Copywriter Doug Adkins
Photographer Rick Dublin
Agency Hunt Adkins
Client Dublin Productions
Country United States

92

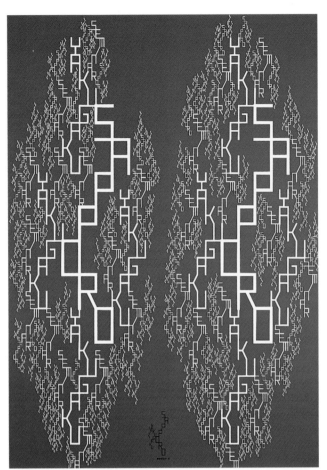

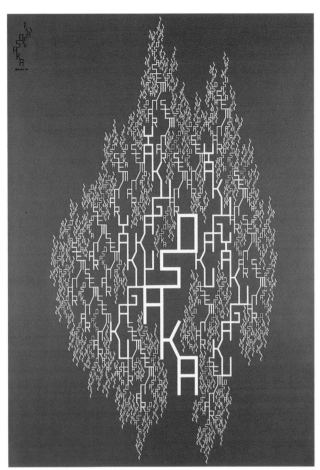

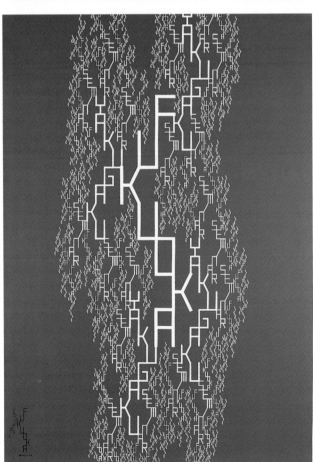

DISTINCTIVE MERIT

**POSTERS AND BILLBOARDS:
PROMOTIONAL**

Pharmaceutical College

Director Norito Shinmura
Designers Mihoko Ichikawa,
Norito Shinmura
Client Yakugaku Seminar
Country Japan

セガは、倒れたままなのか？

SEGA

DISTINCTIVE MERIT

PROMOTIONAL
Is SEGA Still Lying Where He Fell?

Art Directors Seijo Kawaguchi, Noritoshi Nishioka
Creative Director Yasumichi Oka
Copywriter Sho Akiyama
Designers Toshihiro Hyodo, Kengo Kato, Noritoshi Nishioka, Makoto Sawada
Photographer Hatsuhiko Okada
Executive Producer Yasushi Akimoto
Producer Hiroaki Imai
Coordinator Keiichi Shimazu
Agency Dentsu Inc.
Client SEGA Enterprises
Country Japan

DISTINCTIVE MERIT

PROMOTIONAL
With Hakle/Without Hakle

Art Directors Denis Schwarz,
Martin Spillmann
Creative Director Martin Spillmann
Copywriter Martin Spillmann
Photographer Ronald Kroetzer
Agency Advico Young + Rubicam
Client Hakle Toilet Paper
Country Switzerland

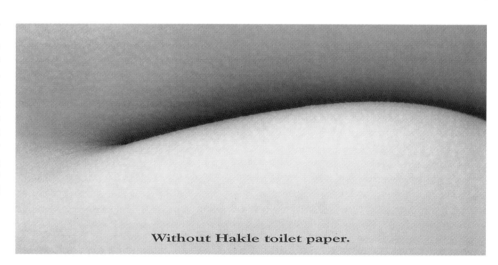

Without Hakle toilet paper.

With Hakle toilet paper.

Copying ❶ – ❺

One of the most important copying techniques is that of making same-size copies from originals (100%). (1) First turn the machine on: to do this, press the master button to its functioning position indicated by a 1 ("One"). (Tip: The machine automatically turns itself to standby mode a short while after the last usage so as to save energy.) Loading the originals: there are two ways to proceed with this: either (2) put multiple originals face upwards in the document feeder, or (3) lay one of the originals face downwards on the glassface (4) Next, enter the required number of copies using the machines interface. (Tip: if you enter the wrong number of copies , press the "C" button to clear.) (5) By pressing the "Start" button, copying will be initiated. Use the "Stop" but to bring the process to an end.

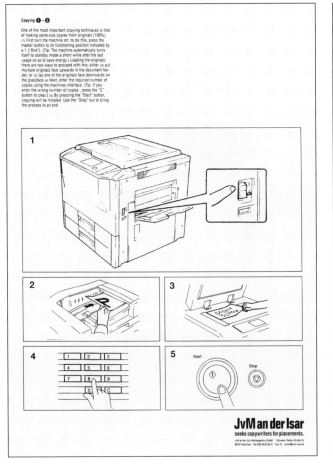

JvM an der Isar

seeks copywriters for placements.

JvM an der Isar Werbeagentur GmbH · Schwere-Reiter-Straße 35
80797 München · Tel. 089/38 6326-0 · Fax-13 · email@jvm-isar.de

Preparing coffee ❶ – ❺

Remove glass jug. Remove lid and pour in water. (1) Open lid of water container and (2) pour water into one of the two water containers (for 1 -3 cups, use **left**- hand side of appliance). (3) Water level can also be read off the indicator. (The graduations on the indicator refer to the fresh water volumes. The subsequent volume of coffee is smaller, since the coffee powder absorbs water.) (4) Swing out the filter holder (5) Insert the filter paper: Type 4 (1x4) (and press in lightly by hand). (6) Put in the ground coffee. The correct quantity can be determined by using a coffee measure. For medium-strong coffee, 1 measure (about 6-7) will be required for each cup. (7) Swing back the filter holder so that it engages properly. Return the glass jug with the lid on to its original position on the appliance. (8) Switch on the appliance. The indicator lamp will light up to show that it is in operation. Remove the glass jug at the end of filtering. (9) Put the glass jug back onto the hotplate to keep the coffee hot.

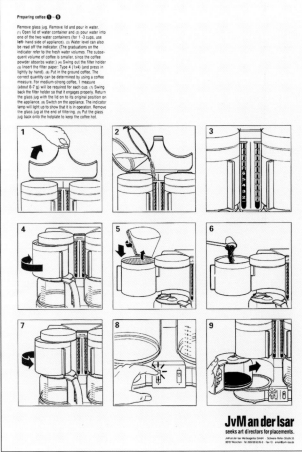

JvM an der Isar

seeks art directors for placements.

JvM an der Isar Werbeagentur GmbH · Schwere-Reiter-Straße 35
80797 München · Tel. 089/38 6326-0 · Fax-13 · email@jvm-isar.de

Binding ❶ – ❼

Before binding, ensure that all papers are as correctly aligned as possible (1) Put the handle in an upright, slightly forward position and guide the sheets into the binder. (Tip: Be careful not to put too many sheets into the binder at once.) (2) Pull the handle down firmly, then replace it to the original position so that punched sheets can be removed. When all sheets have been punched, binding can commence. (3) Place the binding element open-side up behind the metal fingers (4) Push the handle to the rear - the metal fingers will slice into the rings and open them. (5) Now guide the punched sheets onto the binding element, binding them vertically. (6) When all sheets are attached to the binding element, lay them in a horizontal position and pull the handle back to a vertical position. (7) The binding is now complete and the booklet can be removed vertically.

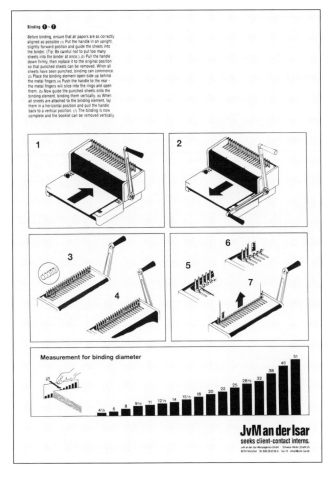

Measurement for binding diameter

JvM an der Isar

seeks client-contact interns.

JvM an der Isar Werbeagentur GmbH · Schwere-Reiter-Straße 35
80797 München · Tel. 089/38 6326-0 · Fax-13 · email@jvm-isar.de

DISTINCTIVE MERIT

PROMOTIONAL, CAMPAIGN
Placement Posters

Art Director Tobias Eichinger
Creative Director Oliver Voss
Copywriter Till Hohmann
Agency Jung von Matt an der Isar
Client Jung von Matt an der Isar
Country Germany

DISTINCTIVE MERIT

PRODUCT OR SERVICE
Camponesa Steak House:
Now Delivering

Art Director Paulo Dhiel
Creative Director Edson Athayde
Copywriters Cassio Jeha, Frederico Saldanha
Photographer Picto
Agency Edson Comunicação
Client Camponesa Restaurant
Country Portugal

DISTINCTIVE MERIT
PRODUCT OR SERVICE
Wave

Art Director Pedro Cappeletti
Creative Directors Nizan Guanaes, Tomás Lorente
Copywriter Jáder Rossetto
Photographer Fabio Bataglia
Producer Elaine Carvalho
Agency DM9 DDB Publicidade
Client Venice
Country Brazil

DISTINCTIVE MERIT

PRODUCT OR SERVICE
Led's Tattoo–Tiger

Art Directors Andre Nassar,
Bruno Prosperi
Creative Director Silvios Matos
Designer Andre Nassar
Illustrator Andre Nassar
Producer Claudio Dirani
Agency FischerAmerica
Client Led's Tattoo House
Country Brazil

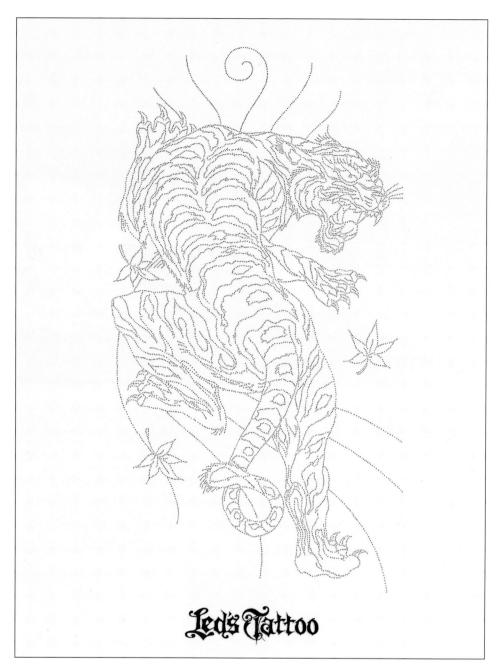

The
tenderest
meat
in town.

DISTINCTIVE MERIT

PRODUCT OR SERVICE
Plastic Cutlery

Art Director Erh Ray
Creative Directors Nizan Guanaes, Tomás Lorente
Copywriter Jose Henrique Borghi
Photographer Rafael Costa
Producer Elaine Carvalho
Agency DM9 DDB Publicidade
Client Esplanada Grill
Country Brazil

New Babylandia. Opening November 18th in Campinas.

BABYLANDIA
the baby store

DISTINCTIVE MERIT

**ENTERTAINMENT
OR SPECIAL EVENT**
Umbilical Cord

Art Director Pedro Cappeletti
Creative Directors Nizan Guanaes, Tomás Lorente
Copywriter Jáder Rossetto
Photographer Richard Kohout
Producer Elaine Carvalho
Agency DM9 DDB Publicidade
Client Babylandia
Country Brazil

DISTINCTIVE MERIT

PUBLIC SERVICE/NON-PROFIT OR EDUCATIONAL
Blows Other Museums Away

Art Director Greg Rowan
Copywriter Bob Hall
Agency J. Walter Thompson Company West
Client USS Hornet Museum
Country United States

IF YOU ARE FALSELY ACCUSED BY THE GOVERNMENT, THEY ISSUE A FORMAL APOLOGY.

UNLESS, OF COURSE, YOU HAPPEN TO BE DEAD.

Human beings are fallible. So is the United States justice system. As long as the death penalty and human error exist, innocent people will be executed. Like the 32 people who were put to death and later found innocent. Or the 47 we've wrongfully imprisoned on death row for the better parts of their adult lives. And guilty or innocent, every execution costs tax payers an average of $11 million, while life in prison costs about $750,000. That's tens of millions of dollars a year that could be used for things like juvenile centers, drug and alcohol treatment, and education. To help us find alternatives to the death penalty, call 1-800-973-6548.

Citizens United for Alternatives to the Death Penalty

DISTINCTIVE MERIT

PUBLIC SERVICE/NON-PROFIT OR EDUCATIONAL

Apology

Art Director Bart Cleveland
Copywriter Cathy Carlisi
Photographer Ken Light
Producer Jeff Evanston
Agency Sawyer Riley Compton
Client Citizens United for Alternatives to the Death Penalty
Country United States

海の魚は、森に育てられる。

性がこわれたら、子孫は残せなくなる。

誰かのゴミが、彼の家。

DISTINCTIVE MERIT

**PUBLIC SERVICE/NON-PROFIT
OR EDUCATIONAL**
Thinking of the Sea a
Hundred Years Ahead

Art Director Norito Shinmura
Copywriter Masakazu Nifuji
Designer Norito Shinmura
Photographer Ko Hosokawa
Client Yamaguchi Federation of
Fisheries Cooperative Association
Country Japan

Multiple Awards

DISTINCTIVE MERIT
TRANSIT, CAMPAIGN
WEND 106.5 FM

and DISTINCTIVE MERIT
TRANSIT
We Wish Celine Dion Had
Been on the Titanic

Art Director John Boone
Creative Directors John Boone,
David Oakley
Copywriter David Oakley
Print Producer Angie Faunce
Agency The Martin Agency
Client WEND FM Radio
Country United States

SURE, WE KNOW
GARTH BROOKS
WASN'T HE IN WAYNE'S WORLD?
106.5 THE END

WE'LL DO A TRIBUTE TO
☆ ELVIS ☆
WHEN HE DIES
106.5 THE END

WE'LL PLAY
HANSON
IF YOU'LL CLEAN UP THE VOMIT
106.5 THE END

WHICH CAME FIRST
THE SPICE GIRLS
OR THE MUTE BUTTON?
106.5 THE END

WE WISH
CELINE DION
HAD BEEN ON THE TITANIC
106.5 THE END

DISTINCTIVE MERIT

TRANSIT

If TV's So Bad for You, Why Is There
One in Every Hospital Room?

Art Director Sara Riesgo
Creative Director Jerry Gentile
Copywriter Raymond Hwang
Agency TBWA Chiat/Day
Client ABC Television Network
Country United States

 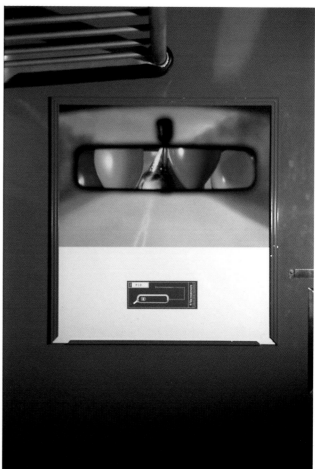

106

Multiple Awards

DISTINCTIVE MERIT

**BILLBOARDS, DIORAMA,
OR PAINTED SPECTACULAR**
Tooth • Balloons • Corn

and DISTINCTIVE MERIT

**BILLBOARDS, DIORAMA,
OR PAINTED SPECTACULAR**
Tooth

Art Directors Greg Bokor,
Gerard Caputo
Creative Directors Edward Boches,
Greg Bokor, Jim Garaventi
Copywriter Jim Garaventi
Photographers Susie Cushner,
Nora Scarlet
Agency Mullen Advertising
Client Swiss Army Brands
Country United States

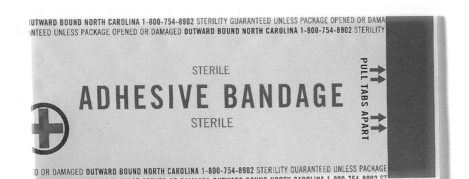

DISTINCTIVE MERIT

BROCHURE
Band-Aid

Art Director Doug Pedersen
Creative Director Jim Mountjoy
Copywriter Curtis Smith
Photographer Pat Staub
Illustrator Floyd Coffey
Agency Loeffler Ketchum Mountjoy
Client Outward Bound
Country United States

DISTINCTIVE MERIT

RADIO: OVER 30 SECONDS
Tomorrow Never Dies

Creative Director Arthur Bijur
Copywriters Adam Chasnow,
Ian Reichenthal
Producer Arlene Adoremos
Engineer Roy Kamen
Studio Kamen Entertainment Group
Agency Cliff Freeman and Partners
Client Hollywood Video
Country United States

108

TOMORROW NEVER DIES

All dialogue and SFX extremely fast throughout

ANNOUNCER: Hollywood Video presents…"Sixty Second Theater." Where we try (unsuccessfully) to pack all the action and drama of a two-hour Hollywood production into sixty seconds. Today's presentation, "Tomorrow Never Dies."

SFX: Bond-style music sting

M: 007, a brilliant but evil madman is…

BOND (Pierce Brosnan sound-alike): …threatening the security of the world, naturally. All right, where's "Q" with my gadgets?

SFX: Footsteps

Q: Bond, here are your gadgets.

Bond: What does this pen do?

Q: Kills people.

Bond: This tie clip?

Q: Kills people.

Bond: What does this whoopee cushion do?

SFX: Whoopee cushion fart

Q: Kills people.

BOND: Nasty. Then I'm off to an exotic destination.

SFX: Bond-style music sting

SFX: Airplane landing

BOND: Ah, here I am.

SEXYPANTS (French accent): Hello, Mr. Bond. I'm Ms. Sexypants.

BOND: Splendid. Shall we get a room?

SFX: Kissing

SFX: Knocking on door

VILLAIN (disguises his voice to sound like a maid): Housekeeping!

SFX: Door handle opening

VILLAIN (German accent): A-ha!

SFX: Bond music sting

SFX: Gun cocking

VILLAIN: I have you now, James Bontt!

BOND: Bond. James Bond.

VILLAIN: What did I say?

BOND: Excuse me, would you like to sit on this whoopee cushion?

VILLAIN (laughs hysterically): Good!

SFX: Whoopee cushion fart then loud explosion

VILLAIN: (screams)

SEXYPANTS: The world is safe again. Oh, James.

BOND: Weren't you in on the plot to kill me?

SEXYPANTS: Yeah.

BOND: Oh, what the heck. You've got nice legs.

SFX: Hollywood Video theme music

ANNOUNCER: If this doesn't satisfy your urge to see "Tomorrow Never Dies," (and we can't say we blame you) then rent it today at Hollywood Video where "Tomorrow Never Dies" is guaranteed to be in-stock, or next time it's free. Welcome to Hollywood. Hollywood Video. Celebrity voices impersonated.

All dialogue and SFX
extremely fast
throughout

ANNOUNCER: Hollywood Video presents..."Sixty Second Theater." Where we try (unsuccessfully) to pack all the action and suspense of a two-hour Hollywood production into sixty seconds. Today's presentation, "Scream 2."

SFX: Scary music chords

SIDNEY: Well, it's just us seven incredibly attractive sorority girls here alone in our nightgowns...

KILLER (gravelly voice): Must kill!

DEBBIE: Did you hear something?

ALISON: I'll go outside alone and investigate!

SFX: Door opening

KILLER: Must kill!

SFX: Woman screaming; slashing sound; bodyfall

SIDNEY: What was that?

DEBBIE: I'll go check!

SFX: Door opening

KILLER: Must kill!

SFX: Woman screaming; slashing sound; bodyfall

HALLIE: There's that noise again. I'm scared!

CICI-HALLIE-LOIS: Let's stick together!

SFX: Scary music up and under

SIDNEY: I've got a better plan! Lois, you hide in the utility shed with the gas-powered cutting and shearing equipment!

LOIS: Okay!

SIDNEY: Cici, you go up to the dark and slippery roof and hide right near the edge!

CICI: All right!

SIDNEY: Hallie, whatever you do, don't leave my side.

HALLIE: Good idea...I have to go the bathroom.

SIDNEY: Ooohh, there's an old outhouse near the swamp!

HALLIE: Perfect!

CICI-HALLIE-LOIS (together): Bye!

SFX: Door opening

KILLER: Must kill! Must kill! Must kill!

SFX: Three women screaming; three slashing sounds; three bodyfalls

SFX: Doorbell

SIDNEY (cheerful): Back already?

SFX: Door opening

KILLER: Must kill!

SIDNEY: Oh my! Good thing I took that kickboxing class! Hi-ya!

SFX: Karate kicks; fighting

KILLER (In pain): Ouch! No, not there!

SFX: Body fall.

Sidney: He sure looks dead.

KILLER: No, I'm not.

SIDNEY: I can't think of a better time to turn my back and put my guard down.

KILLER: Must...

SFX: Karate kick

KILLER (in pain): ...Kill.

SFX: Hollywood Video theme music

ANNOUNCER: If this doesn't satisfy your urge to see "Scream 2," (and we can't say we blame you) then rent it today at Hollywood Video where "Scream 2" is guaranteed to be in-stock, or next time it's free. Welcome to Hollywood. Hollywood Video. Celebrity voices impersonated.

DISTINCTIVE MERIT

RADIO: OVER 30 SECONDS
Scream 2

Creative Director Arthur Bijur
Copywriters Roger Camp,
Adam Chasnow, Ian Reichenthal
Producer Arlene Adoremos
Engineer Roy Kamen
Studio Kamen Entertainment Group
Agency Cliff Freeman and Partners
Client Hollywood Video
Country United States

ADVERTISING RADIO

109

MERIT

**TV: 30 SECONDS OR LESS,
CAMPAIGN**
Rubber Ducky • PG-13 • Snooze

Art Director Sharon Dershin
Creative Directors Tim Kane,
Jon Moore
Copywriter Jody Finver
Photographer Julian Whatley
Line Producer Mary Ann Marino
Director Bob Giraldi
Producer Laurie Irwin
Production Company Giraldi Suarez
Productions
Agency Ammirati Puris Lintas
Client Ameritech
Country United States

RUBBER DUCKY

Camera in hallway looking through doorway of bathroom while dad gives his son a bath.	SFX: Water splashing
	BOY (singing): H I K K L O M E L L O P Q R S T U V W X Y an Z...
SUPER: Would you interrupt this moment for an aluminum siding deal?	
SUPER: Introducing privacy manager, a new service from Ameritech.	BOY: Now I know my ABC, next time won't you sing wiv me?
SUPER: It stops unwanted, unidentified calls before your phone even rings.	
SUPER: Interested? Call 1-800-PRIVACY.	DAD: All right.
SUPER: Privacy Manager 1-800-PRIVACY.	
SUPER: In a world of technology, people make the difference. Ameritech.	

MERIT

TV: 30 SECONDS OR LESS, CAMPAIGN

Blimpie Bloopers: Run • Pop-up • Get the Ball

Art Director Frank Fusco
Creative Directors Brendan Donovan, Bill Oberlander
Copywriters Bob Havlena, Alan Jacobs
Producer Betsy Schoenfeld
Director Harvey Wang
Editor Jordan Green
Production Company Stieffel & Co.
Agency Kirshenbaum Bond & Partners
Client Blimpie Subs & Salads
Country United States

BLIMPIE BLOOPERS: RUN

DAD:
Run Billy, run, run, Billy, run, Billy, run. Oh man, your mom's gonna kill me.

ANNOUNCER:
Got a funny youth baseball video? Enter the Blimpie Blooper contest. Pick up an entry form at your neighborhood Blimpie restaurant.

Multiple Awards

MERIT

**TV: 30 SECONDS OR LESS,
CAMPAIGN**
Horrors • Birds • Credits

and MERIT

TV: 30 SECONDS OR LESS
Credits

Art Director Matt Vescovo
Creative Director Arthur Bijur
Copywriter Eric Silver
Producer Nick Felder
Director Baker Smith
Editor Gavin Cutler
Studio Tate & Partners
Agency Cliff Freeman and Partners
Client Hollywood Video
Country United States

CREDITS

Open inside Hollywood
Video store. Customer
is talking to clerk.

MAN:
So you're saying select new
releases are guaranteed every
single day of the week.

CLERK:
That's right.

Fade to black. Movie
credits start to roll
(listing everyone
responsible for
previous five seconds
of dialogue).

SUPER: Welcome to
Hollywood.

LOGO: Hollywood
Video.

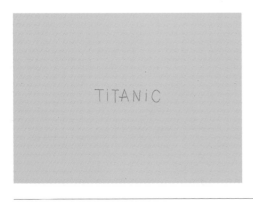

TITANIC

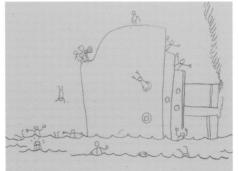

MERIT

**TV: 30 SECONDS OR LESS,
CAMPAIGN**
Titanic • The Godfather •
The English Patient

Art Directors John Shirley,
Cody Spinadel
Creative Director Jerry Gentile
Copywriter Michael Collado
Producer Kara O'Neill
Director Mike Wellins
Agency TBWA Chiat/Day
Client ABC Television Network
Country United States

THE GODFATHER

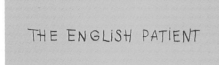

THE ENGLISH PATIENT

THE GODFATHER

SUPER: The Godfather	ANNOUNCER: ABC's Cheap Cinema Theatre Presents…
Open to a guy standing over a dead body.	THUG: They shot Sonny.
Cut to three mobsters shooting one guy.	SHOT GUY: Ow. Ow. Ow.
Open to a guy standing over a dead body.	THUG: They shot Frankie.
Cut to three mobsters shooting one guy.	SHOT GUY: Ow. Ow. Ow.
	ANNOUNCER: Classic movies inexpensively recreated so you can skip the theater and spend more time watching TV.

MERIT

TV: 30 SECONDS OR LESS, CAMPAIGN

Cathlab • Diagnosis • Surgery • Pods • Recovery

Art Director Sharon Harms
Creative Director Kevin Endres
Copywriter Kevin Endres
Photographer Tom Hurwitz
Producer Linda Tesa-Olken
Director Barbara Kopple
Agency Endres & Wilson
Client Saint Thomas Health Services
Country United States

114

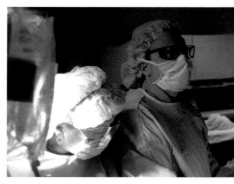

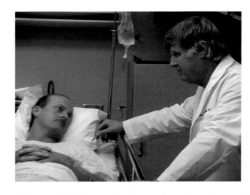

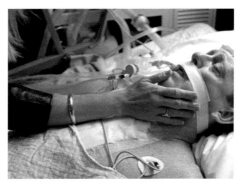

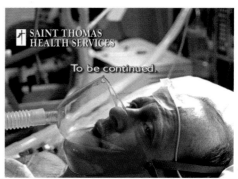

CATHLAB

Shot of doctors and nurses in the middle of a medical procedure, looking at monitors.

SUPER: This story is real. There are no scripts and no actors.

Close-up of Randy. Close-up of monitor.

DOCTOR:
How are you doing Randy?

RANDY:
I'm doing great.

DOCTOR:
We just took a picture of your aorta and it is huge. I want to see what these pictures look like once they're developed, and we'll decide whether in addition to the replacement of the aorta and valve, you may need one bypass.

RANDY:
Thank you.

Doctor reviewing X-ray on monitor.

DOCTOR:
There is a suggestion right here of a dissection flap. I looked at those pictures and...

Doctor talking to Randy.

RANDY:
Yeah...

DOCTOR:
...I think there may be a very small tear in the aorta.

SUPER: Saint Thomas Health Services. Caring for you and those around you.

To be continued.

MERIT

TV: 30 SECONDS OR LESS
Fridge

Art Director Jeff Williams
Creative Director Susan Hoffman
Copywriter Jeff Kling
Producer Jeff Selis
Director Errol Morris
Production Company @radical.media
Agency Wieden & Kennedy
Client Miller Brewing Company
Country United States

Static shot of an old silver metallic fridge at the end of a hallway.

V.O.:
Hear that? That's music to a man's ears. That's the sound of one friend keeping another friend cold. Thank you, refrigerator.

MERIT

TV: 30 SECONDS OR LESS
Kordell Delivers

Art Director Tim Hanrahan
Creative Directors Hal Curtis,
Chuck McBride
Copywriter Canice Neary
Director of Photography
David Stockton
Executive Producer Gregg Stern
Producer Amy Davenport
Line Producer Glenn Rudolph
Director Tenney Fairchild
Editor Peter Wiedensmith
Sound Designer Rich Pavone
Composer Jimmy Haun
Agency Wieden & Kennedy
Client Nike
Country United States

As a wistful, upbeat song plays in the background, football star Kordell Stewart runs through an idyllic suburban community delivering newspapers.

The friendly residents are unprepared for his cheerful but aggressive delivery style. He unwittingly wreaks havoc on the neighborhood as his superhuman throw causes several mishaps.

(What are you getting ready for?)

TV: 30 SECONDS OR LESS
Dances with Dog

Art Director Harvey Marco
Creative Director David Lubars
Copywriter Dean Buckhorn
Producer Julie Hampel
Director Tarsem
Production Company @radical.media
Agency Fallon McElligott
Client Miller Brewing Company
Country United States

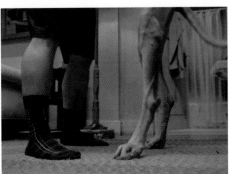

Open on a great dane running into the living room, carrying a Miller Lite in his mouth. The dog places the beer on the table in front of his owner. He looks expectantly at the guy. The guy looks at the dog, then the beer, then the dog again. He ponders, while the dog continues to look at him pleadingly. He gives in.

The dog is on its hind legs with its front paws on the guy's shoulders. They begin to dance. The guy looks embarrassed—he looks at the dog and sort of grimaces. The dog puts its head on the guy's shoulder.

SUPER: The things you do for beer!

SFX:
Miller Lite music

MERIT

TV: 30 SECONDS OR LESS
Soccer

Art Director Walt Connelly
Creative Directors Ron Berger,
Michael Lee, Paul Wolfe
Copywriter Larry Silberfein
Producer Noel Tirsh
Director Gore Verbinsky
Music Elias
Agency Messner Vetere Berger
McNamee Schmetterer/Euro RSCG
Client Intel
Country United States

Open on a soccer player inbounding the ball. As the game ensues, it is revealed that the yellow team's goalie hasn't processed yet. (Much like what happens on your computer when you're waiting for something to process). All we see are his feet frantically running back and forth. Above him appears the processing bar that says "Processing Goalie." Once his teammates realize the situation, they desperately try to keep their opponent from moving the ball downfield. Cut back and forth between the goalie processing a little at a time and the opponents moving closer and closer to the goal. Another processing bar appears above the goalie that says "Still Processing."

Finally the opponent takes a shot at the goal. Our processing goalie, who is still headless, tries to block the shot, but ends up running into the goal post.

A computer message box pops up on the screen: Time for a Pentium II processor?

Cut to Intel logo on soccer ball and Intel bong.

V.O.:
Time for a Pentium II processor?

TV: 30 SECONDS OR LESS
Seance

Art Director Harvey Marco
Creative Director David Lubars
Copywriter Dean Buckhorn
Producer Julie Hampel
Director Tarsem
Production Company @radical.media
Agency Fallon McElligott
Client Miller Brewing Company
Country United States

We see several older women sitting around a table with a psychic.

SFX:
Miller Lite music

MEDIUM:
I feel a presence....
Harold, is that you?

Psychic twitches and her face takes on a whole new expression.

SFX:
Rush of wind

Suddenly, the psychic stands up and walks into the kitchen.

WIFE:
Harold???

The psychic comes back holding a Miller Lite bottle. She walks right past the table and into the living room. She bends over, picks up the remote, and scratches her butt. At that moment a look of recognition comes over the wife's face.

WIFE:
Harold?

WIFE:
Harold!!!!!

SUPER: You always come back for more.

TV: 30 SECONDS OR LESS
Bell (Contender)

Art Director Gary Pacoe
Creative Director Jerry Gentile
Copywriter John Payne
Producer Brigette Whisnant
Director David Dorkin
Agency TBWA Chiat/Day
Client Sony Computer Entertainment
Country United States

Open on traditional monastery with monks walking around.	SFX: Music
One monk pulls on a rope to sound a large bell.	SFX: Bell ringing
Immediately after the bell rings, two monks engage in a fist fight.	SFX: Punching
Cut to two well-dressed women with shopping bags on a busy street corner. As a child rides by on a bike and rings a bell, the women drop their bags and start fighting.	SFX: Bike bell rings
Cut to a hotel lobby with two bellhops and a customer. When the customer rings the service bell, the bellhops begin boxing.	SFX: Punching
	SFX: Bell rings
LOGO: Contender	SFX: Punching
Cut to game footage.	ANNOUNCER (V.O.): Introducing Contender…Once the bell rings, all hell breaks loose.
Cut to women on street corner. One is celebrating victory over the other.	WOMAN #1: Yeah, who's the man?

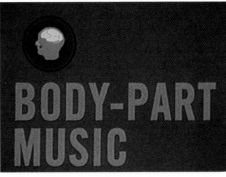

TV: 30 SECONDS OR LESS
Body Part Music

Art Director Taras Wayner
Creative Director David Angelo
Copywriter Kevin Roddy
Graphic Designer Paul McMinean
Producer Maresa Wickham
Director Vaughan Arnell
Editor Doug Walker
Studio Propaganda Films
Agency Cliff Freeman and Partners
Client Cherry Coke
Country United States

SUPER: New thinking from Cherry Coke. Body-part music.

V.O.:
New thinking from Cherry Coke. Body-part music.

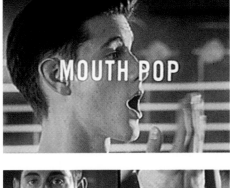

Cut to a full-body shot of teen wearing nothing but boxer shorts.

V.O.:
A useful guide to playing a human symphony.

The teen turns to his right, lifts his leg, puts his hand behind his knee, and squeezes, creating a sound.
SUPER: Kneepit squeeze.

V.O.:
There's the kneepit squeeze.

Cut to a close-up of the teen as he flicks his cheek with his forefinger.
SUPER: Cheek flick.

V.O.:
The cheek flick.

Cut to a close-up of the teen as he opens his mouth and pops it with his hand.
SUPER: Mouth pop.

V.O.:
Mouth pop.

Cut to a close-up of the teen's stomach, he rubs it, up and down, creating a sound.
SUPER: Stomach rub.

V.O.:
The stomach rub.

Cut to a close-up of the teen's armpit area as he sticks his hand into his pit and squeezes.
SUPER: Armpit squeeze.

V.O.:
And the armpit squeeze.

Cut to various quick cuts of the teen repeating several of these actions along with others.

V.O.:
Put 'em together and you can play anything. Try Beethoven's Fifth.

Cut to the screen divided into four squares. Inside each square is a different part of the teen's anatomy. Beethoven's Fifth Symphony begins playing.... And the teen plays different parts of his body along with it.

Cut to a wide shot of the teen standing in a music room while a music conductor paces back and forth conducting the symphony as the teen plays his body.

Cut to shot of Cherry Coke can with atom revolving around it. Pull back to reveal "Do Something Different" title.

V.O.:
This new thought is from Cherry Coke, who encourages you to do something different today.

MERIT

TV: 30 SECONDS OR LESS
Baseball

Art Directors Terry Finley,
Kevin Samuels
Executive Creative Directors
John Doyle, Dave O'Hare
Creative Directors Greg Ketchum,
Dennis Lim
Copywriter Matt Smukler
Producer Tom Foley
Director Peter Care
Music Asche & Spencer
Production Company Satellite
Agency Publicis & Hal Riney
Client Saturn Corporation
Country United States

Medium shot of man asleep in chair. Close-up of man as he hears a thud. Wide shot as man gets out of chair. Close-up on man's face as he looks out the window. Reverse wide shot of kids playing baseball on front lawn. One kid swings, misses, and ball hits car. Cut back to close-up of man looking out window.

Wide shot of man running down stairs.

Medium shot of kid, swings at pitch, misses, ball hits car.

Medium shot as man comes out of front door of house.

Reverse shot of two kids looking up at man. Close-up of kid with bat.

Wide shot as man walks up to kid with bat and takes the bat from him.

Close-up on kid as man walks past with bat in hand.

Low angle shot of man "at the plate" waiting for pitch. Wide shot from side angle with man at bat.

V.O.:
Nature show sounds come from TV

MAN:
Oh, no…no, no, no…
What are you doing?
Gimme the bat.
Your stance is all wrong.

KID:
Huh?

MAN:
Check this out.
Come to papa…

V.O.:
The Saturn wagon, with easy-to-maintain, dent-resistant doors.

MAN:
Good pitch…I'll see you guys

MERIT

TV: 30 SECONDS OR LESS
Spike Lee

Art Director Arty Tan
Creative Directors Hal Curtis, Chuck McBride
Copywriter Mike Folino
Director of Photography Max Malkin
Producers Jennifer Dennis (Wieden & Kennedy), Stephen Orent, John Towse (hungry man)
Director Hank Perlman
Editor Paul Norling (FilmCore)
Production Company hungry man
Agency Wieden & Kennedy
Client Nike
Country United States

SPIKE LEE:
Get her, get her, get her. Get on Miller, get on Miller. Spread out, oh! Regina Miller: You stink!

REGINA MILLER:
Sit down.

SPIKE LEE:
You stink. She ain't got nothing. She ain't got nothing. That was luck.

REGINA MILLER:
Shut up.

SPIKE LEE:
That was luck. You shut up. St. Ignatius eighth grade girl's basketball… it's fantastic!

TAG LINE: Start the season quick.

SPIKE LEE:
Regina, where's your game at?

REGINA MILLER:
Sit down.

SPIKE LEE:
Regina. Where's your game at?

REGINA MILLER:
Sit down.

SPIKE LEE:
Regina, where's your game at?

REGINA MILLER:
Shut up.

TV: 30 SECONDS OR LESS

Homerun (62 & Counting)

Art Director Chris Cereda
Creative Directors Jonathan Cranin,
Joyce King Thomas
Copywriter Eric Goldstein
Producer Greg Lotus
Director Stock Footage
Editor Alan Morris
Music RK Music
Editing House Invisible Dog
Production Company Stock Footage
Agency McCann-Erickson
Client MasterCard
Country United States

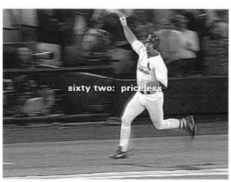

The pitcher has the ball in his hand behind his back, ready to pitch.

He pitches to Mark McGwire.

McGwire swings and hits a homerun.

Next ball is pitched to Sammy Sosa and he hits a homerun.

McGwire hits a homerun. Sosa hits a homerun.

McGwire hits a homerun.

Sosa hits a homerun and it goes out of the stadium, over fans heads, and breaks a car windshield.

McGwire hits a homerun with many camera flashes in the stands.

Sosa hits a homerun.

McGwire takes a victory run around the bases.

Sosa takes a victory run around the bases.

McGwire's team hugs and congratulates him.

Sosa's team hugs and congratulates him.

McGwire and Sosa hug each other.

LOGO: MasterCard designed with baseballs.

Art Director Rob Palmer

Creative Directors Hal Curtis,
Chuck McBride

Copywriter Canice Neary

Producer Jennifer Smieja

Director Ralf Schmerberg

Production Company @radical.media

Agency Wieden & Kennedy

Client Nike

Country United States

The matador enters the arena. The crowd chants in anticipation of "the running of the bulls." The bulls charge and participators run furiously to stay alive.

In front of the arena entrance five football players climb over the fence onto the street.

The football players position themselves in a "line" against the oncoming bulls. From above we see the bulls charge at the players.

The players prepare to "block" the bulls.

Inside the stadium, the matador and crowd peer out the entrance to see what has happened or not happened.

SFX:
Groans, cattle sounds

The matador is confused.

MATADOR:
Donde esta los toros?

SUPER: What are you getting ready for? Nike.

MERIT

TV: OVER 30 SECONDS
Silence

Art Director Eric Urmetzer
Creative Directors Torsten Rieken,
Jan Ritter
Copywriter Reinhard Craseman
Producer Markenfilm
Director Fabrice Carazo
Sound Design Studio Monteur, Paris
Agency Springer & Jacoby
Werbung GmbH
Client Daimler Chrysler AG
Country Germany

The CDI-diesel.
You can't hear a thing.

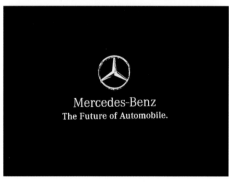

Mercedes-Benz
The Future of Automobile.

An elderly, elegant gentleman is getting ready. The soundtrack is strangely muffled, only becoming sharp and clear when the man places a hearing aid in his ear. He is picked up by his son in a new Mercedes. They drive off. For some reason, the old gentleman once again hears nothing. He increases the volume on his hearing aid. He still can't hear anything, until his worried son asks him if everything is ok. The hearing aid whistles loudly. The son's words sound like a thunder clap.

SUPER: The CDI-diesel. You can't hear a thing.

LOGO: Mercedes-Benz

SUPER: The Future of Automobile.

TV: OVER 30 SECONDS
Swimming Cap

Creative Director Horst Klemm
Copywriter Veikko Hille
Producer Klaus Lind
Director Trevor Robinson
Music Wilbert Hirsch
Studio Cobblestone Pictures Ltd.
Agency BBDO Düsseldorf GmbH
Client Telegate AG
Country Germany

A crowded room in an office, it's a birthday party.

Seriously dressed business people standing around, laughing and staring at a guy who's putting on a great show.

He's loping through the room, baring his teeth, a swimming cap on his head.

His colleagues burst out laughing, but suddenly everyone is quiet, a deadly silence.

Only the showmaker continues, not sensing the change.

The boss has entered the room—a man with a polished bald head and very long teeth.

And he is not amused.

SUPER: Call 11880: More information for Germany. Telegate

V.O.:
For all the job inquiries in Germany?

MERIT

TV: OVER 30 SECONDS
Genius

Art Directors Wayne Best,
Dan Kelleher, Mark Schruntek
Creative Director Arthur Bijur
Copywriters Wayne Best,
Dan Kelleher, Mark Schruntek
Producer Catherine Abate
Director Jeff Gorman
Editor Jerry Fried
Studio Farmland Studios
Agency Cliff Freeman and Partners
Client Staples
Country United States

Yeah, we've got that.

Open on a young office manager sitting in his office.

His boss sticks his head in the door.

BOSS:
Johnson, I'd like to see some ideas on saving the company money. I'll be back first thing in the morning.

Cut to various shots of Johnson working through the night. Hitting himself in the head; throwing a fit; meditating on desk; doing push-ups; calling his mom; pounding his head against the wall.

Cut outside to wide shot of office building at night. The only light is from his office.

As Johnson is asleep at his desk, a mail guy tosses a Staples catalog at him making his head slip off his hand and fall onto the catalog.

BOSS:
Well, Johnson?

His boss enters and immediately notices the Staples catalog stuck to Johnson's face.

Johnson smiles proudly.

BOSS (pleased):
Staples. That will save us a lot of money. You are a genius.

Cut to logo and Staples end treatment.

ANNOUNCER:
For all your supplies at guaranteed low prices, it's Staples. Yeah, we've got that.

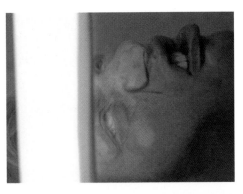

Art Director Julie Lam
Creative Director Bruce Lee
Copywriters Todd Heyman,
Bruce Lee
Producers Jamie Cohen,
Gary Streiner
Director Dewey Nicks
Music JSM Music
Studio Epoch Productions
Agency OgilvyOne
Client Ameritrade
Country United States

MR. P.:
Stuart, can I see you in my
office, please?

MR. P.:
Stuart, I just opened my
Ameritrade account.

STUART:
Let's light this candle. What do
you feel like buying today,
Mr. P.?

MR. P.:
K-Mart.

STUART:
So research it. All this stuff is
provided for you free of charge.

MR. P.:
No cost? Looks like a good
price. Let's buy a hundred
shares.

STUART:
Feel the excitement? You're
about to buy a stock online.

MR. P.:
I'm thrilled. What did that cost?

STUART:
Eight dollars, my man.

MR. P.:
My broker charges me two
hundred dollars to do this.

STUART:
Happy trading. Rock on!

MR. P.:
All right, Stuart.

V.O.:
Ameritrade. Now the market is
really open.

MERIT

TV: OVER 30 SECONDS
Carwash

Art Directors Neil Dawson,
Dino Tzouroutis
Creative Director Larry Barker
Copywriters Paige Nick,
Clive Pickering
Producer Terry Wordingham
Director Johnny Maginn
Music Ain't Love a Kick in the Head
by Dean Martin
Agency DMP DDB Ltd.
Client Shu Uemura
Country England

A man is at the wheel of his car looking miserable.

Water sprays onto the car. We pull back to see he is in a carwash.

The carwash finishes.

The man drives out, around, and back into the carwash.

As he washes his car again and again, he looks completely fed up.

Finally he gets out to inspect his car.

Down the length of the car in big red letters is the word "Bastard."

He gets back into his car and drives through the carwash again.

SUPER: Shu Uemura. Longer Lasting Lipstick.

SFX:
Music throughout

TV: SPOTS OF VARYING LENGTHS, CAMPAIGN

MTV Video Movie Awards–
Samuel L. Jackson

Art Director Lisa Rubisch
Creative Directors Allan Broce,
Christina Norman
Copywriters Tom Kuntz,
Mike Maguire
Director Lisa Rubisch
Agency MTV In-House
Client MTV Movie Awards
Country United States

BAD CAT, BIG BAT

Open on exterior shot of Sam laying outside his trailer. As he speaks to the camera, he is massaged by a large muscular man wearing a mesh midriff, of course.	SAMUEL: Sure, Samuel L. Jackson's a big star. Making feature films. Hosting the MTV movie awards. But hey, it wasn't always like that. I had to get my start just like everyone else. (Sam's voice under) A little job here…
Cut to Sam dressed up as a large pineapple, dancing on a children's show to the tune of *Just Clap Your Hands for Sam*.	(Sam's voice under) A lucky break there…
Cut to Samuel doing a side-by-side comparison of two competing paper towels for a paper towel commercial.	
Cut back to Sam at the massage table.	SAMUEL: Then finally, my big break…
Cut to Sam in the opening scene of the "famous" '70s porn film, "Bad Cat, Big Bat." Starring, of course, Ron Jeremy. SUPER: Bad Cat, Big Bat	
Cut back to Samuel still being massaged at the table.	SAMUEL: Hollywood…iz awl good.
LOGO: MTV Movie Awards	V.O.: It's the 1998 Movie Awards with your host, Samuel L. Jackson.

TV: PUBLIC SERVICE/NON-PROFIT, CAMPAIGN

Pills with Cigarette •
Transplant • My Hope

TV: PUBLIC SERVICE/NON-PROFIT, CAMPAIGN

Pam Can't Breathe • Krystell •
Last Goodbye

Art Director Pete Favat
Creative Directors Pete Favat,
Rich Herstek
Copywriter Rich Herstek
Cinematographer Carlos Bermudez
Producer Amy Feenan
Director Pete Favat
Production Company Picture Park
Productions
Recording Studio SoundTechnics
Agency Arnold Communications, Inc.
Client Massachusetts Department of
Public Health
Country United States

132

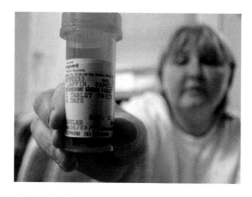
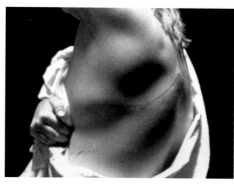

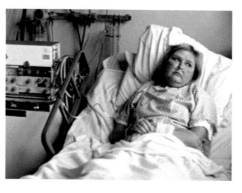

MY HOPE

PAM CAN'T BREATHE

SUPER:
My Hope For You

PAM:
I don't mean to be a pain. I'd give anything just to be a mom instead of some dying reminder of what not to do. Sometimes the only thing that keeps me going is the belief that maybe I can do some good in this world. In the end though, you're gonna decide if all this suffering has been for nothing. I just hope you can learn from my life—before you have to pay with your own.

SUPER:
If You Still Smoke,
Please Quit Now

SUPER:
1-800-TRY-TO-STOP or
call 1-800-TDD-1477

PAM:
Oh my God. The fear of not breathing is worse than anything in the world.

DOCTOR:
This is a healthy human lung.

PAM:
My chest gets tight, my heart begins to beat really fast...

DOCTOR:
This is a lung removed from a patient who had emphysema.

PAM:
I can't think, I try to calm myself down...

DOCTOR:
This is full of carbon from smoking.

PAM:
I start to hyperventilate, and I'm getting no air. There is nothing that is scarier.

SUPER:
This is emphysema

SUPER:
1-800-TRY-TO-STOP
or call 1-800 TDD-1477

MERIT

TV: PUBLIC SERVICE/NON-PROFIT, CAMPAIGN
Basketball • Holding Hands • Hug

Art Director Viv Walsh
Creative Director Bruce Bildsten
Copywriter Riley Kane
Director Doug Menuez
Photographer Mush Emmons
Executive Producer Judy Brink
Producers Ellen Erwitt,
Kristoffer Knutson
Studio Menuez Pictures
Agency Fallon McElligott
Client Camp Heartland
Country United States

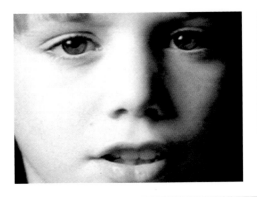

BASKETBALL

Extreme close-up of a boy's face looking into the camera.	BOY: Hi, I have AIDS.
	BOY: Would you play basketball with me?
	BOY: Would you help me go to a place where people will?
SUPER: There's a place where kids with AIDS can get the love and acceptance they need.	
Cut to kids and adult carrying kid piggyback down a wooded path.	SFX: Nature sounds, kid running, adult singing to kids
SUPER: CAMP HEARTLAND	
SUPER: 1-888-724-HOPE www.campheartland.org	

MERIT

POLITICAL COMMERCIAL
Action Figure

Art Director Bill Whitney
Creative Directors Bill Hillsman,
Sue Kruskopf
Copywriter Beth Kinney
Producer Anne Swarts
Director Mark Carter
Music Hest + Kramer Music
Production Company Metropolitan
Hodder Productions
Agency North Woods Advertising
Client Jesse Ventura for Governor
Country United States

134

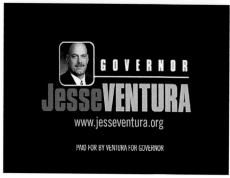

Two boys next to Jesse
Ventura action figure,
flanked by U.S. and
Minnesota state flags.

<u>SFX:</u>
"Jesse's theme" instrumental
under throughout

<u>ANNOUNCER (V.O.):</u>
New, from the Reform Party!

<u>BOYS:</u>
Yeahhh!

<u>ANNOUNCER (V.O.):</u>
It's the new Jesse Ventura
action figure!

Boys play with two
action figures. One has
a dime in its hand.

<u>ANNOUNCER (V.O.):</u>
You can make Jesse battle
special interest groups!

<u>BOY (V.O., imitating Jesse):</u>
I don't want your stupid money!

<u>ANNOUNCER (V.O.):</u>
And party politics!

<u>BOY:</u>
We politicians have powers the
average man can't comprehend!

Shot of action figure
standing tall, American
flag in background.

<u>ANNOUNCER (V.O.):</u>
You can also make Jesse lower
taxes, improve education, and
fight for the things Minnesotans
really care about.

Close-up on kid and
action figure. He
makes Jesse's fist
pound the desk.

<u>BOY (V.O., imitating Jesse):</u>
This bill wastes taxpayer's
money! Redraft it!

<u>ANNOUNCER (V.O.):</u>
Don't waste your vote on
politics as usual!

<u>ANNOUNCER (V.O.):</u>
Vote Reform Party candidate
Jesse Ventura for Governor.

SUPER: Paid for by
Ventura for Governor

SUPER:
www.jesseventura.org

FILM TRAILER/TEASER
Women Never Lie

Art Director Willie Demel
Creative Director Stefan Kolle
Copywriter Thorsten Meier
Producer Bernd Schaem
Agency Kolle Rebbe Werbeagentur GmbH
Client Buena Vista International (Germany) GmbH
Country Germany

A wannabe entertainer introduces the art of Karaoke singing, with the aid of an old German pop song, *Tears Never Lie*, sung to the tune *When a Child is Born*, while at the same time advertising the new cinema film *Women Never Lie*.

V.O.:
Ladies and gentlemen!
We exclusively present today:

Karaoke for beginners.

First the melody.

Come on sing along!

Ahahahah...

...ahahahahahaha...

O.K.! And now with the words!

And don´t forget to sing along!

When you just ask, How do I look today?
When she then says: Like shit my dearest Ray.
She then laughs at you and grins from ear to eye.
That´s when you know, women never lie.

You are great. And now everyone!

When you just ask, Were you once untrue?
When she then says, with Billy, Bob, and Drew.
With Joe, Mike, and Lee, Jimmy and with Guy, that´s when you know, women never lie.

Thanks! You were fantastic!

MERIT

**CONSUMER NEWSPAPER:
LESS THAN A FULL PAGE,
CAMPAIGN**
Marilyn • Elvis • Jerry Garcia

Art Director Ari Merkin
Creative Directors Larry Hampel,
Dean Stefanides
Copywriter Ari Merkin
Agency Hempel Stefanides
Client 5th Avenue Stamp Gallery
Country United States

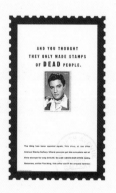

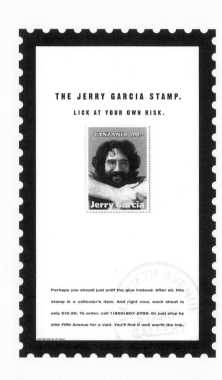

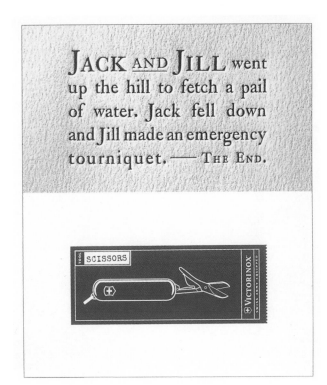

MERIT

CONSUMER NEWSPAPER: LESS THAN A FULL PAGE, CAMPAIGN

Jack and Jill • Muffet • London Bridge

Art Director Greg Bokor
Creative Directors Edward Boches, Greg Bokor, Jim Garaventi
Copywriter Jim Garaventi
Photographer Bruce Peterson
Typographer M&H Type
Agency Mullen Advertising
Client Swiss Army Brands
Country United States

MERIT

TRADE NEWSPAPER: LESS THAN A FULL PAGE, CAMPAIGN

You'll Come • Brains • Two Passions

Art Directors Chucky Monn, Tracy Wong
Creative Director Tracy Wong
Copywriter Chucky Monn
Designers Chucky Monn, Tracy Wong
Producers Kris Latta, Marianna Share
Agency WONGDOODY
Client WONGDOODY
Country United States

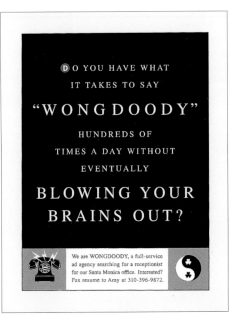

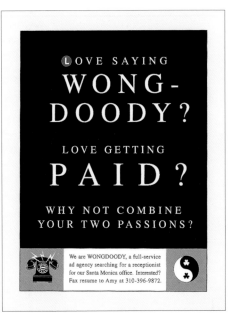

MERIT

**TRADE NEWSPAPER: FULL PAGE,
CAMPAIGN**
Blind • God • Budget

Art Director Christopher Gyorgy
Creative Director Joe Alexander
Copywriter Joe Alexander
Photographers Neal Beidleman,
David Breashears, Ken Kamler,
Robert Schaver, Sumiyo Tsuzuki,
Gordon Wiltsie
Studio Artist Tyson Brown
Print Producer Melissa Ralston
Agency The Martin Agency
Client Science Museum of Virginia
Country United States

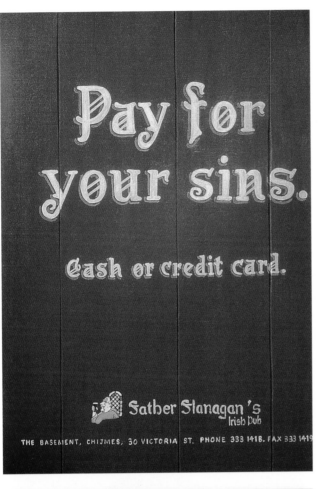

MERIT

CONSUMER MAGAZINE:
FULL PAGE, CAMPAIGN
Credit Card • Collar • Halo

Art Director Scott McCelland
Creative Director Stanley Wong
Copywriters Karl Dunn,
Simon Jenkins
Illustrator Scott McCelland
Agency Bartle Bogle Hegarty Ltd.
(Asia Pacific)
Client Father Flanagan's Irish Pub
Country Singapore

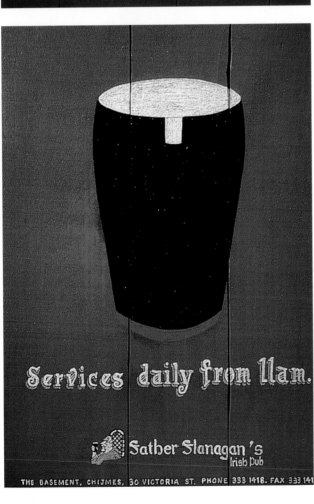

A. Through the head.   B. Through the spinal column.   C. Through the anal vent.

Use a Rapala and minnows will be very grateful.

Factory rule #1: No skinny dipping in the testing tank.

MERIT

**CONSUMER MAGAZINE:
FULL PAGE, CAMPAIGN**

Grateful Minnows • Factory Rule #1 •
Feed His Family

Art Director Frank Haggerty
Creative Directors Kerry Casey,
Jim Nelson
Copywriter Jim Nelson
Photographer Jerry Stebbins
Producer Louia Thompson
Agency Carmichael Lynch
Client Normark Rapala
Country United States

Lauri Rapala invented a lure in order to feed his family.

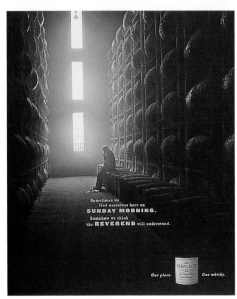

Multiple Awards

MERIT

**CONSUMER MAGAZINE:
FULL PAGE, CAMPAIGN**
The English • Trends • Remote •
Sunday Morning

and MERIT
**CONSUMER MAGAZINE:
FULL PAGE**
The English

Art Director David Carter
Copywriter Chris Ford
Photographer Nadav Kander
Agency TBWA Chiat/Day
Client Seagram/Glenlivet
Country United States

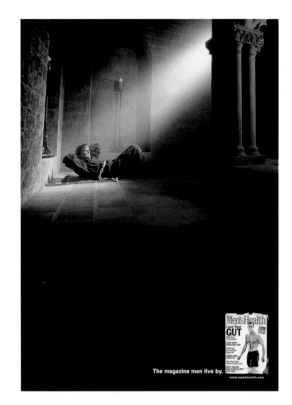

MERIT

**CONSUMER MAGAZINE:
FULL PAGE, CAMPAIGN**
Monk • Dogsled • Snowman • Golf

Art Director Sean Riley
Creative Directors Joe Alexander, Kerry Feuerman
Copywriters Joe Alexander, Christopher Gyorgy, Jonathan Mackler
Photographers Per Breiehagen, Craig Cameron Olsen, Dan Escobar
Studio Artist Mark Brye
Print Producer Edith Arbuckle
Agency The Martin Agency
Client Men's Health
Country United States

MERIT

CONSUMER MAGAZINE:
FULL PAGE, CAMPAIGN

Canine Housekeeper • Bubble
Wrap • Body Part Music

Art Director Taras Wayner
Creative Director David Angelo
Copywriter Kevin Roddy
Designer Charles Anderson
Photographers Charles Anderson,
Howard Burman, Sean Mackenzie
Agency Cliff Freeman and Partners
Client Cherry Coke
Country United States

MERIT

CONSUMER MAGAZINE: SPREAD,
CAMPAIGN

Use Only Original Parts

Art Director Pedro Cappeletti
Creative Directors Nizan Guanaes,
Tomás Lorente
Copywriter Jáder Rossetto
Photographer Alexandre Catan
Producer Elaine Carvalho
Agency DM9 DDB Publicidade
Client Moto Honda Da Amazonia
Country Brazil

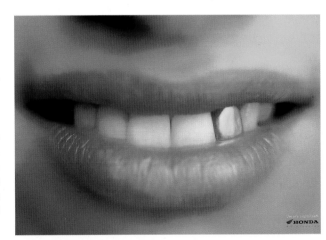

MERIT

**CONSUMER MAGAZINE:
SPREAD, CAMPAIGN**
Secret Recipe • Dinner Plan •
Stressed

Art Director Scott Dube
Creative Directors
Michael McLaughlin, Jack Neary
Copywriter Zak Mroueh
Photographer Per Kristianson
Agency BBDO Canada
Client Campbell Soup Company, Ltd.
Country Canada

CONSUMER MAGAZINE:
SPREAD, CAMPAIGN

TV • Timeclock • Gameboy • Exit

Art Director Jim Henderson
Creative Director Lyle Wedemeyer
Copywriter Tom Kelly
Designer Jim Henderson
Photographers Brian Bailey,
Robin Hood, Gary Kufner,
Douglas Walker
Product Photographer Curtis Johnson
Producer Renee Kirscht
Agency Martin/Williams Advertising
Client Coleman
Country United States

MERIT

**TRADE MAGAZINE:
LESS THAN A FULL PAGE,
CAMPAIGN**
Burly Bear Print Campaign II

Art Directors Cabell Harris,
David Waraksa
Creative Director Cabell Harris
Copywriter Anne Marie Floyd
Designer David Waraksa
Agency Work
Client Burly Bear Network
Country United States

Multiple Awards

MERIT

**PUBLIC SERVICE/NON-PROFIT
MAGAZINE: SPREAD, CAMPAIGN**
Dead Tree • Dead Bird • Dead Fish

and MERIT

**CONSUMER NEWSPAPER: LESS
THAN A FULL PAGE**
Dead Tree

Art Director Cristina Amorim
Creative Director Adilson Xavier
Copywriter Adilson Xavier
Photographer Leonardo Vilela
Illustrator Leonardo Vilela
Special Effects Leonardo Vilela
Producers Paulo Moraes,
Valter Serafim
Agency Giovanni, FCB
Client Greenpeace
Country Brazil

MERIT

**TRADE MAGAZINE:
FULL PAGE, CAMPAIGN**
Drunks • Dominatrix • Gang

and MERIT

TRADE MAGAZINE: FULL PAGE
Drunks

Art Director Steve Mitchell
Creative Directors Doug Adkins,
Steve Mitchell
Copywriter Doug Adkins
Photographer Rick Dublin
Agency Hunt Adkins
Client Dublin Productions
Country United States

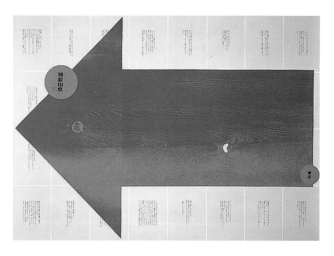
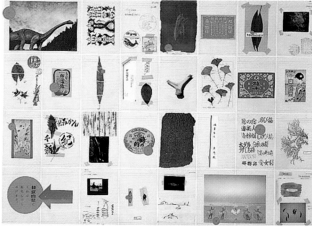

MERIT

PROMOTIONAL, CAMPAIGN
Come to Wakayama • You Can
Go Anywhere

Art Director Hiroaki Nagai
Creative Director Daisaku Fujiwara
Copywriter Daisaku Fujiwara
Designers Hiroaki Nagai, Hiroaki Seki
Photographer Tamotsu Fuji
Studio N.G., Inc.
Client Wakayama Prefecture
Country Japan

MERIT

PROMOTIONAL, CAMPAIGN
Lesson One • Lesson Two •
Lesson Three

Art Director Jason Busa
Copywriter Peterson Mike
Designer Jason Busa
Illustrators Jason Busa,
Peterson Mike
Agency Jam Snob Trees Up
Client Casbah Cinema
Country United States

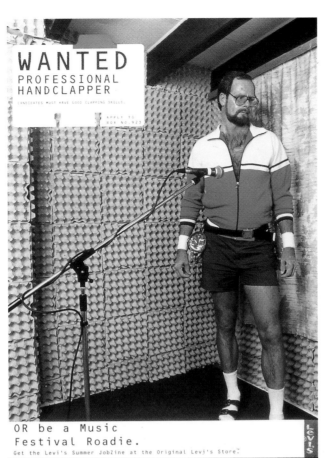

OR be a Music
Festival Roadie.
Get the Levi's Summer JobZine at the Original Levi's Store.

POINT-OF-PURCHASE, CAMPAIGN
Wanted Festival Roadie

Art Director Karen Heuter
Copywriters Dave Bell,
Tyler Whisnand
Photographer Herman Poppelaars
Agency KesselsKramer
Client Levi Strauss & Co.
Country The Netherlands

OR be a Music
Festival Roadie.
Get the Levi's Summer JobZine at the Original Levi's Store.

OR be a Music
Festival Roadie.
Get the Levi's Summer JobZine at the Original Levi's Store.

MERIT

PRODUCT OR SERVICE, CAMPAIGN
Unheard of Style

Art Director Yutaka Murakoshi
Creative Director Toshiro Fumizono
Copywriter Kohtaro Shimada
Designer Yutaka Murakoshi
Photographer Taka Kobayashi
Producer Hirotoshi Yuasa
Agency INTERVISION INC.
Client Sony Marketing, Inc.
Country Japan

MERIT

**PUBLIC SERVICE/NON-PROFIT OR
EDUCATIONAL, CAMPAIGN**

Carpet • Baseball •
Teddy Bear • Teacup

Art Director Rosalinda Graziano

Creative Directors David Rosenberg, Gerald Schoenhoff

Copywriter Trish Kavanagh

Designer Optic Nerve Design

Photographer George Simhoni

Typographer The Composing Room

Agency Publicis SMW

Client Unicef Canada

Country Canada

**PUBLIC SERVICE/NON-PROFIT OR
EDUCATIONAL, CAMPAIGN**

Growing Up in a Small Town •
Golden Years • God-Fearing Man

Art Director Scott Conklin
Copywriter Scott Lynch
Designer Scott Conklin
Photographers Sue Bennett,
Peter Carter
Agency William Eisner Associates
Client Wisconsin Domestic Violence
Country United States

MERIT

PUBLIC SERVICE/NON-PROFIT OR EDUCATIONAL, CAMPAIGN
The Civil Courage Transit

Art Director Paul Snowden
Creative Directors Arndt Dallmann, Guido Heffels
Copywriter Eva Jung
Designer Guido Block
Photographer Gerd George
Agency Springer & Jacoby Werbung GmbH
Client Hamburg Police
Country Germany

153

MERIT

TRANSIT, CAMPAIGN
Daihatsu Inc. Compact Cars Campaign: A Good Car Because of Its Size • Would You Care for One of Our Electric Mini Cars? • Look, That Fire Engine Can Navigate a Street This Narrow • On a Street This Narrow, We Have a Big Advantage of Smallness

Art Directors Masumi Nakazawa, Akira Ouchi
Creative Director Mitsuru Soga
Copywriters Masahiro Kikuchi, Mizuhiro Shindo
Designer Masato Tsuchiya
Photographer Hatsuhiko Okada
Producer Takashi Uehara (Dentsu Inc.)
Client Daihatsu Inc.
Country Japan

MERIT

**BILLBOARD, DIORAMA, OR PAINTED
SPECTACULAR, CAMPAIGN**
Wrangler Camouflage
Jeans–Summer, Fall, Winter

Art Director John Boone
Copywriter David Oakley
Photographer Mike Carroll
Agency The Martin Agency
Client Wrangler
Country United States

154

NEW DEALERSHIP
NOW OPEN AT

28° 13' 30" S
28° 18' 20" E

HOCHLAND

MERIT

**CONSUMER NEWSPAPER:
LESS THAN A FULL PAGE**
New Dealership

Art Director Jan Jacobs
Creative Director Tony Granger
Copywriter Clare McNally
Illustrator Jan Jacobs
Agency TBWA Hunt Lascaris
Client Land Rover
Country South Africa

**CONSUMER NEWSPAPER:
LESS THAN A FULL PAGE**
Snow Angel

Art Director Tim Vaccarino
Creative Directors Lance Jensen,
Alan Pafenbach
Copywriter Shane Hutton
Photographer Steve Bronstein
Illustrator Peter Levins
Production Manager Kelli Howe
Agency Arnold Communications, Inc.
Client Volkswagen of America
Country United States

ADVERTISING PRINT

156

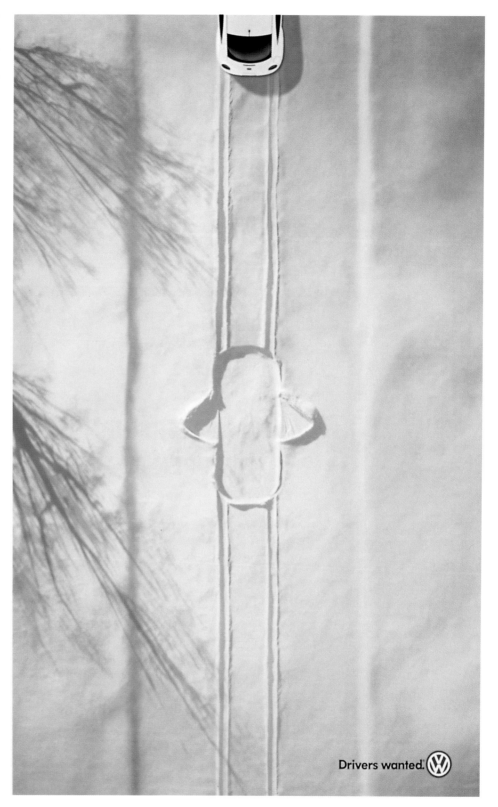

Multiple Awards

MERIT

CONSUMER NEWSPAPER, FULL PAGE
and MERIT

ENTERTAINMENT OR SPECIAL EVENT
Comrades 90km Road Race—Durban
To Pietermaritzburg

Art Director Vanessa Pearson
Creative Director Graham Warsop
Copywriter Lawrence Seftel
Agency The Jupiter Drawing Room
Client Nike South Africa
Country South Africa

157

MERIT

CONSUMER NEWSPAPER, SPREAD
Chest

Art Director Chris Garbutt
Creative Director Ashley Bacon
Copywriter Ashley Bacon
Photography In House
Agency Lindsay Smithers–FCB
Client Boy Scouts of South Africa
Country South Africa

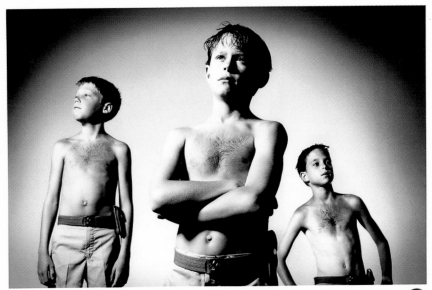

CONSUMER MAGAZINE, SPREAD
Digitally Remastered

Art Director Will Uronis
Creative Director Lance Jensen
Copywriter Lance Jensen
Separator Uni-Graphic/Anderson
Printer Uni-Graphic Inc.
Agency Arnold Communications, Inc.
Client Volkswagen of America
Country United States

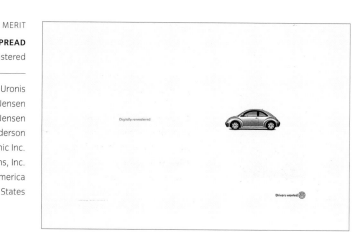

CONSUMER MAGAZINE, SPREAD
Clocks

Art Director Doug Pedersen
Creative Director Jim Mountjoy
Copywriter Curtis Smith
Photographer Jim Arndt
Agency Loeffler Ketchum Mountjoy
Client Biltmore
Country United States

CONSUMER MAGAZINE, INSERT
Scratch

Art Director Anton Crone
Creative Director Tony Granger
Copywriter Derek Shevel
Photographer David Prior
Agency TBWA Hunt Lascaris
Client Pharma Natura
Country South Africa

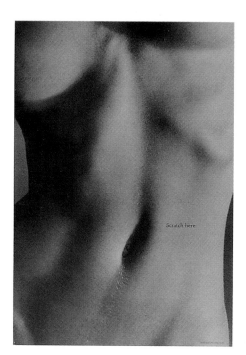

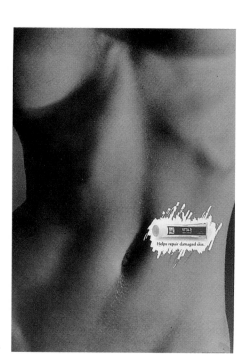

THE TRUTH BEHIND TV DEMOGRAPHICS:

Some networks have been known to count Alexander and Daniel as two separate viewers to inflate their ratings estimates. During the seven hour block of Super Bowl Pregame programming, FOX will deliver more adult viewers, 18-34 and 18-49, than the four networks' average during Primetime* And you can be sure each and every one of them will have their own brain stem.

The FOX Super Bowl Pregame block of programming, January 31, 1999, 11:00 am to 6:18 pm ET. For more information contact Jim Burnette, Senior Vice President of Sales, at 212-556-2431.

MERIT

TRADE MAGAZINE, FULL PAGE
Twins

Art Directors Rossana Bardales, Taras Wayner
Creative Director Eric Silver
Copywriter Adam Chasnow
Agency Cliff Freeman and Partners
Client FOX Sports
Country United States

THE TRUTH BEHIND TV DEMOGRAPHICS:

While forecasting the audience of adult viewers for our seven hour block of Super Bowl Pregame programming, we discovered that other networks have been counting this hermaphrodite as both a male and female viewer. At FOX, we find this misleading tactic reprehensible. That's because we know we'll deliver more adults, 18-34 and 18-49, than the NBA, NHL and MLB combined* Besides, our researchers easily concluded that this is indeed a woman. The pouty lips were a dead giveaway.

The FOX Super Bowl Pregame block of programming, January 31, 1999, 11:00 am to 6:18 pm ET. For more information contact Jim Burnette, Senior Vice President of Sales, at 212-556-2431.

MERIT

TRADE MAGAZINE, FULL PAGE
Hermaphrodite

Art Directors Rossana Bardales, Taras Wayner
Creative Director Eric Silver
Copywriter Adam Chasnow
Agency Cliff Freeman and Partners
Client FOX Sports
Country United States

MERIT

TRADE MAGAZINE, FULL PAGE
Writing Tools

Art Director Kevin Daley
Creative Directors Gary Greenberg, Peter Seronick
Copywriter Craig Johnson
Photographer Jack Richmond
Agency Greenberg Seronick O'Leary & Partners
Client Portfolio
Country United States

Multiple Awards

MERIT

TRADE MAGAZINE, SPREAD
and MERIT

POSTERS AND BILLBOARDS, PROMOTIONAL
Nobody Does So Much for
a Good Photo

Art Directors Rodrigo de Almeida,
Marcello Serpa
Creative Directors
Eugenio Mohallem, Marcello Serpa
Copywriters Tales Bahu,
Rondon Fernandes
Photography Manolo Moran,
Stock Photos
Producer Jose Roberto Bezerra
Agency Almap BBDO
Client Stock Photos
Country Brazil

160

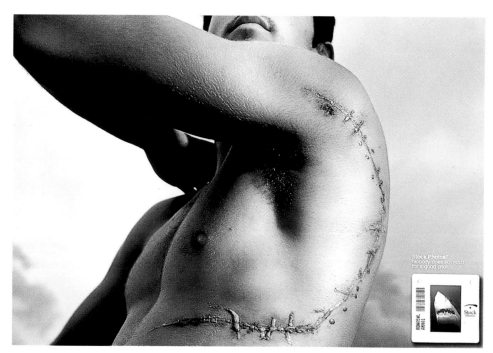

MERIT

PROMOTIONAL
My Other SAAB Is a Car

Art Directors Jonathan Mackler,
Noel Ritter
Creative Directors Kerry Feuerman,
Rob Schapiro
Copywriter Kerry Feuerman
Photographer Clint Clemens
Studio Artist Laurie Christopher
Print Producer Jenny Schoenherr
Agency The Martin Agency
Client SAAB Cars USA, Inc.
Country United States

MERIT

POINT-OF-PURCHASE
Prison

Art Directors Greg Bokor,
Gerard Caputo
Creative Directors Edward Boches,
Greg Bokor, Jim Garaventi
Copywriter Jim Garaventi
Photographer William Huber
Agency Mullen Advertising
Client Swiss Army Brands
Country United States

MERIT
POINT-OF-PURCHASE
Wuss

Art Director Stephen F. Goldblatt
Copywriter Lennon Courtney
Photographer Scott Harben
Agency DDB Needham Dallas
Client Laser Quest
Country United States

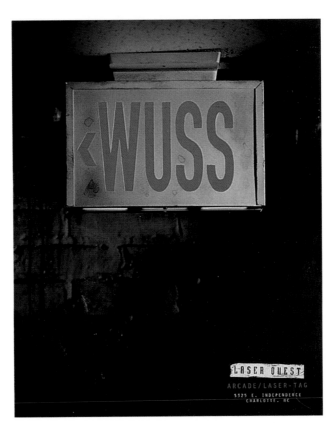

MERIT

POINT-OF-PURCHASE
H

Art Directors Pedro Cappeletti,
Sibely Silveira
Creative Directors Nizan Guanaes,
Tomás Lorente
Copywriter Jáder Rossetto
Photographer Richard Kohout
Producer Elaine Carvalho
Agency DM9 DDB Publicidade
Client Honda Automóveis do Brasil
Country Brazil

MERIT

POINT-OF-PURCHASE
Driving Range

Art Director Paul Laffy
Creative Director Edward Boches
Copywriter Edward Boches
Agency Mullen Advertising
Client Money Magazine
Country United States

MERIT

PRODUCT OR SERVICE
Pick This Up

Art Director David Nien-Li Yang
Copywriter David Nien-Li Yang
Photographer Bill Rogers
Agency Cramer-Krasselt/Chicago
Client Brad Wilken Chiropractor
Country United States

The advertising medium here is the sticker shown.

MERIT

PRODUCT OR SERVICE
Rats? Call Insetisan Now

Art Directors Andre Nassar,
Bruno Prosperi
Creative Director Silvios Matos
Copywriter Renato Simoes
Designer Bruno Prosperi
Illustrator Bruno Prosperi
Producer Claudio Dirani
Agency FischerAmerica
Client Insetisan
Country Brazil

MERIT

PRODUCT OR SERVICE
Parents

Art Director Sean Farrell
Creative Director Spencer Deadrick
Copywriter Colin Nissan
Photography Cheryl Clegg, Stock
Agency Clarke Goward Advertising
Client Eastpak
Country United States

MERIT

PRODUCT OR SERVICE
Burgers

Art Director Pedro Cappeletti
Creative Directors Nizan Guanaes,
Tomás Lorente
Copywriter Jáder Rossetto
Producer Elaine Carvalho
Agency DM9 DDB Publicidade
Client Venice
Country Brazil

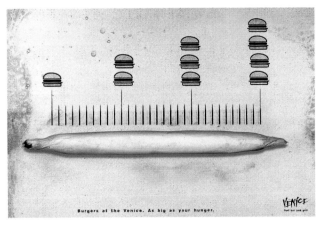

MERIT

PRODUCT OR SERVICE
New Rowenta Professional

Art Director Jack Ronc
Creative Director Gilberto Dos Reis
Copywriter Wanderley B. Doro
Photographer Freitas
Producer Margarete Travaglin
Agency Publicis Norton
Client Rowenta
Country Brazil

MERIT

PRODUCT OR SERVICE
Blueprint

Art Director Ed Parks
Creative Directors Paul Silverman, Amy Watt
Copywriters Jim Elliott, Bill Roden
Photographer Michael Indresano
Agency Mullen Advertising
Client Stanley
Country United States

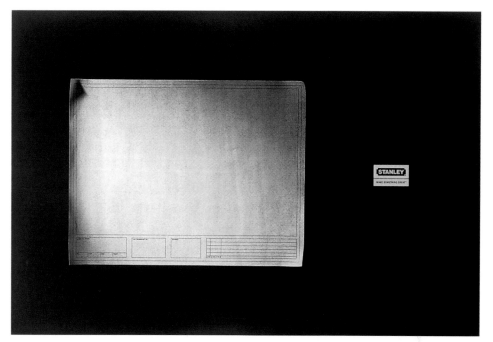

PRODUCT OR SERVICE
Summer Is Coming

Art Directors Jim Carroll,
Andrea McAdams
Creative Director Eddie Van Bloem
Copywriters Jim Carroll,
Andrea McAdams
Photographer Robert Ammirati
Agency OMC Creative
Client Diet Center
Country United States

MERIT
PRODUCT OR SERVICE
Physics Book

Art Director Sean Farrell
Creative Director Spencer Deadrick
Copywriter Colin Nissan
Photography Cheryl Clegg, Stock
Agency Clarke Goward Advertising
Client Eastpak
Country United States

MERIT
ENTERTAINMENT OR SPECIAL EVENT
Gay Film Festival

Art Director Lapeace Kakaza
Creative Director Tony Granger
Copywriter Trevor McKenzie
Photographer Eben Barnard
Agency TBWA Hunt Lascaris
Client Out of Africa
Country South Africa

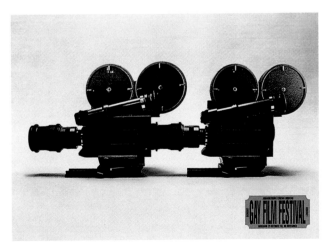

MERIT

**ENTERTAINMENT OR SPECIAL
EVENT**
Residence Theatre: T-Crash

Art Director Tobias Eichinger
Creative Director Oliver Voss
Photographer Peter Weber
Agency Jung von Matt an der Isar
Client Bayerisches Staatsschauspiel
Country Germany

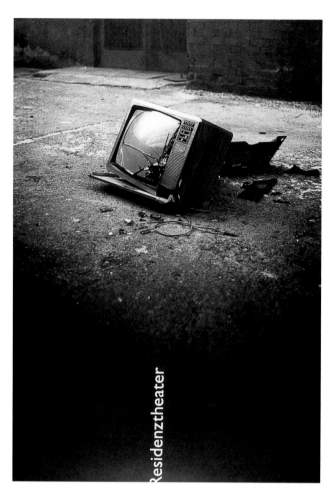

MERIT

**ENTERTAINMENT OR SPECIAL
EVENT**
The Monster Will Appear

Art Directors Yasuhiro Hayashi,
Naoki Nakano
Creative Director Takeshi Matsumoto
Copywriter Takeshi Matsumoto
Designer Yasuhiro Hayashi
Photographer Masao Chiba
Agency Dentsu Inc.
Client Asahi Broadcasting Co., Ltd.
Country Japan

MERIT

ENTERTAINMENT OR SPECIAL EVENT
Cry Loud

Art Director Rodrigo Butori
Creative Director Alexandre Gama
Copywriter Alexandre Gama
Photographer Fototeca
Agency Young & Rubicam Brazil
Client Air Extreme Bungee Jump
Country Brazil

MERIT

PUBLIC SERVICE/NON-PROFIT OR EDUCATIONAL
77%

Art Directors Aaron Eiseman,
Abi Aron Spencer
Creative Director Sal DeVito
Copywriters Aaron Eiseman,
Abi Aron Spencer
Design Inspired By Barbara Kruger
Photographer Henry Leutwyler
Agency DeVito/Verdi
Client The Pro-Choice Public
Education Project
Country United States

MERIT

PUBLIC SERVICE/NON-PROFIT OR EDUCATIONAL
Fingerprint

Art Directors Cabell Harris, David Waraksa
Creative Director Cabell Harris
Copywriter Anne Marie Floyd
Designer David Waraksa
Agency Work
Client Richmond Clean City Commission
Country United States

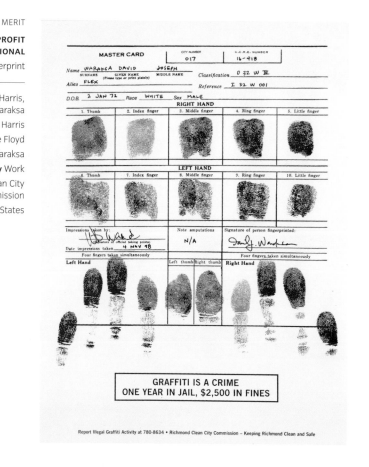

MERIT

PUBLIC SERVICE/NON-PROFIT OR EDUCATIONAL
I Miss My Lung, Bob

Art Director Nancy Steinman
Creative Director Bruce Dundore
Copywriter Jeff Bossin
Photographer Myron Beck
Production Manager Anita Lee
Typographer Nels Dielman
Agency Asher & Partners
Client California Department of Health Services
Country United States

MERIT

PUBLIC SERVICE/NON-PROFIT OR EDUCATIONAL
Gear Lever

Art Director Andreas Geyer
Creative Directors Detlef Krüger, Ulrike Wegert
Copywriter Ulrich Zünkeler
Graphic Design Silke Baltruschat, Bettina Fuhrmann, Katrin Mielke
Photographer Werner Hinniger
Agency KNSK, BBDO
Clients Matthias Machnig, Bernd Schoppe (SPD)
Country Germany

MERIT

PUBLIC SERVICE/NON-PROFIT OR EDUCATIONAL
Soccer World Cup

Art Director Andreas Geyer
Creative Directors Detlef Krüger, Ulrike Wegert
Copywriter Ulrich Zünkeler
Graphic Design Silke Baltruschat, Bettina Fuhrmann, Katrin Mielke
Agency KNSK, BBDO
Clients Matthias Machnig, Bernd Schoppe (SPD)
Country Germany

MERIT

PUBLIC SERVICE/NON-PROFIT OR EDUCATIONAL
Help Fight Traffic in Illegal Organs

Art Director Márcio Ribas
Creative Directors Nizan Guanaes, Tomás Lorente
Copywriter Drausio Graganani
Photographer Rafael Costa
Producer Elaine Carvalho
Agency DM9 DDB Publicidade
Client Hospital Israelita Albert Einstein
Country Brazil

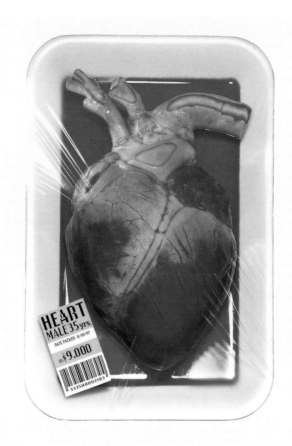

 Help fight traffic in illegal organs. Report to 0800-611997.

MERIT | **Art Director** Michihiro Ishizaki
TRANSIT | **Creative Directors** Satoru Miyata
Volare | **Copywriter** Hiroshi Mitsui
| **Designer** Noboru Naito
| **Photographer** Bishin Jumonji
| **Agency** Dai-Ichi Kikaku Co., Ltd.
| **Client** Kirin Brewery Co., Ltd.
| **Country** Japan

MERIT

TRANSIT
Donbei

Art Director Takeshi Yamamoto
Creative Director Katsuya Sato
Copywriter Hideo Kobayashi
Designer Takeshi Yamamoto
Photographer Hitoshi Ohte
Illustrator Noriyuki Kikuchi
Producer Hiroshi Sakaushi
Agency Asatsu-DK
Client Nissin Food Products Co., Ltd.
Country Japan

MERIT

TRANSIT
X-Ray

Art Director Rodd Isberto
Creative Directors David Apicella,
Ted Barton
Producer Annie O'Neill
Chief Creative Officer Rick Boyko
Agency Ogilvy & Mather
Client Kodak
Country United States

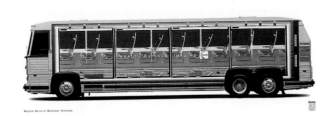

MERIT

TRANSIT
Eggs

Art Director Theo Ferreira
Creative Director Mike Schalit
Copywriter Alistair Morgan
Agency NET#WORK
Client Virgin Atlantic
Country South Africa

MERIT

TRANSIT
Bus Wrap

Art Director Paul Shields
Creative Director Steve Crane
Copywriter Steve Crane
Photographer Nick Veasey
Agency Emmerling Post
Advertising, Inc.
Client White Plains Hospital Center
Country United States

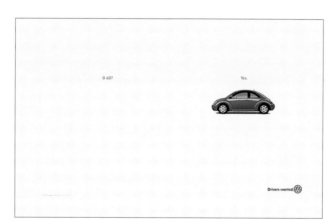

MERIT

BILLBOARD, DIORAMA, OR PAINTED SPECTACULAR
0–60

Art Director Lance Paull
Creative Director Alan Pafenbach
Copywriter Lance Jensen
Photographer Bill Cash
Illustrator Peter Levins
Production Managers
Karen Hennessey, Hannah Holden
Printer Uni-Graphic
Agency Arnold Communications, Inc.
Client Volkswagen of America
Country United States

MERIT

BILLBOARD, DIORAMA, OR PAINTED SPECTACULAR
Waiting–Couple in Chair

Art Director Jonathan Mackler
Creative Directors Kerry Feuerman,
Rob Schapiro
Copywriter Kerry Feuerman
Photographer Robert Mizono
Studio Artist Donnie Garland
Print Producer Linda Locks
Agency The Martin Agency
Client SAAB Cars USA, Inc.
Country United States

MERIT

**BILLBOARD, DIORAMA, OR PAINTED
SPECTACULAR**

Twister

Art Directors Theo Ferreira,
Debbie Gyngell
Creative Director Mike Schalit
Copywriter Alistair Morgan
Agency NET#WORK
Client Virgin Atlantic
Country South Africa

173

MERIT

**BILLBOARD, DIORAMA, OR PAINTED
SPECTACULAR**

Before TV, Two World Wars.
After TV, Zero.

Art Director John Shirley
Creative Director Jerry Gentile
Copywriter Rich Siegel
Agency TBWA Chiat/Day
Client ABC Television Network
Country United States

MERIT

BROCHURE OR CATALOG
How to Sell Out

Art Director Scott MacGregor
Creative Director Lee Clow
Copywriter Mike McKay
Photographer Smith/Nelson
Agency TBWA Chiat/Day
Client Beldings
Country United States

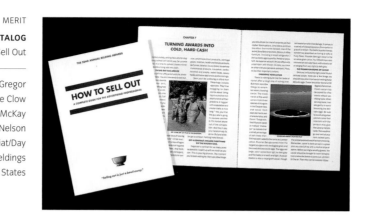

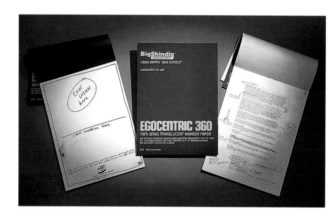

MERIT

BROCHURE OR CATALOG
Kansas City Ad Club Omni Call
for Entries

Art Director Subashini Nadarajah
Creative Director Steve Wood
Copywriters Sean O'Dell, Steve Wood
Designer Subashini Nadarajah
Illustrators Subashini Nadarajah,
Sean O'Dell
Senior Print Production Manager
Emily Wilcox
Executive Creative Director
Jeff Bremser
Agency Bernstein Rein
Country United States

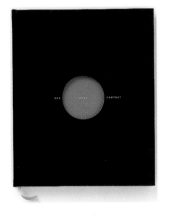

MERIT

BROCHURE OR CATALOG

Das Hebe Porträt (The Hebe Portrait)

Art Director Joerg Bauer
Creative Director Reiner Hebe
Copywriter Reiner Hebe
Designer Joerg Bauer
Photographers Werner Pawlok, Nils Schubert
Producer Reiner Hebe
Agency Hebe, Werbung & Design
Client Hebe, Werbung & Design
Country Germany

MERIT

BROCHURE OR CATALOG

Toy Car/Auto Show

Art Director Cliff Wong
Creative Directors Lance Jensen, Alan Pafenbach
Copywriter Lance Jensen
Printer Anderson Lithograph
Agency Arnold Communications, Inc.
Client Volkswagen of America
Country United States

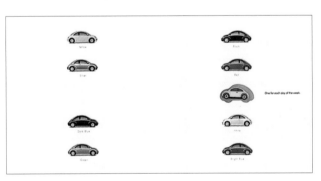

MERIT

MIXED MEDIA CAMPAIGN
Blonde, Built & Beautiful

Art Director Mark Mason
Copywriters Andrew Durkan,
Mark Mason
Designers Wesley Lewis,
Mark Mason
Illustrator Wesley Lewis
Agency Saatchi & Saatchi
Country South Africa

Multiple Awards
see also Graphic Design section,
p. 293

MERIT
BROCHURE OR CATALOG
Check In–Check Out

Art Director Erik Kessels
Copywriters Johan Kramer,
Tyler Whisnand
Photographers Anuschka Blommers,
Niels Schumm
Agency KesselsKramer
Client The Hans Brinker Budget Hotel
Country The Netherlands

AS GOOD AS IT GETS

All dialogue and SFX
extremely fast
throughout

ANNOUNCER: Hollywood Video presents…"Sixty Second Theater." Where we try (unsuccessfully) to pack all the action and drama of a two-hour Hollywood production into sixty seconds. Today's presentation, "As Good As It Gets."

SFX: Doorbell

MELVIN (Jack Nicholson sound-alike): All right. Who is it?

SFX: Many locks being unlocked quickly

SIMON (Grey Kinnear sound-alike): It's your artistic neighbor. Have you seen my little doggie?

MELVIN: Yeah. I stuffed the yapper down the trash chute.

SIMON: You are a cruel man!

MELVIN: I'm a hungry cruel man. I'm going to breakfast.

SFX: Door swings open with bells

SFX: Restaurant sounds

MELVIN: You look bad today, even for a waitress.

CAROL (Helen Hunt sound-alike): You are a cruel, obsessive-compulsive man.

MELVIN: You forgot rich.

CAROL: Get out!

SFX: Gets up from chair. opens door

CAROL: Did you say rich?

SFX: Door closes. Bells ring

MELVIN: See ya.

SFX: Doorbell

MELVIN: All right.

SFX: Many locks being unlocked quickly

MELVIN: Well, if it isn't my "artistic" neighbor.

SIMON: You are a cruel man. Will you drive me to my parents' house?

MELVIN: Okay, can I bring the waitress?

SIMON: Does she like show tunes?

SFX: Tires screeching out; Car driving

SFX: Show tunes play on car stereo

SFX: Tires screech to a stop

MELVIN: We're here.

CAROL & SIMON (together): We don't like you. Let's go home.

SFX: Tires screeching out; Car driving

SFX: Show tunes play on car stereo

SFX: Tires screech to a stop

MELVIN: We're home. Now can I be your boyfriend?

SIMON: Well, okay.

MELVIN: Not you. Her.

SIMON: What about me?

MELVIN: Well, you can be my roommate.

SFX: Hollywood video theme music

ANNOUNCER: If this doesn't satisfy your urge to see "As Good As It Gets" (and we can't say we blame you) then rent it today at Hollywood Video. Where "As Good As It Gets" is guaranteed to be in-stock, or next time it's free. Welcome to Hollywood. Hollywood Video. Celebrity voices impersonated.

MERIT

RADIO: OVER 30 SECONDS
As Good as it Gets

Creative Director Arthur Bijur
Copywriters Wayne Best,
Adam Chasnow
Engineer Roy Kamen
Producer Arlene Adoremos
Agency Cliff Freeman and Partners
Studio Kamen Entertainment Group
Client Hollywood Video
Country United States

ADVERTISING RADIO

177

Multiple Awards

178

PUNK ROCK PARROT

ANNOUNCER:
Cherry Coke Theater presents...

SFX:
Dramatic musical introduction

ANNOUNCER:
...Cherry Coke Theater (flute music),
showcasing those who do something
different. We invite you now to mosh
along with Aaron Goode and Polly
Rotten, his punk rock parrot.

AARON:
Lots of parrots can sing. (SFX: parrot
squawks), I taught mine to sing punk
rock. Ready, Polly?

SFX:
Squawk

PARROT:
One, two, three...

Punk music begins

PUNK ROCKER SCREAMS:
You've got to fight authority!!

PARROT (mimics):
Fight authority!

PUNK ROCKER:
Smell the rotten garbage!!

PARROT:
Smell the rotten garbage!

PUNK ROCKER:
Headless chickens runnin'!!

PARROT:
Headless chickens runnin'!

PUNK ROCKER:
Fight, fight, fight, fight, fight!

PARROT:
Fight, fight!

PUNK ROCKER:
Go crazy, crazy, crazy!

PARROT:
Crazy, crazy, crazy!

PUNK ROCKER:
Yeah!!! (Parrot squawks loudly in
unison)

SFX:
Music ends and wings flap as parrot
flies away

ANNOUNCER (flute music):
That's all for today's Cherry Coke
Theater presentation. If you do
something different, please visit us
at Cherrycoke.com.
Until next time, bye-bye.

SFX:
Chime and then flute instrumental accompanies our host's introduction

ANNOUNCER:
For the next sixty seconds we invite you to sit back and surrender yourself to those who have done something different as Cherry Coke Theater presents Wayne Best and the smooth sounds of his car alarm melodies.

WAYNE:
Hi! Most people hate the sound of a car alarm. Not me. Check this out! One, two, a one, two, three…

Groovy guitar strumming accompanies variable and well-known car alarm sirens creating a rather palatable melody

WAYNE:
Uh, thank you.

ANNOUNCER (flute music):
And so closes today's performance of Cherry Coke Theater. Please do visit us on the web at Cherrycoke.com. Until next time, Cherry Coke reminds you to do something different.

ARMPIT ORCHESTRA

SFX:
Flute instrumental accompanies our host's introductory remarks

ANNOUNCER:
Good day, friends. This is your host, and welcome to Cherry Coke Theater, dedicated to saluting those who do something different.Today's performance? Tchaikovsky's 1812 Overture, featuring Wilmington, Delaware's very own armpit orchestra.

Music stops; man clears his throat and taps conductor's baton against music stand

SFX:
A quartet of armpit musicians orchestrate an explosive version of Tchaikovsky's masterpiece

SFX:
Flute music returns

ANNOUNCER:
This concludes today's performance of Cherry Coke Theater. If you do something different, why don't you contact us on the Web at Cherrycoke.com?

**RADIO: OVER 30 SECONDS,
CAMPAIGN**

Lou 1, 3 and 4

Creative Director Duncan Bruce
Copywriter Aubrey Singer
Producer Pat Lyons
Agency TBWA Chiat/Day
Client The Billy Graham Mission
Country United States

180

LOU 1

ANNOUNCER:
We interrupt this program to
bring you a special message from
the prince of darkness, the
master of evil, the inventor of
PBS, Lucifer.

MUSIC:
From "The Omen"

LUCIFER:
This is a warning NOT to go to the
free concert at the Corel Centre,
featuring the music of Michael W.
Smith and the band Jars of Clay.
So what if they won a Grammy!
Besides, Grammy spelled
backwards is Ymmarg—that's an
evil Latin word for...uh... can't
remember. Got a lot on my mind.
But it's not good!
And also, if you play Jars of Clay's
hit song "Flood" backwards, you
can hear evil messages. Listen
and hear the darkness...

SFX:
Music playing backwards—we
hear the message "Plenty of parking."

LUCIFER:
Oh, never mind.

MUSIC:
Crescendos

LUCIFER:
But if you DO go to the free
concert on June 27th, I'll make
sure elevator music follows you
wherever you go...Da-da-da-da
de-dadadada. You'll never be
able to get it out of your head!
You're singing it now! So heed my
warning and stay away from the
free concert at the Corel Centre
on June 27th... Ha-ha-ha-
ha—(starts coughing). That was a
bagel.

ANNOUNCER:
So there you have it, folks. Don't
miss the free concert at the Corel
Centre on June 27th, 7:30 p.m.,
with Jars of Clay and Michael W.
Smith. Everyone's going to be
there. Well, almost.

LOU 3

ANNOUNCER:
Well, once again, folks, please welcome my special guest, Lucifer.

SFX:
Loud "Exorcist"-type sounds

LOU:
Call me Lou.

ANNOUNCER:
So Lou, I hear you're upset about that free concert that's happening on June 27th at the Corel Centre.

SFX:
Doors slamming

ANNOUNCER:
Speaking of "slammin," the Grammy-Award-winning band Jars of Clay's gonna be playing, along with Michael W. Smith. Not to mention that special appearance by Billy Graham.

SFX:
"Exorcist"-type sounds

ANNOUNCER:
Whoa, looks like I hit a soft spot there, huh, Lou?

MUSIC:
Haunting crescendo as Lou talks

LOU:
Heed my warning. If you go to that free concert, I guarantee... your bathwater will never be the right temperature again. No, it'll be a little too hot or a little too cold, you'll add some hot water, that's logical, but then it'll be a little too hot, so you'll add some cold and it'll be a little too cold, and it will be your own private hell!

ANNOUNCER:
So if I'm hearing you, Lou, this is not going to be good.

LOU:
Oh, it'll be so ungood. So you'll add a little more hot, a little more cold, a little more hot, a little more cold, and you'll think, "I better call a plumber," but you'll get a machine, and they're evil.

MUSIC:
Jars of Clay kicks in

ANNOUNCER:
So there you have it, folks. Don't miss the free concert at the Corel Centre on June 27th, 7:30 p.m., with Jars of Clay and Michael W. Smith. Everyone's going to be there. Almost.

LOU 4

ANNOUNCER:
Well once again folks, Lucifer, the prince of darkness, is here in the studio—and he's really upset...

SFX:
Puking

ANNOUNCER:
...with an upset stomach. So Lou, it's about that free concert featuring the Grammy Award-winning band Jars of Clay and Michael W. Smith, isn't it?

LOU:
I am going to do everything in my power to make sure that free concert doesn't happen.

ANNOUNCER:
Oh yeah, like what?

SFX:
Doors slamming

ANNOUNCER:
Oooo, the old door-slamming trick. Ooo.

LOU:
Shut up.

ANNOUNCER:
Look, why don't you just admit there's nothing you can do to stop the show, huh?

MUSIC:
Haunting crescendo as Lou talks

LOU:
Nothing??

ANNOUNCER:
No.

LOU:
Nothing!

ANNOUNCER:
No.

LOU:
If you go to that free concert, I'll...I'll make sure that every time you eat mixed nuts...you'll never find any cashews... just lots of Brazil nuts...Brazilians don't even like those.

ANNOUNCER:
Ooooo, I'm so scared...

LOU:
And when you reach into the cereal box to find the toy...it won't be there...even though it says so on the box—there's this really cool little artist's rendering of an action pose. Why?

SFX:
Choking

LOU:
I have all the toys!!

SFX:
Choking

LOU:
Swallowed my gum.

MUSIC:
Jars of Clay kicks in

ANNOUNCER :
So there you have it, folks, don't miss the free concert at the Corel Centre on June 27th, 7:30 p.m., featuring Jars of Clay, Michael W. Smith, and the words of Billy Graham. Everyone's going to be there. Almost.

new

media

I n this rapidly growing and changing field, competitions such as these lend insight into trends within the form. Judging from the entries, this was the year New Media matured. While excellence has been recognized in previous years, this year's judges unanimously insisted that John Maeda's homage to the keyboard *Tap, Type, Write,* be singled out for special recognition, and so the Judges' Special Citation was born.

In addition to the continued explosive growth of entries in the New Media category, other recognizable trends included a proliferation of Internet banner ads. This will necessitate the continued adjustment of categories for next year's competition. Another surprise was the number of excellent CD-ROMs entered. While only a couple of years ago the creative use of this medium seemed to be waning, its benefits in certain distribution channels is clearly sustaining their usefulness.

In addition to the continued explosive growth of entries in the New Media category, other recognizable trends included a proliferation of Internet banner ads.

Because of the interactive nature of New Media entries, judging is a time-consuming enterprise. This year's judges deserve great thanks for the many hours they devoted to this process both in the preliminary and final rounds of judging. Special thanks goes to Brian Wu who was available for consultation when necessary, and, of course, to the Art Directors Club staff whose tireless efforts make this yearly gift possible.

CHARLES ALTSCHUL is a consultant specializing in the use of technology in art. He is currently chair of a committee of the Yale University Council formed to study the future of the Yale School of Art. He recently created the nation's first BFA program in multimedia at the University of the Arts in Philadelphia. Altschul's interests in technology and design stem from contemporary as well as historical perspectives. As founder and president of The New Overbrook Press, he has published handcrafted books including Samuel Beckett's *The Lost Ones* with intaglio prints by Charles Klabunde, and *The Last Lionel Electric Train Store,* a book of poems and illustrations by Roy Villa.

—Charles Altschul,
THE COOPER UNION
NEW MEDIA CHAIR

ROY ANDERSON, JR. left his position at Ogilvy & Mather Portland in 1993, and started his own multimedia production boutique, iCom. He and his small team have created over seventy CD-ROMs and Web sites for a broad client base that includes Hewlett-Packard, Intel, Jannsen Pharmaceutica, and The Art Directors Club for its first CD-ROM which was included in the 77th *Annual*.

HEIDI DANGELMAIER founded Hi-D to make technology accessible to non-geeks. Her interactive applications bring people together to strengthen brand loyalty, and help organizations with customer service, product development, promotion, public service, entertainment, education, and activism. Heidi has worked with organizations including Ameritech, Samsung, MetLife, Time Warner, and Sega, as well as social institutions such as The Smithsonian Institution, C.U.N.Y., and the Pew Foundation.

JIM GASPERINI has been designing, writing, and programming interactive media since the early '80s. His multimedia work "ScruTiny in the Great Round," a collaboration with collage artist Tennessee Rice Dixon and composer Charlie Morrow, won the Grand Prix du Jury Milia D'Or at MILIA '96 in Cannes. He is currently creative director of the SimCity project for Maxis/Electronic Arts.

ISAAC VICTOR KERLOW is an artist/designer and is currently director of digital talent and development at The Walt Disney Company. Prior to this post, Kerlow led the group of digital artists and animators at Disney Interactive responsible for developing and producing CD-ROM, on-line, and platform games. He is the author of several books including *The Art of 3-D Computer Animation and Imaging* published in 1996 by John Wiley and Sons.

CLEMENT MOK and his Studio Archetype are involved with everything from cyberspace theme parks to expert publishing systems and major identity programs. Clients have included IBM, Nintendo, QVC, UPS, American Express, and Netscape. Mok is also a founder of two other software companies, CMCD's Visual Symbol Library and NetObjects.

Since 1996, **TIFFANY SHLAIN** has served as the creative director and executive producer of The Webby Awards. In April 1998, Shlain founded The International Academy of Digital Arts and Sciences (IADAS), an organization dedicated to advancing creativity on the Web. Shlain is also an accomplished Web site and CD-ROM designer and an award-winning filmmaker.

ANNETTE WEINTRAUB is professor of art at The City College of New York and director of the Robinson Center for Graphic Arts and Communication Design. Her work explores the architectural environment as metaphor and investigates the dynamics of urban space. Weintraub's Web works (*Pedestrian* and *Realms*) and her digital still images have been shown in museums and galleries nationwide.

BRIAN WU is an information designer and the principal of Inside Out Design in New York City. The Company's work includes Web sites, intranet sites, interface design for software applications, document design, and publications in print for Xerox, Union Pacific, Bank of America, Zagat Survey, Cactus, and others. Formerly, Wu was a designer and systems manager at Chermayeff & Geismar, art director at Callaway Editions, and design director at BAM! Software.

DAVID SIEGEL'S Siegel Vision builds strategic direction and integrates technology with the on-line world for clients such as Sony, the U.S. Government, and Amazon.com. His books include *Secrets of Successful Web Sites: Project Management on the World Wide Web*, and *Creating Killer Web Sites*. He is chairman of Studio Verso, a high-end site design consultancy that has produced Web sites for clients such as Hewlett-Packard, Sony, and Office Depot.

LYNDA WEINMAN is an author, instructor, and designer specializing in graphics for screen-based media. Recent books include <Designing Web Graphics.3>, and *Dreamweaver 2.0 Hands-On-Training*. With her husband Bruce Heavin, Weinman opened the Ojai Digital Arts Center which is geared to the training of graphic artists in digital design.

GOLD

JUDGES' SPECIAL CITATION

**WEBSITE/CD-ROM DESIGN:
ART/EXPERIMENTAL PROJECTS**

Tap, Type, Write

Art Director John Maeda
Designer John Maeda
Illustrator John Maeda
Producer Naomi Enami
Studio MaedaStudio
Client Digitalogue Co., Ltd.
Country United States

Tap, Type, Write pays tribute to one of the great writing implements of all time–the typewriter. Despite an inability to simulate the inky smudge of the ribbon or the tactile response of the keys, *Tap, Type, Write* turns typing at the keyboard into a carefully choreographed audio-visual experience.

188

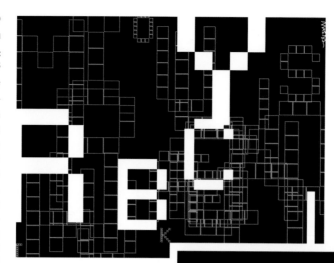

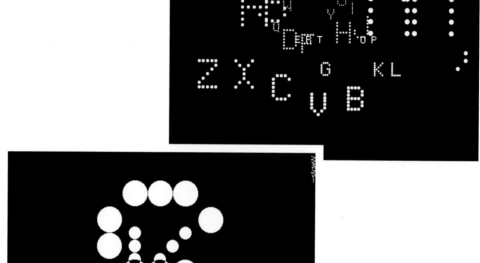

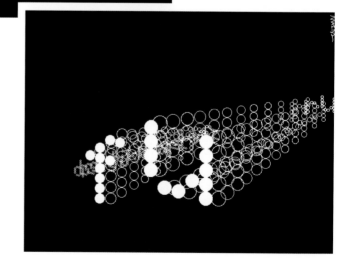

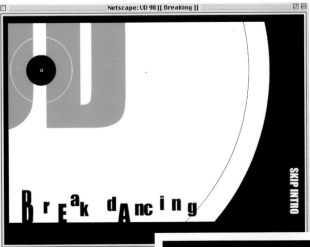

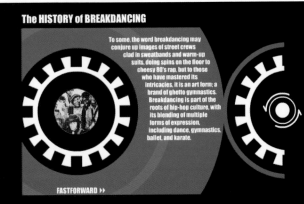

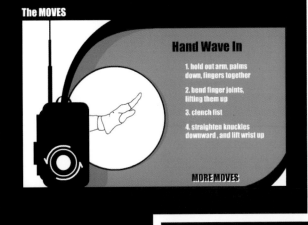

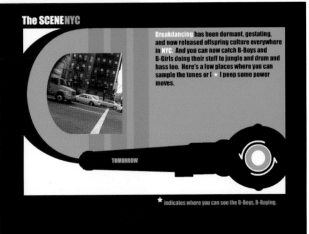

**WEBSITE/CD-ROM DESIGN:
ART/EXPERIMENTAL PROJECTS**

Urban Desires Featuring Breaking
(www.desires.com/features/breaking)

Art Director Khoi Uong
Creative Director PJ Loughran
Editor-In-Chief Gabrielle Shannon
Writers Laurie Linder, Khoi Uong
Designer Khoi Uong
Flash Design Kiley Bates, Khoi Uong
Digital Artist Khoi Uong
Illustrator Khoi Uong
Programmers Khoi Uong,
Dheeraj Vasishta
Producers Kiley Bates, James Plath
Publishers Chan Suh, Kyle Shannon
Agency AGENCY.COM
Client Urban Desires
Country United States

The designer, Khoi Uong, has this to
say about the site: It's a free-form
master jam in the old-school style,
wedding form with content.

GOLD

**WEBSITE/CD-ROM DESIGN:
ART/EXPERIMENTAL PROJECTS**

Urban Feedback Tokyo

Art Director Giles Rollestone
Creative Director Giles Rollestone
Designers Sophie Greenfield,
Giles Rollestone
Producer Giles Rollestone
Programmer Julian Baker
Studio Royal College of Art
Agency Urban Feedback
Client Too Corporation, Japan
Country England

Urban Feedback Tokyo is an abstract, atmospheric, interactive work that aims to capture and relay a sense of the city of Tokyo from a distant perspective in London. The interface was developed to focus on the fragmentary experience of day-to-day urban life. As viewers move through the site's spaces, different juxtapositions of media can be created which reflect an atmospheric journey through streets and city spaces and includes the chaos of overheard conversations, texts, sounds, symbolic and subliminal imagery. *Urban Feedback Tokyo* will be the second release in a series of multiple media experiences focusing on different cities.

190

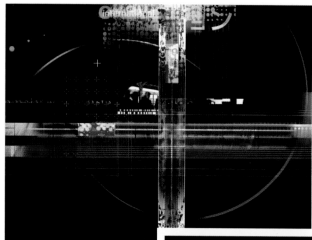

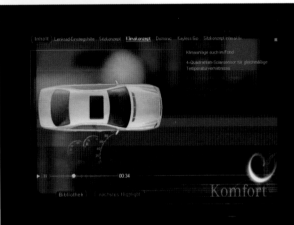

**WEBSITE/CD-ROM DESIGN:
ADVERTISING/SALES**

Die neue S-Klasse. Sinn und
Sinnlichkeit (The New S-Class.
Sense and Sensibility)

Art Directors Anette Scholz,
Michael Volkmer

Copywriters Matthias Färber,
Mareike Schmiedt

Screendesign Katja Rickert,
Susanne Schwalm

Videodesign Christiano Civitillo,
Markus Hermanni, Holger Hirth,
Florian Kraft, Anna Saub,
Christoph Schuhmacher

Programmer Thorsten Kraus

Music Ralf Wengenmayr

Agency Scholz & Volkmer

Client Daimler-Benz AG

Country Germany

The purpose of *The New S-Class.
Sense and Sensibility* CD-ROM,
produced on behalf of Daimler-Benz
AG, is to introduce the new
Mercedes S-Class to potential
buyers. While the layout of this
application paves the way for
focusing on the design and the
aesthetics of this upper-class
model, detailed product
information conveys all the facts
worth knowing about the car.

GOLD

**WEBSITE/CD-ROM DESIGN:
ADVERTISING/SALES**
nonstøck.2

Art Director Hans Neubert
Creative Director Hans Neubert
Designers Jutta Kirchgeorg,
Hans Neubert
Programmers Matt Anacleto,
Bryan Yee
Executive Producer Alberta Jarane
Music Jarryd Lowder
Agency Belk Mignogna
Associates/Nuforia, Inc.
Client nonstøck. inc.
Country United States

BMA was commissioned to create nonstøck's first interactive catalogue, *nonstøck.2*, which has since been distributed in eighteen countries. The challenge was to redefine the marketplace by providing a level of design and technical sophistication unmatched by any of nonstøck's competitors. BMA's approach was simple: create a useful search tool that is easy to use, but also entertaining and thought provoking. The result is a CD-ROM that works not unlike a software application or virtual desktop in which the experience of the search takes into consideration the way creative people think and play. It was our intention to strike a balance between useful tool and playful toy.

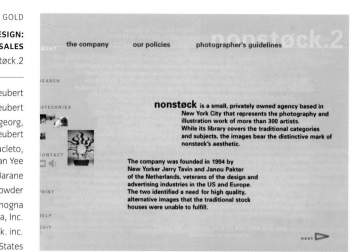

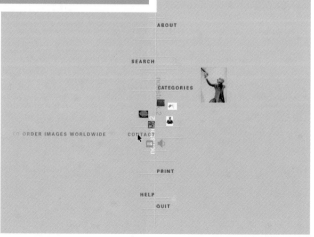

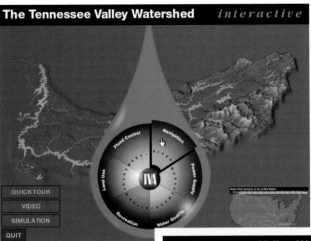

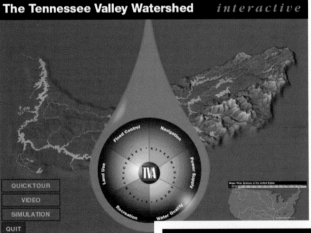

GOLD

WEBSITE/CD-ROM DESIGN: CORPORATE

The Tennessee Valley Watershed

Art Director Scott Colthorp
Creative Director Craig Colthorp
Copywriters Scott Colthorp,
Kate Marx, Alan Silverman
Designers Craig Colthorp,
Bill Dahlinger
Executive Producer Kate Marx
Producer Jeffrey Woods
Agency Atmosphere Pictures
Client Tennessee Valley Authority
Country United States

The Tennessee Valley Watershed CD-ROM was developed to demonstrate to members of congress, Tennessee residents, and utilities companies how the Tennessee Valley Authority manages the many competing demands placed upon the Tennessee River and the Tennessee Valley Watershed.

The Watershed CD has been instrumental in educating politicians and the public about the important role the TVA has played in the history and prosperity of the region. It effectively outlines the TVA's purpose, responsibilities, and objectives.

The CD demonstrates TVA functions with educational animation, interactive simulations, and three movies. The watershed map highlights power facilities and recreation areas, complete with statistics and phone numbers.

**WEBSITE/CD-ROM DESIGN:
ART/EXPERIMENTAL PROJECTS**

Dance with Me
(www.interport.net/~odley)

Creator Jonathan Gottlieb

Copywriter Jonathan Gottlieb

Designer Jonathan Gottlieb

Graphic Designers Jonathan Gottlieb,
Angela Greene

Producer Jonathan Gottlieb

Programmer Jonathan Gottlieb

Dancers Dorothy Drew,
John Lucchese

Sound Designer Jonathan Gottlieb

Casting/Graphic Elements
Angela Greene

Studio Odley Productions/
rhythmImage

Client Odley Productions/
rhythmImage

Country United States

194

Dance with Me is an interactive
dance number for anyone who ever
wanted to jump inside their TV set
when *Soul Train* came on.

The goal of the Web site is to bring
rhythm to the interactive experience,
and go beyond the push-button
interface. To provide something on
the Web that is more than just a
vending machine or brochure. *Dance
with Me* is designed to give people
in the on-line community something
to do beyond checking their e-mail
and stock quotes, something
entertaining to explore when
they're tired of playing games.

It will show advertisers they can
re-purpose their wildest TV spots
in truly interactive ways without
humongous download times.

The main goal is to make people
smile.

SILVER

**WEBSITE/CD-ROM DESIGN:
ART/EXPERIMENTAL PROJECTS**

Gardens in Kyoto

Art Director Naomi Enami
Designer Masaki Kimura
Photographer Tadayuki Naito
Producer Naomi Enami
Music Hiroki Okano
Programmer Shinji Sagiya
Agency Digitalogue Co., Ltd.
Client Digitalogue Co., Ltd.
Country Japan

Gardens in Kyoto is a collection of 500 photographs depicting what the experts believe to be the forty-nine most captivating gardens in the old capital city of Japan. Photos of temple gardens and private courtyards of old inns provide a three-dimensional textbook on the history, landscape form, and appreciation of Japanese garden construction. The musical score was composed by Hiroki Okano, an artist active in Europe who experiments with meditation sound using folk instruments from around the world.

SILVER

**WEBSITE/CD-ROM DESIGN:
GAME/ENTERTAINMENT**

YOU DON'T KNOW JACK®
Volume 4: The Ride

Art Direction Curium Design
Creative Director David Houghtalling
Art and Animation Stephen Ekstrom,
Lucas Kuzma, Liz Newell,
Adina Nystrom, Mike O'Connor,
Brian Perkins, Jamie Ruderman,
Troy Shelton, Evan Sornstein,
Tim Sniffen, RC Williams
Producers Michele Lindzy,
Julie Stroud
Director/Architect Harry Gottlieb
Agency Curium Design
Client Berkeley Systems & Jellyvision
Country United States

In early 1998, two gaming legends–
Berkeley Systems and Chicago's
Jellyvision–challenged Curium
Design to give Volume 4 of
YOU DON'T KNOW JACK®
(appropriately titled, *The Ride*)
a complete graphic overhaul.

Curium met the challenge by
designing *The Ride* with a hip, edgy,
industrial look that reflects the
irreverent content of the popular
trivia game, whose target audience
is 18-36-year-olds, with constant
movement, exciting 3-D graphics,
arresting realism, and of course,
lots of game show fun.

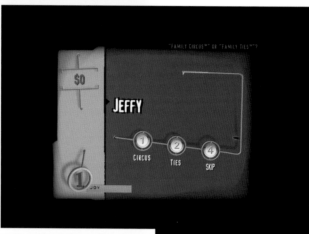

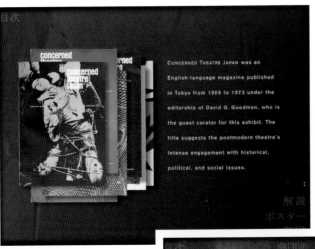

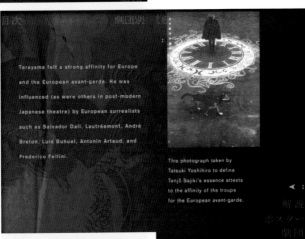

SILVER

**WEBSITE/CD-ROM DESIGN:
INSTITUTIONAL**

Concerned Theatre Japan:
The Graphic Art of Japanese
Theatre 1960 to 1980

Art Director John V. Clarke
Author David G. Goodman
Designer John V. Clarke
Design Assistant Jennifer Rhim
Production Krannert Art Museum
Co-Production Musashino Art
University, Japan
Production Assistants Young Suh,
Susannah Toro
Programmer Rose Marshack (XCO)
Studio Clarke Communication Design
Clients Krannert Art Museum,
Kinkead Pavilion, University of Illinois
at Urbana-Champaign
Country United States

Concerned Theatre Japan had its first
showing at the Krannert Art Museum
at the University of Illinois at Urbana-
Champaign. The exhibit consists of
seventy-three posters from a variety
of Japanese designers including
Tadanori Yokoo and Hirano Koga. It
has since traveled to New York City,
where it appeared at the AIGA
Gallery, and will open in Tokyo at the
ggg Gallery in September of 1999.

The CD-ROM began as an alternative
to a traditional exhibition catalogue,
serving as a lasting record of the
assembled body of work. It was
designed to be used as an electronic
kiosk where viewers could research
the historical background of each of
the posters featured in the exhibit.
What ultimately emerged, however,
was an invaluable reference tool for
exploring an often unrecognized
period of artistic expression in
Japanese art.

The disk offers a detailed history
of this underground theatre
movement from artistic, cultural,
and sociological points of view,
and with dynamic links to
appropriate posters, biographies,
videos, and critical commentaries.
Of particular interest are the various
and extensive indexes which allow
the user to locate posters and video
visually, and other information
textually. Additionally, each poster
can be inspected with a zoom
and scroll option.

SILVER

WEBSITE/CD-ROM DESIGN:
ADVERTISING/SALES

IBM e-culture Campaign

Art Directors Juan Gallardo,
Warren Kemp

Creative Director Jan Leth

Copywriter David Levy

Producers Jude Raymond Fish,
Kate Kehoe

Agency Ogilvy Interactive

Studio Compound

Client Todd Watson (IBM)

Country United States

The goal of the IBM *e-culture* campaign was to show how IBM e-business solutions have helped a range of large and small companies energize their businesses by taking advantage of the Internet. Internally, the campaign was dubbed e-culture because the broader intention was to tout how Internet-based solutions have pervaded countless aspects of contemporary life.

Since e-business is all about pushing the electronic envelope, it was necessary to do the same with this campaign by developing intriguing interactivity for the Enliven banners, and whizzy RealFlash mini-spots for the pop-up interstitial, thus offering a bit of fun before the serious sell. We created a series of interactive visual metaphors, for example for REI, a retailer of outdoor gear, in which the cursor becomes a flashlight that helps the user search for a campsite. It was also important to integrate the imagery used in the print work, as well as the essence of each company helped by IBM.

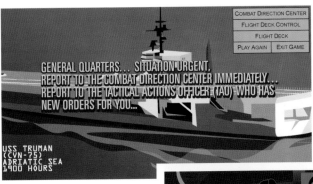

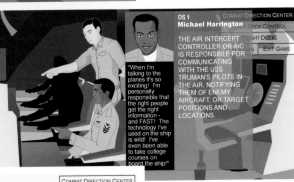

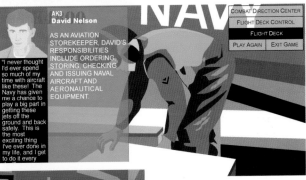

SILVER

**WEBSITE/CD-ROM DESIGN:
ADVERTISING/SALES**

The Mission
(www.navyjobs.com/under_15/HTML
/sub_game.HTML)

Art Director Nick Cogan
Designer Ryan Edwards
Executive Producer Josh Kimberg
Studio Bullseye Art Ltd.
Agency Organic
Client U.S. Navy
Country United States

This project was designed to teach 8-15-year-old children about the daily workings of a U.S. Navy aircraft carrier. *The Mission* was built in Flash and is presented in a linear format with some game-playing options. It can be found in the "15 and under" section of the www.navyjobs.com Web site. Imagery for the game was drawn from photographs taken on an aircraft carrier, and the music and sound were created by Bullseye specifically for the U.S. Navy.

SILVER

**WEBSITE/CD-ROM DESIGN:
CORPORATE**

Niemetz

Art Director Phil Dean
Copywriter Louise Miller
Designers Simon Krystal,
Andy Shillito, Paul Waddington
Producer Andy Shillito
Agency The Attik
Client Heavenly Moments
Corporation GmbH
Country England

The overall design brief for creating
the Niemetz CD-ROM was to
develop an interactive, multilingual
sales tool that clearly illustrated the
company's one hundred years of
heritage and expertise while
demonstrating its current core
business propositions.

This CD-ROM was developed for the
Niemetz sales team to sell the
revolutionary new process of cake
production and packaging using a
captivating design combining 3-D
animation and video footage.

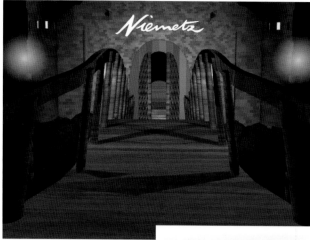

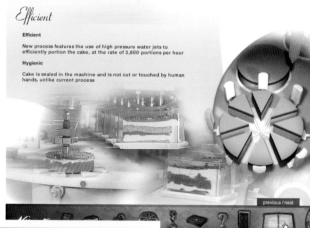

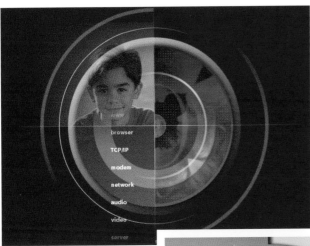

**WEBSITE/CD-ROM DESIGN:
INSTITUTIONAL**

Ohio SchoolNet Tools

Art Director Andrew Ricard
Copywriter Gail Harbaugh
Designers Mike Huntry,
Dan Ledman, Andrew Ricard
Illustrators Mike Huntry,
Dan Ledman, Andrew Ricard
Music Andrew Ricard
Agency Out of the Box Designs, Inc.
Client Ohio SchoolNet
Country United States

For use by Ohio's K–12 educators, the Ohio SchoolNet Tools CD provides an introduction to the Internet, its terminology, and essential Internet software. Designed for both novice and advanced users, the CD features easy navigation and helpful animated illustrations. Ohio SchoolNet gained favorable recognition as an organization committed to keeping Ohio's schools on the cutting edge of technology.

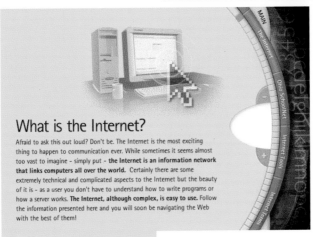

What is the Internet?

Afraid to ask this out loud? Don't be. The Internet is the most exciting thing to happen to communication ever. While sometimes it seems almost too vast to imagine - simply put - **the Internet is an information network that links computers all over the world.** Certainly there are some extremely technical and complicated aspects to the Internet but the beauty of it is - as a user you don't have to understand how to write programs or how a server works. **The Internet, although complex, is easy to use.** Follow the information presented here and you will soon be navigating the Web with the best of them!

DISTINCTIVE MERIT

**WEBSITE/CD-ROM DESIGN:
PROMOTION/SELF-PROMOTION**

Gr8

Art Director Lisa Wurfl-Roeca
Creative Directors Morton Jackson,
Lisa Wurfl-Roeca
Designers Morton Jackson,
Steve Palmieri, Lisa Wurfl-Roeca
Producer Steve Palmieri
Music Josh Mobley
Agency Gr8
Client Gr8
Country United States

The purpose of the *Gr8* CD-ROM is
to provide an interactive tool that
highlights the agency's work. The
interface allows users to see the
results of Gr8's business process in
integrating design, technology, and
marketing. The CD-ROM illustrates
the progressive nature of Gr8's
design philosophy and enables
clients to experience the impact
projects have when marketing,
design, and technology skills are
combined in equal shares.

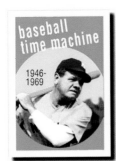

**WEBSITE/CD-ROM DESIGN:
EDUCATIONAL**

The Science of Baseball
(www.exploratorium.edu/baseball)

Art Director Jim Spadaccini
Writers Ellen Klages, Noel Wanner
Designer John Fowler
Photographer Amy Snyder
Illustrator David Barker
Executive Producer Robert Semper
Video Kurt Keppler
Interactives Lowell Robinson
Studio The Exploratorium
Client The Exploratorium
Country United States

The Science of Baseball explores the history and science behind America's favorite pastime. Packed with video and audio interviews with major league players and scientists, the site takes visitors inside the game while interactive exhibits let users test their own skills. *The Science of Baseball* was created by The Exploratorium, San Francisco's museum of science, art, and human perception.

WEBSITE/CD-ROM DESIGN: ADVERTISING/SALES

www.ferretcompany.com

Art Director Georgann Cartwright
Creative Director Leslie Godbe
Design The Design Team at Godbe Communications
Copywriter Jeanne Carley
Photographer Jeanne Carley
Agency Godbe Communications
Client The Ferret Company
Country United States

The Ferret Company Web site (www.ferretcompany.com) was developed to showcase ferret-themed gift items which feature the award-winning photography of Jeanne Carley. The Web site was designed with the concept of developing a community for owners and fans of this popular pet. Upon visiting the site, ferret lovers are encouraged to lend their support to legalization efforts and to submit their favorite pictures of their ferret companions to the gallery on the site. In addition to the clever photography, this site captures the ferret's whimsy and playful nature with animations such as the "ferret flop."

**WEBSITE/CD-ROM DESIGN:
ADVERTISING/SALES**
Herman Miller for the Home
(www.hmhome.com)

Art Director Kevin Budelmann
Creative Director Kevin Budelmann
Designers Kevin Budelmann,
Alison Popp
Programmer Jeff Sikkema
Copywriter Julie Ridl
Photographers Various
Illustrator Steven Joswick
(front page collage)
Producers Kevin Budelmann,
Julie Ridl
Studio BBK Studio
Client Ray Kennedy
(Herman Miller for the Home)
Country United States

Herman Miller's retailing effort,
Herman Miller for the Home,
wanted to establish a Web presence
that was independent from the
parent company. BBK Studio,
which developed the division's print
collateral and identity, designed this
on-line version of Herman Miller for
the Home's printed catalog. The site
includes information about their
classic furniture designs, home
office furniture, ergonomic chairs,
list of retailers, product designers,
and links to the corporate on-line
store. The Web site's unique
horizontal navigation and design
suggests taking a walking tour of a
real product showroom or
exhibition space.

**WEBSITE/CD-ROM DESIGN:
ADVERTISING/SALES**

BMW 7 Series (www.bmwusa.com)

Art Director Kevin Flatt
Creative Director Dan Olson
Designers Kevin Flatt, Nhan Nguyen
Multimedia Programmer
Mark Sandau
Programming Duffy Programming
Team, Selectica Programming Team
HTML Heather Gowdy
Copywriter Chuck Carlson
Agency Duffy Design and Interactive
Client BMW of North America
Country United States

The BMW Web site is designed to
mirror the performance of BMW
cars. The recent improvements
to the BMW 7 Series fueled a
performance upgrade of the 7 Series
section of bmwusa.com. The entire
section was redesigned, resulting in
a cleaner interface, more intuitive
navigation, and the addition of new
functions. You can now completely
configure a 7 Series sedan on-line,
obtain accurate pricing, apply for a
lease or loan, and transmit your
choices to your preferred BMW
center to place your order.

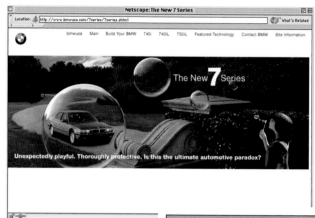

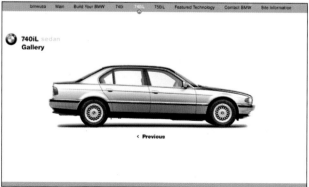

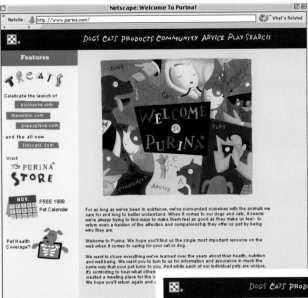

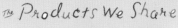

MERIT

WEBSITE/CD-ROM DESIGN: ADVERTISING/SALES

Purina (www.purina.com)

Art Director Dan Olson
Creative Director Dan Olson
Designers Nhan Nguyen, Jason Strong
Programmers Margaret Bossen, Matt Jannusch, Brad Olson, Kore Peterson, Colin Schaub
Copywriter Deborah Gold
Illustrator Greg Clarke
Producer Jen Nord
Agency Duffy Design and Interactive
Client Ralston Purina
Country United States

The *Purina* Web site was designed to create a community by and about pet lovers that establishes *Purina* as an authority on pet nutrition and as a partner in caring for the pets people love. The site's goal is to become the most popular pet care resource on the Web. The text and design work together to create a warm understanding of the emotions people feel toward their pets.

MERIT

**WEBSITE/CD-ROM DESIGN:
ADVERTISING/SALES**

Mercedes-Benz 2000 S-Class
On-line Showroom
(www.mbusa.com/s-class)

Art Director Jason Delichte
Creative Directors Michel Clairo,
Ted Hellard
Designers Benno Masanori,
Carolyn Rouse
Copywriter Heather Fitzgerald
Production Managers
Stephanie Chamberland,
Chris Gokiert, Candace Matviw
Agency Lowe Interactive
and Critical Mass
Client Mercedes-Benz
of North America
Country United States

The Mercedes-Benz 2000 S-Class
Preview Program On-line is a
relationship marketing program
designed to communicate
information to the car-buying public
about the year 2000 S-Class series in
the hope of driving traffic to
Mercedes-Benz Centers for test
drives, and, ultimately, purchases.

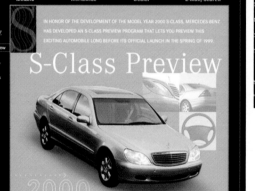

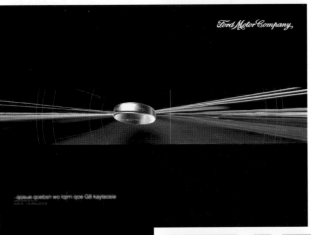

MERIT

WEBSITE/CD-ROM DESIGN: ADVERTISING/SALES
Ford Detroit Autoshow Kiosk

Art Director John Mamus
Executive Creative Director Jan Leth
Creative Director Mach Arom
Designer John Mamus
Technical Design Supervisor Wolfgang Von Stuermer
Programmer Mark Hofschneider
Copywriter Donna Oetzel
Illustrator Terrance Peng
Producers Kari Altman, Fashawna Hall
Production Manager Rachael Heapps
Agency Ogilvy Interactive
Client Ford Motor Company
Country United States

Entitled *F6*, this kiosk application invites autoshow visitors to embark on a virtual road trip—an imaginary drive defined by their own choices. To begin, each user chooses a theme that establishes a look and feel for their trip. They can then select from various vehicle, food, lodging, luggage, and companion types while stopping along the way to read various banners about key Trustmark messages. At the end of the trip users are registered to win a real road trip inspired by one of the themes from *F6*.

MERIT

**WEBSITE/CD-ROM DESIGN:
CORPORATE**

www.momgroup.com

Art Director Rod Zylstra
Creative Director Mark Ury
Designer Rod Zylstra
Programmer Oliver Bett
Copywriters Joy Parks, Mark Ury
Photographer Jim Cochrane
Producer James Fox
Agency Animatics Interactive Corp
Client M.O.M. Printing
Country Canada

How do you make an intangible Web page feel like paper? Our answer was to meld type, tightly cropped images, and color into a shifting matrix. This created a visible texture that reinforced the client's reputation as meticulous commercial printers. We also fussed over how to celebrate the staff and customers, both renowned for their work. Using their work turned out to be the answer. Dozens of people were interviewed about their craft from which a dialogue was created that highlighted the passion everyone felt for M.O.M. After the site launched, one of their pressmen complained that it didn't look like a printer's Web site. We were so pleased.

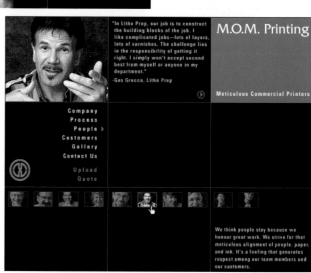

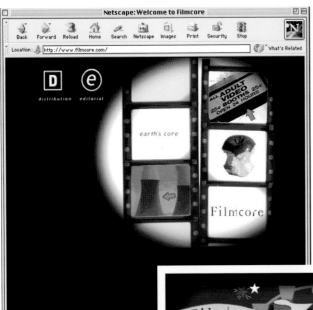

WEBSITE/CD-ROM DESIGN:
CORPORATE

www.filmcore.com/editorial

Art Director Rick Morris
Designer Rick Morris
Programmer/Animator Phil Acosta
Copywriter Steve Sandoz
Illustrator John Parra
Producer Sylvia Kahn
Studio Producer's Source
Client FilmCore
Country United States

In graphically designing this site, a totally unconventional approach was used. It was important to find solutions that made the media used compatible with the Internet. A freelance illustrator was commissioned to execute the "midway" in oil painting. Using a series of compression experiments, a method was developed to reach the lowest possible file size while maintaining the nuances of the brushstrokes in the illustrator's artwork. Animations were treated as three-position cycling movies to produce the perfect mad carnival effect.

MERIT

**WEBSITE/CD-ROM DESIGN:
CORPORATE**

www.audi-tt.com

Creative Directors Alex Baumgardt,
Thomas Noller
Designer Daniel Jennett
Programming Büro am Draht
Copywriter Karin Müller
Photographer Quirin Leppert
Concept Development Stephan Platt,
Vicky Tiegelkamp
Video Production Patrick Boltz,
Jörg Schultze
Producer Marion Laurinat
Music Rashad Becker
Agency Meta Design Plus GmbH
Client Audi AG
Country Germany

The *TT Web Event* is part of a total
concept market launch of the
Audi TT from the model's first
appearance under wraps to its
presentation at the Paris Auto
Show on October 1, 1998.

The *TT Web Event*, on-line since
September 17, 1998, focuses on
three main themes: design,
technology, and vision. It uses a
story-telling mode to place the
Audi TT in an exploratory and
experimental context to optimize
the emotional impact of the
automobile on the viewer.

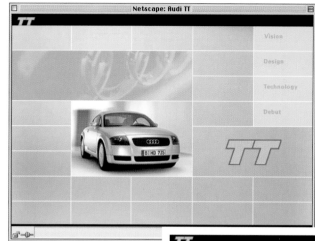

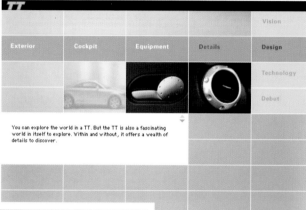

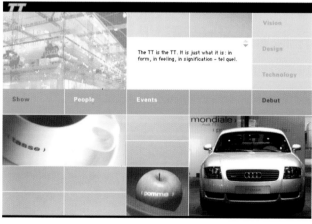

MERIT

WEBSITE/CD-ROM DESIGN: CORPORATE

Denny's Restaurants
(www.dennysrestaurants.com)

Art Director Jason Delichte
Creative Director Michel Clairo
Designer Chantelle Koolick
Illustrator Clay Weishaar
Producers Dan Goodman,
Adam Q. Holden-Bache
Production Manager Leah Wood
Agency Lowe Interactive
and Critical Mass
Client Denny's Restaurants
Country United States

The Denny's Restaurants Corporate
Web site is an interactive brand
presence and resource for
information and promotional events
concerning Denny's Restaurants.

MERIT

WEBSITE/CD-ROM DESIGN: CORPORATE

Online Magic
(www.onlinemagic.com)

Design Director Januzzi Smith
Art Director Darren Navier
Creative Director Alex Wright
Designer Jim Curry
Agency AGENCY.COM
Client Online Magic
Country England

The Online Magic site was created to establish and communicate the strong brand identity created for this award-winning Web company by Januzzi Smith. The concept of the Online Magic brand was based on messaging. The unique bold, flat color "Omid" letterforms thus formed the basis of the site design.

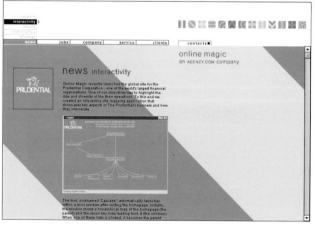

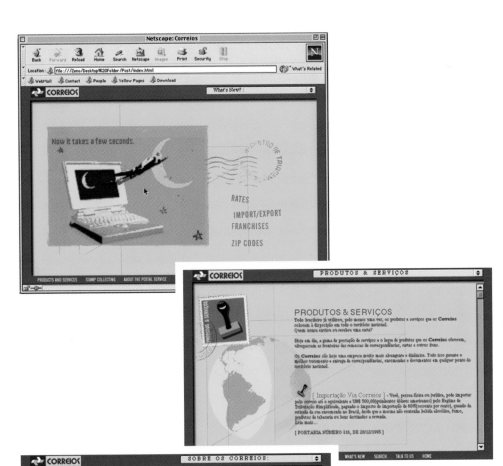

**WEBSITE/CD-ROM DESIGN:
CORPORATE**

www.dm9.com.br/post

Art Director PJ Pereira
Creative Directors Nizan Guanaes,
Tomás Lorente
Designer Daniel Brum
Programmer Pedro Mozart
Copywriter PJ Pereira
Illustrator Daniel Brum
Producer PJ Pereira
Multimedia Company Urbana
Webmakers
Agency DM9 DDB Publicidade
Client Correios (Brazilian Post Office)
Country Brazil

The purpose of this Web site
produced for the Brazilian Post Office
was to develop and launch its official
site in Brazil. It is designed to bring
people information on the company
and the on-line services it offers,
such as letters and telegrams via
the Internet.

MERIT

**WEBSITE/CD-ROM DESIGN:
CORPORATE**
Star Trek Digital Style Guide

Art Directors Pär Larsson,
Henry Vizcarra
Designers Pär Larsson,
Peggy Martin, Rickard Olsson,
Suppasak Viboonlarp
Illustrator Pär Larsson
Agency 30sixty design
Client Viacom Consumer Products
Country United States

The *Star Trek Digital Style Guide*
CD-ROM was created for licensees
of Viacom Consumer Products.
It enables the user to access
information, fonts, logos, ready-to-
use line art, and high-resolution
images from every existing *Star Trek*
television show and feature film. The
design objective was to incorporate
the visual material of each Star Trek
TV show and film into an easy-to-use
interface, while maintaining the
unique color and graphic scheme of
the individual properties.

WEBSITE/CD-ROM DESIGN: CORPORATE

FedEx Automation Interactive

Art Director Cynthia Henry
Creative Director Cynthia Henry
Designers Merry Perry, Mike Saurer
Copywriters Vince Giorgi, Dave Smith
Illustrator Mike Kasun
Producer Mike Pease
Agency Hanley-Wood Custom Publishing
Client Federal Express
Country United States

217

The *FedEx Shipping Automation Interactive* presentation was designed to help FedEx sales professionals sell FedEx shipping-automation systems. With a visually appealing, easy-to-use demo on their laptops, account executives can engage prospects and customers (ranging from Fortune 500 chief information officers to start-up entrepreneurs) in the simplicity and efficiency of automated shipping. Given the client's request for a decidedly "non-techy" tool with which to sell tech solutions, Hanley-Wood Custom Publishing used a "cityscape" motif to create a familiar, welcoming graphical user interface.

**WEBSITE/CD-ROM DESIGN:
CORPORATE**

Women's World Cup Graphic
Standards Manual

Art Director Alan Colvin
Creative Director Joe Duffy,
Dan Olson
Designer Alan Colvin
Multimedia Programmer
Mark Sandau
Copywriter Various
Agency Duffy Design and Interactive
Client FIFA 1999 Women's World Cup
Organizing Committee
Country United States

218

The *Women's World Cup Graphic
Standards Manual* CD-ROM was
designed to provide artwork and
guidelines for the 1999 FIFA
Women's World Cup Identity System.
The foundation for establishing the
1999 Women's World Cup as a brand
is being laid; creating standards for
the use of this identity will assure
that the brand being built is destined
for greatness. To achieve this goal,
all communications surrounding the
event must be of the highest caliber.

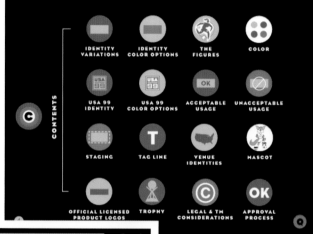

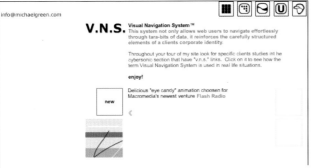

MERIT

**WEBSITE/CD-ROM DESIGN:
PROMOTION/SELF-PROMOTION**
Michael Green: Theory of Visual
Navigation Systems

Art Director Michael Green
Creative Director Michael Green
Designer Michael Green
Programmer Michael Green
Copywriter Michael Green
Producer Michael Green
Music Michael Green
Agency Michael Green, LLC
Client Michael Green
Country United States

Theory of Visual Navigation Systems
allows Web users to navigate
effortlessly through tara-bits of data
while reinforcing the carefully
structured elements of clients'
corporate identities.

WEBSITE/CD-ROM DESIGN: PROMOTION/SELF-PROMOTION
SmellFunny Software
(www.smellfunny.com)

Art Director Dean Terry
Designers Terran Kim,
Chris Rodriguez
Copywriters Irl Nathan,
Chris Rodriguez
Illustrators Kwesi Kennedy,
Terran Kim, Chris Rodriguez
Producers Irl Nathan, Dean Terry
Sound Design Dean Terry
Consultant Terrill Thomas
Agency PixelWave Design
Client PixelWave Design
Country United States

SmellFunny Software is a self-promotional streaming media showcase site developed by PixelWave Design. The Web site presents a fictional software company with highly questionable products. The circular, mechanical interface is completely done in Flash 3 and the product presentations are RealFlash movies.

220

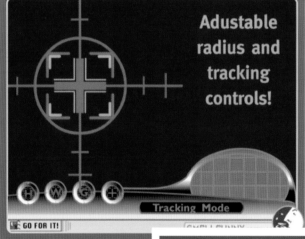

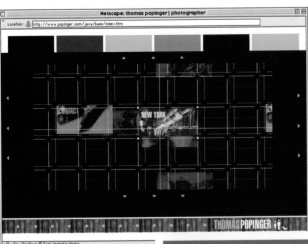

Art Director Jeremy Abbett
Creative Director Jeremy Abbett
Designers Anne Eickenberg,
Andrea Mittmann
Screen Designer Anne Eickenberg
Programmers Nicole Kenguel,
Jan Studt
Photographer Thomas Popinger
Producers Manuel Funk, Ralf Kemmer
Sound Sascha Merg
Agency Fork Unstable Media
Client Thomas Popinger
Country Germany

Fork Unstable Media aims to create
alternatives to the way people
normally experience a Web site. By
presenting a variety of options to the
client, the end user may experience
an engaging navigation system or a
narrative in which a journey from
point A to point B is achieved. For his
Web site, Viennese photographer
Thomas Popinger wanted a platform
where he could display his work and
update portions of it himself. He also
wanted to represent the three cities
in which he works in such a way that
visitors would get a feel for each city
even if they have never been there.

MERIT

**WEBSITE/CD-ROM DESIGN:
PROMOTION/SELF-PROMOTION**
Synthetic Pleasure
(www.thermofish.com)

Art Director Juliane Hadem
Designer Juliane Hadem
Illustrator Juliane Hadem
Copywriter Juliane Hadem
Translator Toni Gielessen
Producer Juliane Hadem
Studio Juliane Hadem
Country United States

Thermofish is about the experience of the individual. It offers the user a journey composed of meditative clicks through the world of the goddess Kali Kha, featuring an art project area and a gallery which invites the user into a variety of digital worlds.

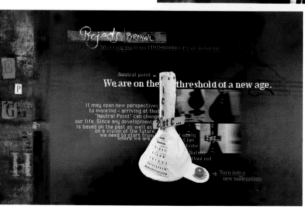

Creative Director Mike Melia
Designers David Hewitt, Mike Melia,
Sven Oberstein
Programmer Lydia Sharp
Photographer David Hewitt
Studio Melia Design Group
Client Melia Design Group
Country United States

Our Web site showcases our design
and programming skills while
providing some insight as to who we
are and projects we have had the
opportunity to work on.

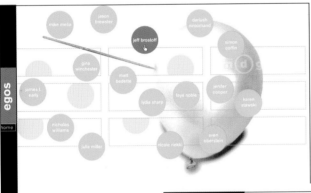

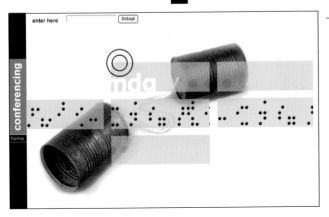

**WEBSITE/CD-ROM DESIGN:
PROMOTION/SELF-PROMOTION**

Underline (www.underline.com)

Art Director Lin Ong
Creative Directors D.J. Edgerton,
Paul Geczik
Designer Nina Ong
Programmer Nina Ong
Copywriter D.J. Edgerton
Illustrator Paul Geczik
Producer Laura Favorito
Agency Underline
Client Underline
Country United States

The goal in producing the *Underline*
Web site was to create an on-line
portfolio using traditional design
materials and natural media while
presenting it in this new medium,
proving that it is possible to provide
Web users with a comfortable,
familiar experience even in a
Web-based environment.

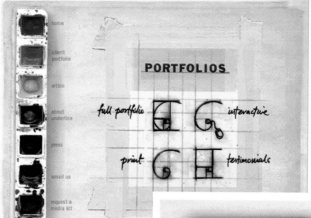

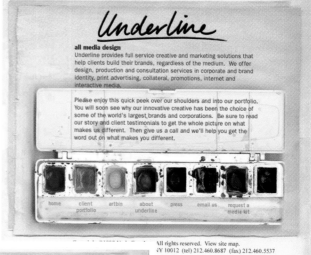

WEBSITE/CD-ROM DESIGN: PROMOTION/SELF-PROMOTION

www.choppingblock.com

Art Director Rob Reed
Designers Mike Essl, Rob Reed, Matthew Richmond, Tom Romer
Copywriter Rob Reed
Illustrators Rob Reed, Brian Romero
Producer Chris Darner
Studio The Chopping Block, Inc.
Client The Chopping Block, Inc.
Country United States

Rather than settling for a single static corporate identity, The Chopping Block regularly changes its Web site in tribute to a variety of graphic design languages and looks. Prior to the firm's recent incarnation as "design scouts," the company has lived on-line as racecar drivers, famous horror movie monsters, and NASA astronauts. Site fans should note that The Chopping Block is hard at work on the next on-line identity. Expect something big to hit a small screen near you in summer 1999.

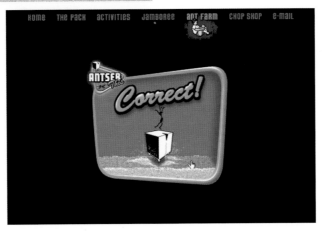

**WEBSITE/CD-ROM DESIGN:
PROMOTION/SELF-PROMOTION**

www.johnrees.com

Art Director Dave Groom

Designer Sean Bates

Programmer Sean Bates

Photographer John Rees

Studio John Rees
Photographic Images

Client John Rees

Country United States

The purpose of this Web site is
to give designers and art
directors a quick overview of
my photography work.

**WEBSITE/CD-ROM DESIGN:
PROMOTION/SELF-PROMOTION**
Felderman+Keatinge
(www.fkadesign.com)

Art Director Richard Parr

Designers Brad Benjamin,
Steve Mausolf, Gavin Wu

Programmer
Anissa Barton Thompson

Illustrator Stanley Felderman

Producer Richard Parr

Studio Guidance Solutions

Client Felderman+Keatinge

Country United States

www.fkadesign.com introduces the
architectural interior design firm
Felderman+Keatinge Associates to
interested viewers by offering a
window into the company's culture
and its mission to unite art and
technology. The Web site engages
the viewer by revealing the firm's
process through the dynamic
manipulation product portfolio.

227

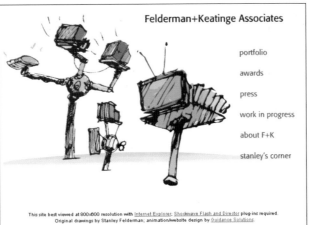

MERIT

**WEBSITE/CD-ROM DESIGN:
PROMOTION/SELF-PROMOTION**
Dickson's Access (CD-ROM)

Creative Director Mike Melia
Designers David Hewitt, Mike Melia,
Nicole Riekki
Programmer Nicholas Williams
Copywriter Cally Curtis
Photographers David Hewitt,
Joel Marcus
Illustrator Gina Binkley
Studio Melia Design Group
Client Dickson's
Country United States

Melia Design Group developed a
direct-mail CD-ROM targeting
national designers and corporations
so that they could "access"
Dickson's. Our approach was to
create a virtual tour via a playful
and elegant interface.

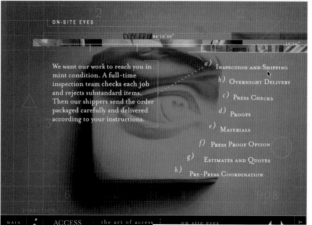

**WEBSITE/CD-ROM DESIGN:
PROMOTION/SELF-PROMOTION**
Road Trip

Copywriter Tim Dundon
Designer Betsy Masi
Programmer John Lau
Photographers (video footage)
Scott Lauder, Valerie Salez
Production Managers
Colleen Gaudet, Cher Novinc
Music Koko Productions
Studio Detroit Creative Group
Client Detroit Creative Group
Country Canada

Road Trip is a five-panel folding
case that houses a CD-ROM, a
fourteen-page booklet, and
several interchangeable insert
sheets. The objective of the piece
was to showcase the graphic
design and multimedia capabilities
of Detroit Creative Group. The
CD-ROM component features
offbeat video footage of a retro
couple on a meandering road trip,
their often nonsensical dialogue and
navigation leading the viewer into
key features of Detroit Creative
Group such as Mileage (history),
Performance (portfolio), and Specs
(amenities). Type and graphic
elements in both the CD-ROM and
the print materials are reminiscent of
both the graphic simplicity of
highway signage and the forward
motion of streams of traffic.

Art Director Trey Harrell
Creative Director Melanie J. Husk
Designer Trey Harrell
Programmer Trey Harrell
Copywriters Mary McDonald,
Carl Smith
Illustrator Trey Harrell
Director Carl Smith
Music Trey Harrell
Producer Trey Harrell
Production Assistants Bruce Cooke,
Varick Rosete
Agency Husk Jennings Advertising
Client People 3, Inc.
Country United States

The purpose of the *People 3* CD-ROM was to introduce a trade show audience to our client's information technology and human resources consulting services. Since the target group was the information technology industry, we used their medium of choice to showcase the benefits of optimizing their employees with People 3's services.

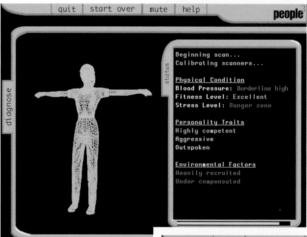

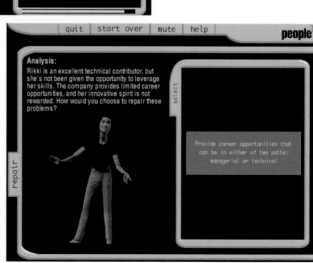

WEBSITE/CD-ROM DESIGN:
BOOK/MAGAZINE
Folha de São Paulo '98

Art Director Paulo Marques
Creative Director Mauro Cavaletti
Designer Paulo Marques
Engineer/Programmer
Alexandre Maylinch
Producer Abel Reis
Agency Midialog
Client Publifolha
Country Brazil

Created by Midialog, the CD-ROM
Folha de São Paulo '98 revolutionized
the storage of news, articles, and
pictures published by the newspaper
during the year. Modern graphic
design and advanced multimedia
tools allow users to interact with the
information in an unusual and
exciting way.

231

MERIT

WEBSITE/CD-ROM DESIGN: EDUCATIONAL

NOVA Online (www.pbs.org/nova)

Art Director Kim Ducharme
Designer Kim Ducharme
Programmer Brenden Koatsey
Copywriter Karen Hartley (Hot Science section)
Senior Producer Lauren Aguirre
Producer Peter Tyson
Assistant Producer Rob Meyer
Studio WGBH Educational Foundation
Client NOVA
Country United States

NOVA Online supports the long-running PBS show's weekly broadcasts with innovative and interactive content related to the program's themes. It is designed for people of all ages who are interested in exploring the world of science. The Web site is visually compelling and features an intuitive navigation system and structure that allows users to easily and seamlessly move through the editorial content.

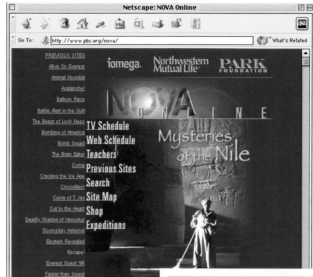

THE PEAK OF HIS CAREER

THE WALTZ OF ALL WALTZES

In 1865, to celebrate the opening of the Vienna Ring-strasse, Strauss wrote a Polka as a musical homage to his home city: 'S gibt nur a Kaiser-stadt, 's gibt nur a Wien. And 1867 saw him finally at the peak of his dance composing career, with the composition of The Blue Danube Waltz, the epitome of the waltz, the not-so-secret Austrian national anthem and the world's first hit melody.

PREVIOUS PAGE   NEXT PAGE

CONTENTS   BIOGRAPHY   CHRONOLOGY

THE PEAK OF HIS CAREER

... AND BACK TO PARIS

In October 1877, Paris was once again longing for Strauss to return. He had become the trend setter; there were Strauss hats, Strauss ties and Strauss stockings – in every respect, Strauss was "in".

Paris around 1880

Foster for the Paris performance of Fledermaus.

A cartoon: Strauss as prime minister – and everyone's happy.

"At the Strauss concert".

PREVIOUS PAGE   NEXT PAGE

LIST OF WORKS   HELP   BACK   QUIT

CHRONOLOGY

1852

INVOLVEMENT AT THE COURT BALLS
Strauss plays with the Court Ball Orchestra, and composes the Liebeslieder Waltz and the Annen Polka.

1853

JOSEF JOINS THE STRAUSS BUSINESS
Schani is seriously ill, and his brother Josef has to conduct the orchestra for the first time. Johann composes the Kaiser Franz Joseph I Rettungs-Jubel march on the occasion of the Emperor's "miraculous escape".

THE ATTEMPTED ASSASINATION
On February 18, Emperor Franz Joseph, during his usual walk along the Bastions, only escapes violent death thanks to a quirk of well-meaning fate. The Emperor is the victim of an assault by a Hungarian journeyman tailor, but is merely injured.

1804   1852   1899

CONTENTS   BIOGRAPHY   CHRONOLOGY

CHRONOLOGY

THE YEAR OF TRAGEDY
A year of misfortune, with the death of his mother on February 23, and his brother Josef on July 22.

THE FIRST OPERETTA
Strauss makes his debut as an operetta composer. Indigo und die vierzig Räuber is premiered at the Theater an der Wien.

1870

OPENING OF THE MUSIKVEREIN
The Musikverein Building, constructed by Theophil Hansen from 1867 to 1870, is opened in January.

1871

THE TRAVELLING EMPRESS
Empress Elisabeth, increasingly unhappy in Vienna, begins to travel more and more from the 1870s on. During these years, she spends most of her time primarily in the Gödöllö Palace in Hungary. 1870 is the first year in which she is not in Vienna at all.

1804   1870   1899

CONTENTS   BIOGRAPHY   CHRONOLOGY   LIST OF WORKS   HELP   BACK   QUIT

MERIT

WEBSITE/CD-ROM DESIGN: EDUCATIONAL
Johann Strauss the Younger–
The King of Waltz

Art Director Irmi Walli

Creative Director
Werner Petricek

Designer Irmi Walli

Programmers Jochen Fill,
Alexander Kölbl, Alexander Schälss,
Alexander Ullrich

Copywriter Barbara Sternthal

Recording MG Sound, Vienna

Sound Effects Foster Kent, Salzburg

Music (Audio) Special Projects,
Polygram Austria,
by courtesy of Deutsche
Grammophon GmbH, Hamburg

Music (CD-ROM) Deutsche
Grammophon GmbH, The Decca
Record Company Limited

**Music Dramaturgy and Sound
Director** Stefan Müller

Producer Michael Zeiller

Agency 01 EDV–Consulting und
Development GmbH

Clients City of Vienna, Polygram
(Universal Music Austria)

Country Austria

The audio portion of this Enhanced CD–Johann Strauss the Younger– contains seven excerpts from Neujahrskonzerte of the Wiener Philharmoniker. The CD-ROM features an interactive presentation of the life of Johann Strauss the Younger consisting of his biography, a chronology, and a list of works. Explore the life, music, and historical background of the waltz king in four languages (English, German, French, and Italian).

MERIT

**WEBSITE/CD-ROM DESIGN:
ART/EXPERIMENTAL PROJECTS**

Balloon Hat Experience
(www.balloonhat.com)

Art Director Andrew Wermuth

Designers Charlie Eckert,
Andrew Wermuth

Programmers Nancy Dillon,
Rob Stupary

Copywriter Addi Somekh

Photographer Charlie Eckert

Balloon Hat Twister Addi Somekh

Studio Vermouth Designskidoodle

Client The Varieties of the Balloon
Hat Experience

Country United States

The Balloon Hat Experience Web site
projects the haphazard and romantic
image of the world traveler. The
purpose of this photo-based site is to
show that laughter and amusement
can bond people throughout the
world and transcend barriers such as
language and national border.
Because the Web was chosen as the
project's medium, these barriers
continue to be transcended, allowing
participants access to the photos
from anywhere in the wired universe.

234

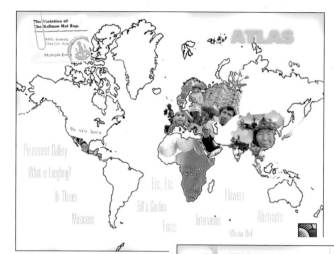

back to threes

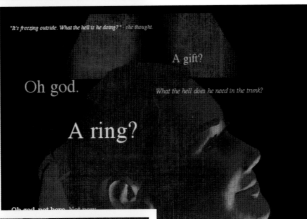

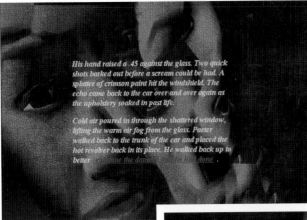

MERIT

WEBSITE/CD-ROM DESIGN:
ART/EXPERIMENTAL PROJECTS
Fuel
(www.bornmag.com/friction/fuel)

Art Director Auriea Harvey
Designer Auriea Harvey
Programmer Marc Antony Vose
Illustrator Auriea Harvey
Author Neil Simon
Studio Entropy8 Digital Arts
Client Born Magazine
Country United States

Fuel is a disturbing tale of a disturbed romance. Entropy8 utilized DHTML, 3-D imagery, and digital painting to create an interactive story with atmosphere and suspense.

235

MERIT

**WEBSITE/CD-ROM DESIGN:
ART/EXPERIMENTAL PROJECTS**
The Experimental Files
(www.lightofspeed.com)

Art Director David Crawford
Designer David Crawford
Agency David Crawford
Client David Crawford
Country United States

The Experimental Files
(www.lightofspeed.com) houses
over twenty Flash experiments
ranging from the purely visual to
the semi-narrative. For the past year
this site has served as a showcase
for new ideas; now it also chronicles
my progression as a Web artist.

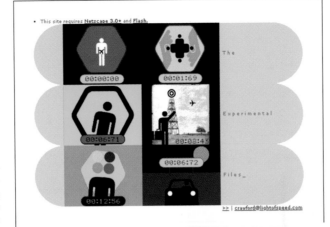

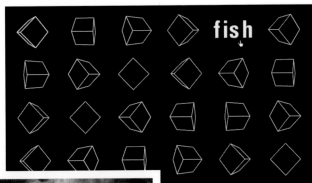

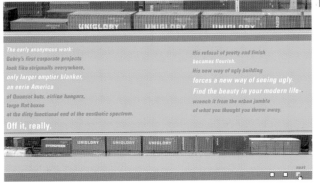

MERIT

**WEBSITE/CD-ROM DESIGN:
ART/EXPERIMENTAL PROJECTS**
Azimuth 360°–The Site Specific
Work of Frank O. Gehry

Creative Director Ray Wood
Designer Ray Wood
Copywriter Will Aitken
Programmers André Beaudry,
Ray Wood
Still Photographer Diana Shearwood
Quicktime VR Photographers
Ramona Ramlochand,
Diana Shearwood
Producer Theo Diamantis
Agency Behaviour
Client Behaviour New Media: Scroll
Country Canada

Azimuth 360° is an interactive
exploration of the architecture of the
Guggenheim Museum in Bilbao,
Spain. The feature fuses traditional
and panoramic photography, text,
and modern graphic design to create
a unique portrait of Frank O. Gehry's
aesthetic. The Web site's target
audience is anyone who enjoys
interactive content on the Web that
focuses on photography, design, and
architecture.

237

MERIT

**WEBSITE/CD-ROM DESIGN:
ART/EXPERIMENTAL PROJECTS**

I-Section
(www.turbulence.org/WORKS/
i-section)

Art Director Friederike Paetzold
Designer Friederike Paetzold
Programmer Uwe Kristen
Copywriter Friederike Paetzold
Illustrator Friederike Paetzold
Studio 11K
Client 11K
Country United States

I-Section is an experimental Web site exploring the emotional resonance associated with internal organs, the possibility of an aesthetic of dissection, and what is left when the body has been taken apart. Utilizing the interactive capabilities of DHTML, the piece takes the form of an on-line anatomy lesson in which metaphorical associations rather than scientific explanations are the result. *I-Section's* inspiration was an eighteenth-century anatomically correct mannequin displayed in Vienna's Museum of Medical History: an idealized wax figure that disturbingly blurs the line between scientific observation and pleasure/power-oriented looking.

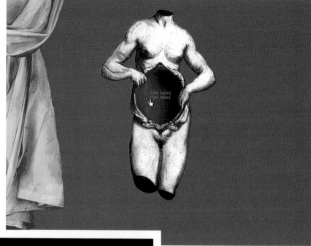

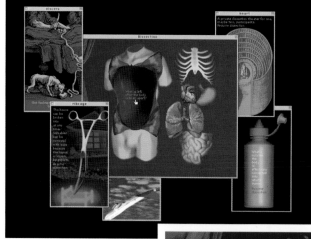

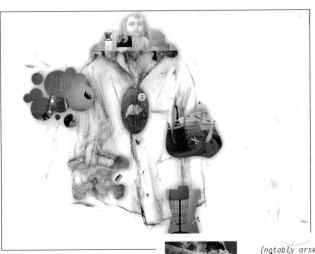

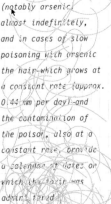

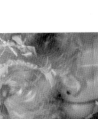
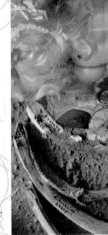
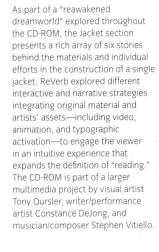

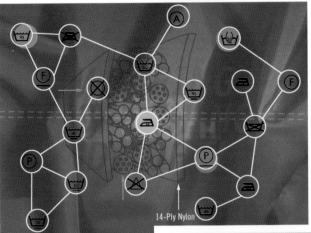

MERIT

WEBSITE/CD-ROM DESIGN: ART/EXPERIMENTAL PROJECTS
Fantastic Prayers–Jacket section

Art Direction Constance DeJong, ReVerb
Designers Beth Elliott, Somi Kim
Photographer Tony Oursler
Illustration Constance DeJong, Tony Oursler, ReVerb
CD-Rom Artists Constance DeJong, Tony Oursler, Stephen Vitiello
Music Stephen Vitiello
Engineering Walkabout Visualization Resources
Producer Karen Kelly
Agency ReVerb
Client Dia Center for the Arts
Country United States

239

As part of a "reawakened dreamworld" explored throughout the CD-ROM, the Jacket section presents a rich array of six stories behind the materials and individual efforts in the construction of a single jacket. ReVerb explored different interactive and narrative strategies integrating original material and artists' assets—including video, animation, and typographic activation—to engage the viewer in an intuitive experience that expands the definition of "reading." The CD-ROM is part of a larger multimedia project by visual artist Tony Oursler, writer/performance artist Constance DeJong, and musician/composer Stephen Vitiello.

graphic

design

We've all seen them. Award shows by the pound. Page after page of entries. Ink as thick as tar. Shows that are not the least bit discriminating. You send it in, they put it in.

When the Art Directors Club invited me to chair this year's show, I had an idea: to tell the judges that if an entry wasn't a progressive, forward-thinking, kick-ass, mind-boggling example of great communications, it shouldn't be in the show. I know, it's hard to imagine. But getting into this show should be almost impossible. The judges stuck to the directive, and if you *are* in it, you know you've created a small piece of genius.

I know, it's hard to imagine. But getting into this show should be almost impossible.

The next few pages contain the cream, the sweet spot, that little place in the woods where the birds are always singing—you get the picture. A deep, heart-felt thanks goes out to all who participated in this inspiring event.

Enjoy. And for those of you who got in, congrats.

NEIL POWELL joined Joe Duffy and his group as an intern in March 1991, and seven years later is design director of Duffy NYC. Neil's work includes national and international branding, corporate identity, and Web site development for clients such as BMW, Giorgio Armani, The Lee Apparel Company, Jim Beam Brands, Tidy Cat, The Stroh Brewery Company, *Time* Magazine, The Coca-Cola Company, Hart Skis, and Faith Popcorn's BrainReserve. Neil is on the faculty of the School of Visual Arts where he is teaching a senior portfolio class.

—Neil Powell,
DUFFY DESIGN AND INTERACTIVE, NYC
DESIGN DIRECTOR

244

CURTIS SCHREIBER is principal and creative director at VSA Partners, Inc. in Chicago. He is best known for his annual report and poster design work for clients such as Harley Davidson, Inc., General Motors, Sram, and the Chicago Board of Trade. He is involved in the creative direction of his firm's major communication programs, and in the development of its growing portfolio of Internet and Web site design programs.

JENNIFER GREY is a creative director/designer at Pittard Sullivan. Her design solutions incorporate all techniques, including cel animation, computer graphics, miniatures, motion control, live action, stop motion, film effects, and video and digital compositing. She has designed the main titles for many motion pictures, including *Dumb and Dumber*, *The Indian in the Cupboard*, and *Forget Paris*.

DREW HODGES is creative director of Spot Design and SPOTCo. Spot Design clients include ABC Television, MTV Networks, and Calvin Klein. Projects include DreamWorks Records' *Prince of Egypt*, and Universal Pictures' upcoming Andy Kaufman biopic, *The Man on the Moon*, starring Jim Carrey. SPOTCo is a full service advertising agency specializing in the theater industry with shows such as *Rent*, *The Diary of Anne Frank*, *Chicago*, and *De La Guarda*.

HUGH KRETCHMER graduated from Arts Center College and traveled to Southeast Asia. The portfolio that resulted from this trip earned him recognition as a finalist in the National Geographic internship program, but deciding photojournalism wasn't his forte, Kretchmer went back to the studio. His work now reflects the movements of the Russian Constructivist, Surrealist, and Dadaist movements.

PAUL SAHRE is a graphic designer based in Brooklyn, currently working for Warner Brothers Records, Random House, and Soho Repertory Theatre. He teaches graphic design and typography at Parsons School of Design and The Cooper Union, and often designs posters which he prints himself for non-profits such as The Fells Point Corner Theatre.

PAUL VENAAS is art director of *Bikini* magazine, a division of RayGun Publishing. Previously, in Nashville, he was vice president of marketing and sales for Via records and art director for *7 Ball* magazine. Venaas also worked for Major Broadcasting Music Group as director of creative services before moving to Los Angeles where he currently resides.

J. ABBOTT MILLER is a designer and writer whose projects are concerned with the cultural role of design. Among Miller's extensive exhibition and publication design work are the award-winning *2wice*, a magazine of visual culture; a book of his essays co-written with Ellen Lupton called *Design Writing Research: Writing on Graphic Design*; and major exhibitions with clients including Geoffrey Beene, *Rolling Stone*, and the Library of Congress. Since 1997, Miller has been co-chair, with Lupton, of the program in graphic design at the Maryland Institute College of Art in Baltimore. In 1999, Miller joined the New York office of the international design consultancy Pentagram as a partner.

WARD SUTTON designs and illustrates concert posters for bands including Pearl Jam, Beck, and Radiohead. In 1998, he created the poster artwork for the Broadway show *Freak* starring John Leguizamo. His illustrations have appeared in *Rolling Stone*, *Esquire*, and *New York Magazine*. His portrait of Prince Charles appeared on the cover of *The New York Times Magazine*. "Schlock 'n' Roll," Sutton's comic strip, runs in *The Village Voice* and many other U.S. newspapers.

ROBYNNE RAYE is co-founder of Modern Dog, a small Seattle-based design studio. Her early projects were in support of Seattle's tightly budgeted fringe theater community. She continues to do work for theater and entertainment companies, both local and national, and considers her poster designs to be some of her favorite work. Clients include *U&LC* Magazine, Microsoft, Long Wharf Theatre, Simon & Schuster, K2 Snowboards, and Hollywood Records.

STEVE SANDSTROM is creative director and a principal of Sandstrom Design, a fifteen-person firm in Portland, Oregon. Clients include Levi Strauss & Co., Nike, ESPN, Microsoft, Tazo Tea, Reebok, Nissan Pathfinder, Seagram's, Wieden & Kennedy, and TBWA Chiat/Day. Prior to founding the firm in 1988, Sandstrom was senior art director for Nike Design, primarily responsible for corporate image pieces and collateral materials for the apparel division.

JOELLE NELSON is an illustrator who first gained visibility through illustrations created for *RayGun* magazine. Current clients include Verve/Polygram Records, Old Navy, The United Way, Target, and the *Philadelphia Inquirer*. Nelson finds inspiration in synthesis, and frequently blends acrylic paint, pieces of abstract photography, and bits of textured scraps and paper. Her style often incorporates retroactive elements that integrate simple shapes and ideas with layers of meaning.

HERBERT WINKLER is art director of *Wallpaper* magazine. He has art directed many magazines including *Cash Flow*, *Gault Millau*, *Ego* Austria and *Ego* Germany, *Ahead*, and *IQ*. In 1998, he founded a design office, section.d, in Vienna with partners Max Haupt-Stummer and Robert Jasensky. He is currently working on a redesign of *Carnet* magazine for deAgostini Rizzoli Periodici publishing house in Milan.

In 1996, **TODD PIPER-HAUSWIRTH** accepted a partnership with Charles Anderson Design, a firm specializing in product design and development, consulting, naming, identity, and package design, and also with the CSA Archive, a subsidiary company specializing in stock imagery. His clients have included The French Paper Company, Coca-Cola, Photonica, Paramount Pictures, Agfa, Target, and Isuzu Motors.

ALLISON MUENCH WILLIAMS and partner JP Williams head Design: M/W, a New York City-based company specializing in establishing the images of clients through collateral and packaging. They have done extensive work for Takashimaya New York, including several direct mail catalogs, advertising, and packaging programs for the private label fragrance, cosmetics, and The Tea Box. Other clients include Banana Republic, Chronicle Books, Isabella Rossellini Cosmetics, and Saks Fifth Avenue. Allison was formerly a design director at Carbone Smolan Associates.

JENNIFER STERLING is principal of Jennifer Sterling Design based in San Francisco. The firm specializes in packaging, product design, book and major collateral communications, annual reports, corporate and product identity, Web services, and film titles. Recently Jennifer was selected as one of Absolut's advertising campaign features. She is best known for the concept and creation of Fox River's Confetti line of design promotional materials for the paper industry.

JONATHAN BARNBROOK has tried to "stay small," by working independently and in many fields, including graphic design, font design, and television commercial directing. Recently, he worked in collaboration with artist Damien Hirst on the book *I Want to Spend the Rest of My Life Everywhere with Everyone, One to One Always, Forever Now*, and on the design of the London restaurant Pharmacy. He designed two fonts for Emigre, *Exocet* and *Manson*, and set up his own font design company, Virus. He has directed commercials for companies including Nike and Toyota.

GOLD

**ENTERTAINMENT OR
SPECIAL EVENT, SERIES**
Graphic Wave '98

Art Director Tatsuo Ebina
Designer Tatsuo Ebina
Photographer Tadashi Tomono
Illustrator Tatsuo Ebina
Producer Kumiko Nagasawa
Studio E Co., Ltd.
Client Ginza Graphic Gallery
Country Japan

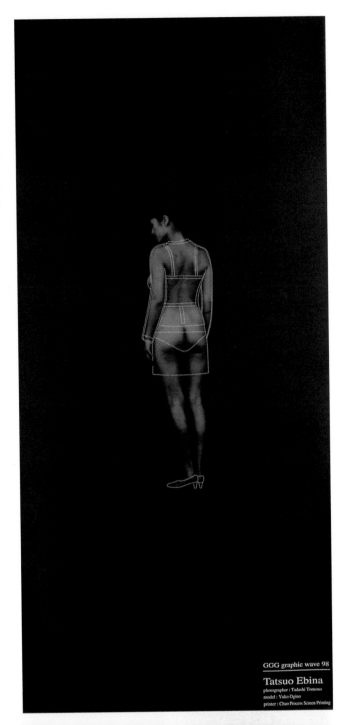

GGG graphic wave 98
Tatsuo Ebina
photographer : Tadashi Tomono
model : Yuko Ogino
printer : Chuo Process Screen Printing

GGG graphic wave 98
Tatsuo Ebina
photographer : Tadashi Tomono
model : Yuko Ogino
printer : Chuo Process Screen Printing

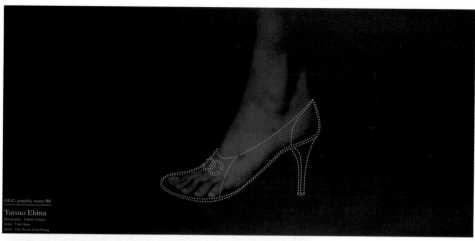

GGG graphic wave 98

Tatsuo Ebina
photographer : Tadashi Tomono
model : Yuko Ogino
printer : Chao Process Screen Printing

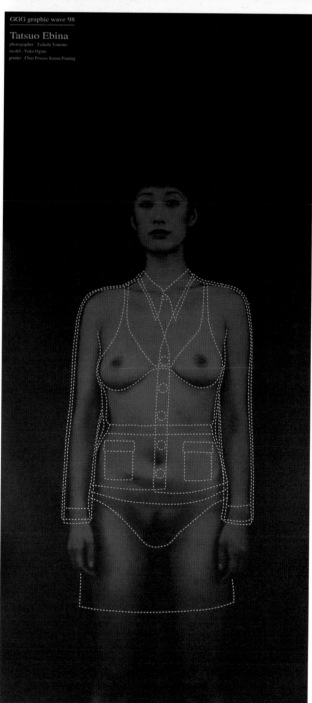

GOLD

**CONSUMER MAGAZINE,
FULL ISSUE**

BIG Magazine, EDC! Tokyo Issue

Art Direction Tycoon Graphics

Design Tycoon Graphics

Editor Koji Yoshida (soft m@chine)

Copywriters David d'Heilly,
Takashi Murakami, Towa Tei

Photographers Junji Hata,
Itaru Hirama, Higashi Ishida
(Aloha State), Kenji Miura
(Lightsome), Kazunali Tajima,
Aya Tokunaga (KiKi Inc.), Shoji Uchida

Illustrators Keiji Itoh (UFG Inc.),
Terry Johnson (Flamingo Studio),
Yoko Kawamoto, Yutanpo Shirane,
Hiro Sugiyama (Enlightenment),
Ichiro Tanida (John & Jane Doe Inc.)

Lighting Director Masayuki Ozawa

Hair & Make-up Hiromi Chinone (Jet),
Katsuya Kamo (Mod's Hair),
Shinji Konishi (KiKi Inc.),
Mika Mitani (A.K.A.), Masaki Tanimori
(Kay Office Plus), Isao Yamada (Jet)

Props Design Kaoru Tomita

Translators Miki Hayashi,
Mito Tachikawa, Kaori Yoshida,
Ray Yoshimoto

Stylists Kyoko Fushimi, Kaz Ijima
(Balance), Takashi Kumagai,
Sonya S. Park (Aloha State),
Hiroko Umeyama

Client BIG Magazine

Country Japan

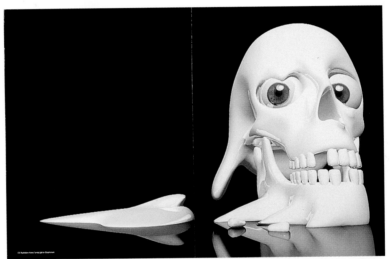

Multiple Awards
see also Illustration section, p.376

GOLD

**SPECIAL TRADE BOOKS
(IMAGE DRIVEN)**
Blue Mode

Art Director Hideki Nakajima
Creative Director Taka Kawachi
Designer Hideki Nakajima
Illustrator Hiroshi Tanabe
Studio Nakajima Design
Client Korinsha Press & Co., Ltd.
Country Japan

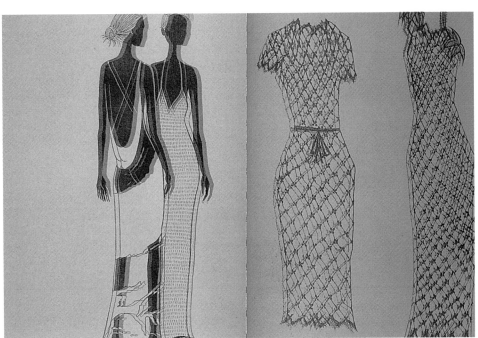

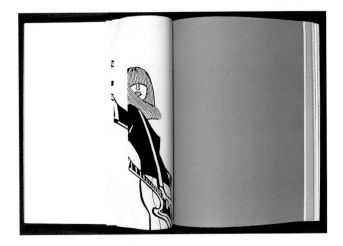

SILVER

**CONSUMER MAGAZINE,
INSERT, SERIES**
Cut Magazine, June 1998 Issue

Art Director Hideki Nakajima
Designer Hideki Nakajima
Editor-in-Chief Ken Sato
Editor Hiroshi Inada
Photographers Katsuo Hanzawa,
George Hoiz, Fabio Lovino,
Kyoji Takahashi
Studio Nakajima Design
Client Rockin' On Inc.
Country Japan

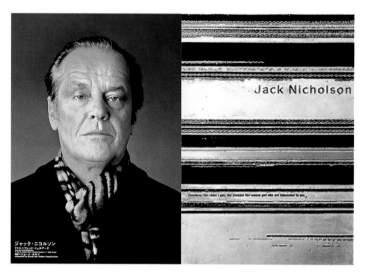

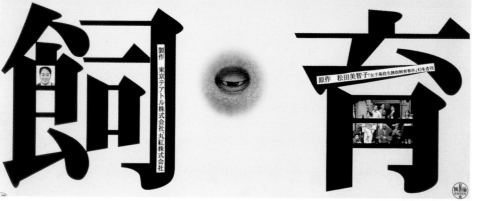

SILVER

**ENTERTAINMENT
OR SPECIAL EVENT**
Perfectly Breeding

Art Director Tadanori Yokoo
Designer Tadanori Yokoo
Copywriter Junko Narusawa
Photographer Mitsuru Tabei
Producer Yoshihisa Ichii
Agency Media Box Co., Ltd.,
Studio Tadanori Yokoo Studio
Clients Tokyo Theatres Co., Ltd.,
Marubeni Corporation
Country Japan

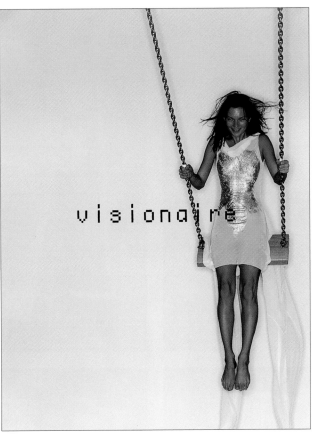

SILVER

**LIMITED EDITION,
PRIVATE PRESS, OR SPECIAL
FORMAT BOOKS**
Visionaire 27 Movement

Art Director Greg Foley,
Peter Saville (cover)
Creative Director Stephen Gan
Design Visionaire,
the apartment (cover)
Photographer Nick Knight (cover)
Styling Katy England,
Alexander McQueen (cover)
Imaging Chris Levine (iC Holographic)
Studio Visionaire
Country United States

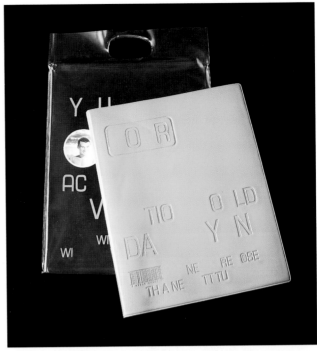

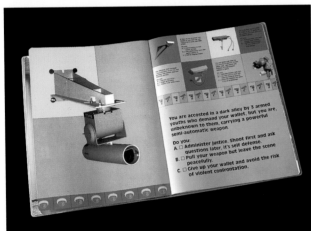

SILVER

**MUSEUM, GALLERY,
OR LIBRARY BOOKS**
Your Action World by David Byrne

Art Directors David Byrne, Stefan Sagmeister
Designers Hjalti Karlsson, Stefan Sagmeister
Copywriter David Byrne
Photographer David Byrne
Illustrators Hjalti Karlsson, Stefan Sagmeister
Producer Michele Concina
Publisher Edimar
Agency Sagmeister, Inc.
Client Todo Mundo
Country United States

01. BATTERSEA
02. ONE WAY RIDE
03. DICTIONARY
04. CLUB MONTEPULCIANO
05. EDEN
06. LUNG
07. ELECTRO SHOCK FADERS
08. OUT OF TUNE
09. THIS STRANGE EFFECT
10. RENAISSANCE AFFAIRE
11. TUNA
12. MAGENTA

SILVER	**Art Director** Erwin Gorostiza
ENTERTAINMENT	**Designer** Erwin Gorostiza
Blue Wonder Power Milk,	**Client** Epic Records/Sony Music
Hooverphonic	**Country** United States

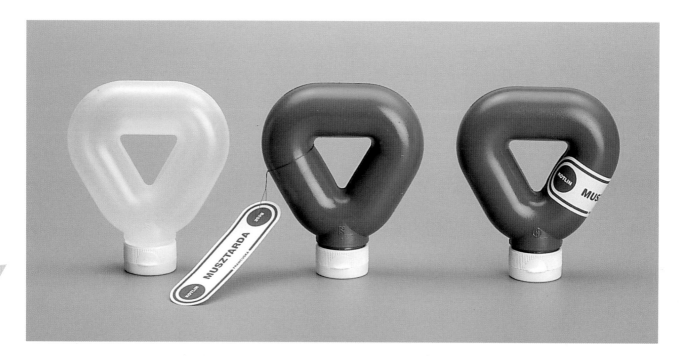

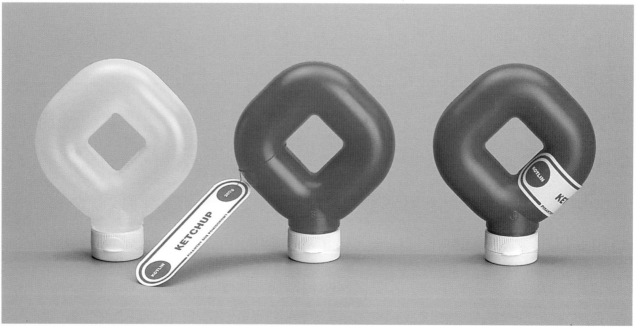

SILVER

FOOD/BEVERAGE, SERIES
Mustard and Ketchup Packages

Art Director Tadeusz Piechura
Creative Director Tadeusz Piechura
Designer Tadeusz Piechura
Copywriter Tadeusz Piechura
Photographer Piotr Tomczyk
Producer Suwary S.A.–Pabianice
Agency Atelier Tadeusz Piechura
Client Suwary S.A.–Pabianice
Country Poland

**GALLERY OR MUSEUM
EXHIBIT/INSTALLATION**
Structure and Surface:
Contemporary Japanese Textiles

Curators Cara McCarty,
Matilda McQuaid
Graphic Designer Ed Pusz
Architects Sheila Choi, Toshiko Mori,
Mark Steigelman
Photographer Paul Warchol
Fiber Optics Lighting Designer
Shozo Toyohisa with Asahi Glass Co.
and S.G.F. Associates Inc.
Client The Museum of Modern Art
Country United States

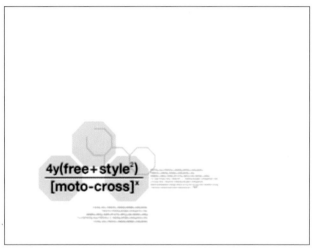

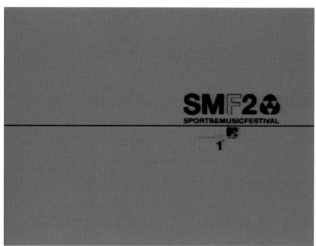

SILVER

TV IDENTITIES, OPENINGS, OR TEASERS

MTV Sports

Art Directors Greg Hahn, Jordan Nogee, Todd St. John
Creative Director Jeffrey Keyton
Designer Greg Hahn
Illustrator Pakorn Buppahavesa
Executive Producer Christina Norman
Music Dust Brothers
Agency MTV Design
Client MTV
Country United States

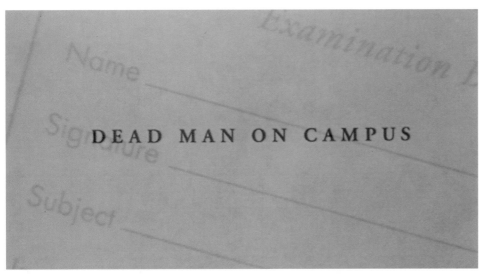

SILVER

CINEMA: OPENING TITLE SEQUENCE
Dead Man on Campus

Art Director Karin Fong
Creative Director Peter Frankfurt
Designers Adam Bluming, Karin Fong
Copywriters Adam Bluming,
Karin Fong
Editors Doron Dor, Kurt Mattila,
Larry Plastrik
Illustrator Wayne Coe
Producer Maureen Timpa
Director Alan Cohn
Studio Imaginary Forces
Clients MTV Films, Paramount
Country United States

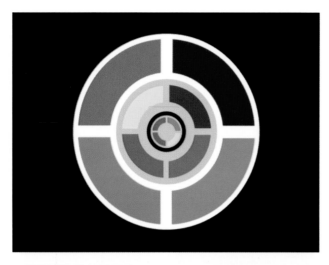

SILVER

CORPORATE/PROMOTIONAL VIDEO

Boycott '98 A/W

Art Direction Tycoon Graphics
Creative Director Takeshi Nakamura (KIEV)
3-D Computer Graphics Gen Nishikawa
Photographer Kiyonori Okuyama (O.K.Y. Photos)
Illustrator Hiro Sugiyama (Enlightenment)
Executive Producer Atsuro Tayama
Director Takeshi Nakamura (KIEV)
Animator Ichiro Itano
Music Kiyoshi Hazemoto
Digital Effects Itaru Inoue, Junichi Nakajima
Miniature Model Design Takashi Kume
Clients Tycoon Graphics, World Co., Ltd.
Country Japan

DISTINCTIVE MERIT

POINT-OF-PURCHASE, SERIES
Shiseido Successful Aging Seminar

Art Director Naomi Yamamoto
Creative Director Naomi Yamamoto
Designer Saiko Kawahara
Photographer Kaz Kiriya
Producers Wakako Ishii, Toshihiro Semura
Studio Shiseido Co., Ltd.
Client Shiseido Co., Ltd.
Country Japan

DISTINCTIVE MERIT

**ENTERTAINMENT
OR SPECIAL EVENT, SERIES**
Laforet Grand Bazar '99

Art Director Katsunori Aoki
Creative Directors Katsunori Aoki,
Ichiro Tanida
Designer Katsunori Aoki
Copywriters Katsunori Aoki,
Ichiro Tanida
Illustrator Ichiro Tanida
Producer Ryu Matsumoto
Agency Sun-Ad Company Limited
Client Laforet, Harajuku
Department Store
Country Japan

DISTINCTIVE MERIT

**ENTERTAINMENT
OR SPECIAL EVENT, SERIES**
'98 Tokyo City Keiba

Art Director Koji Mizutani
Creative Director Hiroyuki Nomaru
Designer Hiroshi Ohmizo
Copywriter Takashi Saito
Illustrator Keiji Ito
Agency Asatsu-DK
Studio Mizutani Studio
Client Tokyo Metropolitan
Racing Association
Country Japan

263

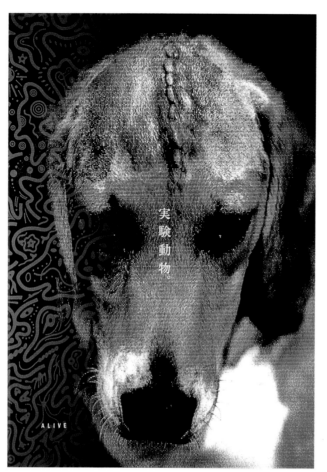

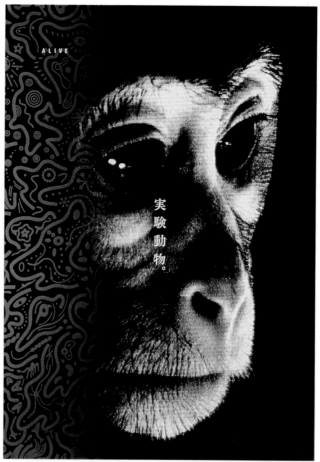

DISTINCTIVE MERIT

**PUBLIC SERVICE, NON-PROFIT,
EDUCATIONAL, SERIES**
A Guinea Pig 1

Art Directors Kengo Lizuka,
Hisamoto Naito
Designer Kengo Lizuka
Copywriter Shinzo Higurashi
Illustrator Hiromi Inayoshi
Agency T.G.V. Inc.
Client ALIVE (All Life in a Viable
Environment)
Country Japan

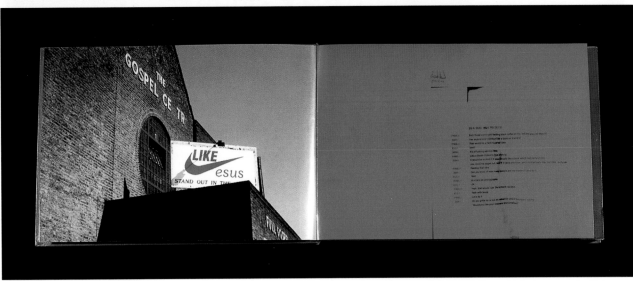

DISTINCTIVE MERIT

**GENERAL TRADE BOOKS
(TEXT DRIVEN)**

Sneakers: Size Isn't Everything

Art Direction Milk Projects Ltd.

Creative Direction Milk Projects Ltd.

Design Milk Projects Ltd.

Copywriting Milk Projects Ltd.

Photography Milk Projects Ltd.

Illustration Milk Projects Ltd.

Production Milk Projects Ltd.

Publisher Booth-Clibborn Editions

Country England

DISTINCTIVE MERIT

**SPECIAL TRADE BOOKS
(IMAGE DRIVEN)**
CSA Archive Book Volume 2

Art Director Charles S. Anderson
Designers Charles S. Anderson,
Todd Piper-Hauswirth
Studio Charles S. Anderson
Design Company
Client CSA Archive
Country United States

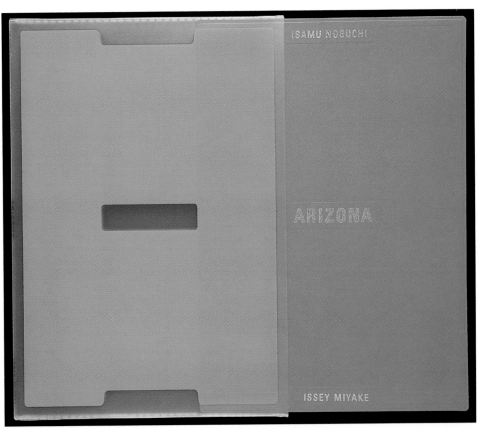

**LIMITED EDITION, PRIVATE PRESS,
OR SPECIAL FORMAT BOOKS**

Arizona,
Isamu Noguchi and Issey Miyake

Art Director Noriyuki Tanaka
Designers Hideo Kawamura,
Noriyuki Tanaka
Photographer Kazuyasu Hagane
Artists Issey Miyake, Isamu Noguchi
Studio Noriyuki Tanaka Activity
Client Marugame Genichiro-Inokuma
Museum of Contemporary Art
Country Japan

DISTINCTIVE MERIT

**MUSEUM, GALLERY,
OR LIBRARY BOOKS**
The Hugo Boss Prize 1998
Exhibition Catalog

Art Director Lisa Billard
Designers Lisa Billard, Ting Ting Lee
Studio Lisa Billard Design
Client The Guggenheim Museum
Country United States

DISTINCTIVE MERIT

ANNUAL REPORT
Technology Music, 1997

Art Director Neal Ashby
Designer Neal Ashby
Copywriter Neal Ashby
Photographer Mike Northrup
Illustrator John Moore
Studio Recording Industry
Association of America
Client Recording Industry
Association of America
Country United States

DISTINCTIVE MERIT

BOOKLET/BROCHURE

Champion Excerpts

Art Directors Mats Hakansson,
Allison Muench Williams, JP Williams
Designers Mats Hakansson,
Allison Muench Williams
Producer Dicksons Inc.
Agency Design: M/W
Client Champion International
Country United States

DISTINCTIVE MERIT

PROMOTION/SELF-PROMOTION
French Family Portraits

Art Director Charles S. Anderson

Designers Charles S. Anderson,
Kyle Hames, Erik Johnson,
Todd Piper-Hauswirth

Illustrator Charles S. Anderson

Studio Charles S. Anderson Design Company

Client French Paper Company

Country United States

DISTINCTIVE MERIT

PROMOTION/SELF-PROMOTION
Nenn' es doch 880

Art Director Gilmar Wendt
Creative Directors Rainer Groothuis,
Victor Malsy, Gilmar Wendt
Designer Gilmar Wendt
Agency Groothuis + Malsy
Client Groothuis + Malsy
Country Germany

272

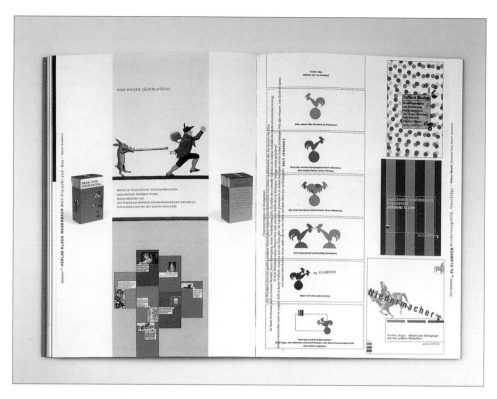

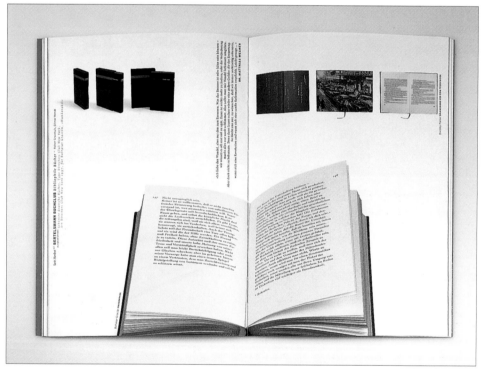

DISTINCTIVE MERIT

ENTERTAINMENT
Trust Me

Art Director Jennifer Sterling
Creative Director Jennifer Sterling
Designer Jennifer Sterling
Illustrator Jennifer Sterling
Copywriter Deonne Kahler
Producer/Printer Rohnerletterpress
Agency Jennifer Sterling Design
Client Bhoss
Country United States

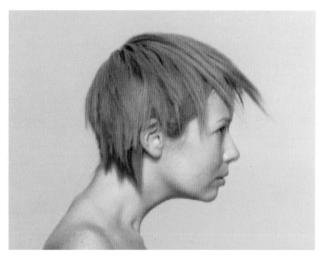

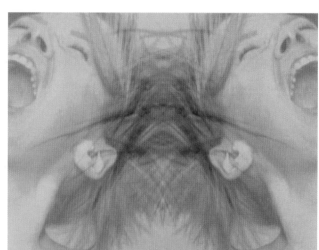

Multiple Awards	**Art Directors** Catherine Chesters, Jenny Rask
	Creative Director Jeffrey Keyton
DISTINCTIVE MERIT	**Designer** Catherine Chesters
	Director Catherine Chesters
TV IDENTITIES, OPENINGS, OR TEASERS	**Executive Producer** Christina Norman
	Producer Catherine Chesters
and MERIT	**Agency** MTV Design
ART DIRECTION	**Client** MTV Networks
MTV's Fashionably Loud Miami	**Country** United States

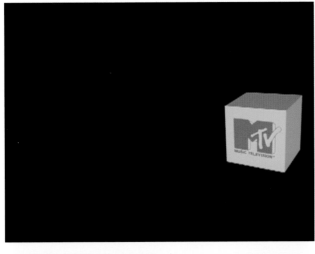

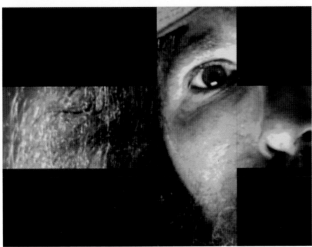

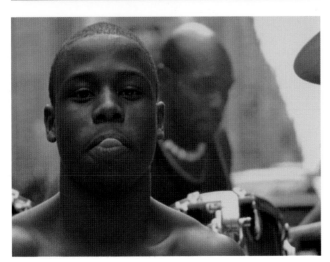

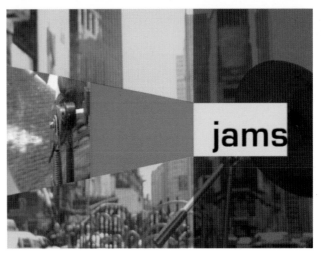

DISTINCTIVE MERIT

**TV IDENTITIES,
OPENINGS, OR TEASERS**

Times Square, MTV Channel
Re-design '98

Art Directors Rodger Belknap, Catherine Chesters
Creative Director Jeffrey Keyton
Designer Catherine Chesters
Director Catherine Chesters
Executive Producer Christina Norman
Producer Catherine Chesters
Illustrator Pakorn Buppahavesa
Sound Design Olivier Spencer
Agency MTV Design
Client MTV Networks
Country United States

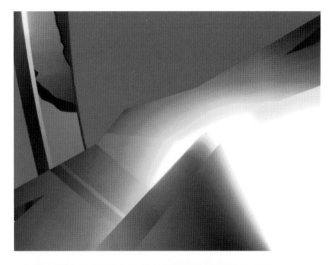

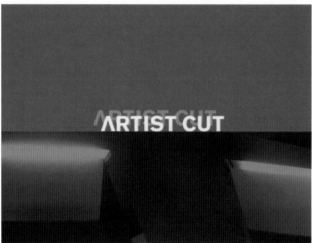

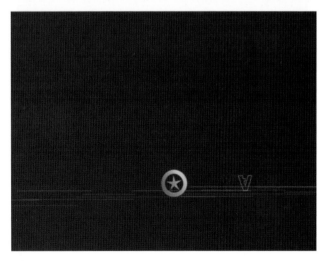

DISTINCTIVE MERIT

**TV IDENTITIES,
OPENINGS, OR TEASERS**
MTV 1998 Music Video Awards

Art Directors Rodger Belknap, Tracy Boychuk
Creative Director Jeffrey Keyton
Designers Tracy Boychuk, Nurit Naddas
Design Director Romy Mann
Illustrator Pakorn Buppahavesa
Executive Producer Christina Norman
Sound Design Olivier Spencer
Agency MTV Design
Client MTV Networks
Country United States

DISTINCTIVE MERIT

MUSIC VIDEO

God Lives Underwater,
From Your Mouth

Creative Director Randy Sosin
Producer Eric Mathes
Director Roman Coppola
Agency The Directors Bureau
Client 1500/A&M Records
Country United States

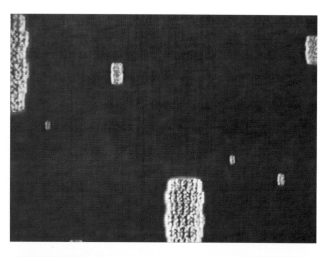

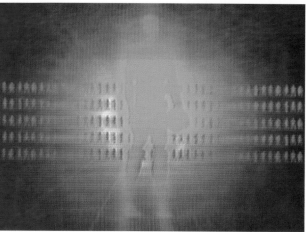
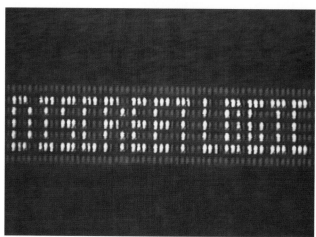

Multiple Awards

DISTINCTIVE MERIT

CORPORATE/PROMOTIONAL VIDEO

and MERIT

ART DIRECTION

You Don't Know Us

Art Director Patrick Giasson

Designer Patrick Giasson

Digital Artists Ludovic, Frank Black, Annie Conn, Christopher Friedberg

Producer Frank Black

Music David Kristian

Agency Behaviour

Client Discreet Logic

Country Canada

Multiple Awards
see also Advertising section, p.47

DISTINCTIVE MERIT

ANIMATION
Hete-Roy

Designer J.J. Sedelmaier
Copywriter Robert Smigel
Animators Don McGrath,
J.J. Sedelmaier, Mike Wetterhahn
Composer Steven M. Gold
Audio Post Mike Fisher
Voices Andrew Daly, Carey Prusa,
Robert Smigel
Agency NBC
Client Saturday Night Live
Country United States

279

MERIT

**CONSUMER MAGAZINE,
FULL PAGE, SERIES**
What Makes "Me" Anyway?

Art Director Satoji Kashimoto
Designers Daizou Fukuda,
Satoji Kashimoto
Copywriter Yuhei Nayuki
Photographer Yoshiaki Tutui
Producer Junko Kawano
Agency Recruit Co., Ltd.
Client Recruit Co., Ltd.
Country Japan

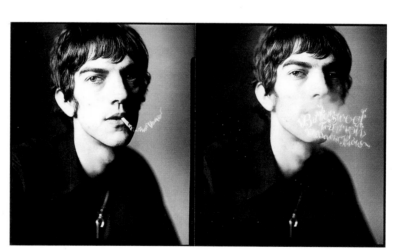

MERIT

CONSUMER MAGAZINE, SPREAD
The Verve

Art Director Fred Woodward
Designers Gail Anderson,
Fred Woodward
Photographer Mark Seliger
Photo Editor Rachel Knepfer
Client Rolling Stone
Country United States

Multiple Awards
see also Photography section, p.356

MERIT

CONSUMER MAGAZINE, SPREAD
Johnny Depp's Savage Journey

Art Director Fred Woodward
Designers Gail Anderson,
Fred Woodward
Photographer Dan Winters
Photo Editor Rachel Knepfer
Client Rolling Stone
Country United States

MERIT

**CONSUMER MAGAZINE,
MULTI-PAGE**
Bodenschätze (Natural Treasures)

Art Directors Petra Langhammer,
Hans Günter Schmitz
Creative Director Hans Günter Schmitz
Designer Hans Günter Schmitz
Photographer Hans Günter Schmitz
Agency Schmitz Visual
Communication
Client Süddeutsche Zeitung
(The Magazine of Southern Germany)
Country Germany

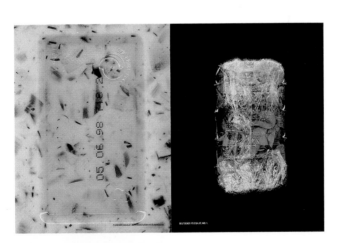

MERIT

**CONSUMER MAGAZINE,
MULTI-PAGE, SERIES**
Oasis (Buzz)

Art Director Yuko Kasuga

Designers Yuko Kasuga, Mayo Seki,
Rikiya Tanaka

Editor-In-Chief Koji Miyazaki

Photographers Davies+Davies,
Yuko Kasuga

Studio Rockin' On Inc.

Client Rockin' On Inc.

Country Japan

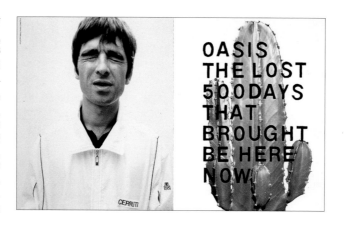

MERIT

CONSUMER MAGAZINE, SPREAD
Back to the Future

Art Director Peter Yates

Creative Director F. Darrin Perry

Design Director F. Darrin Perry

Designer Peter Yates

Illustrator Hiroshi Tanabe

Client ESPN Magazine

Country United States

MERIT

**CONSUMER MAGAZINE,
MULTI-PAGE, SERIES**
National Football League Preview

Art Director Peter Yates

Creative Director F. Darrin Perry

Design Director F. Darrin Perry

Designer Peter Yates

Photographers Kwaku Alston,
Davis Facter

Illustrators Andy Lackow, Hiroshi Tanabe

Client ESPN Magazine

Country United States

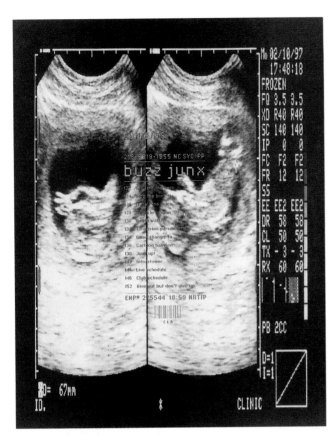

MERIT

**CONSUMER MAGAZINE,
MULTI-PAGE, SERIES**

Buzz Junx

Art Director Yuko Kasuga

Designers Yuko Kasuga, Mayo Seki,
Rikiya Tanaka

Editor-in-Chief Koji Miyazaki

Photography Go Relax E More

Client Rockin' On Inc.

Country Japan

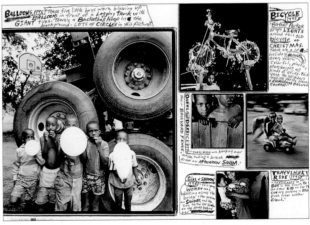

MERIT

**CONSUMER MAGAZINE,
MULTI-PAGE, SERIES**

Weeping Mary

Art Director D.J. Stout

Creative Director D.J. Stout

Designers Nancy McMillen, D.J. Stout

Copywriter Anne Dingus

Photographer O. Rufus Lovett

Studio Texas Monthly Magazine

Country United States

MERIT

CONSUMER MAGAZINE, INSERT, SERIES
Cut Magazine, May 1998 Issue

Art Director Hideki Nakajima
Designer Hideki Nakajima
Editor-In-Chief Ken Sato
Photographers Bob Frame, Neil Kirk, Stéphane Sednaoui, Cliff Watts
Studio Nakajima Design
Client Rockin' On Inc.
Country Japan

MERIT

CONSUMER MAGAZINE, INSERT, SERIES
Cut Magazine, January 1999 Issue

Art Director Hideki Nakajima
Designer Hideki Nakajima
Editor-In-Chief Ken Sato
Photographers Steven Klein, Akira Matsuo, Herb Ritts
Studio Nakajima Design
Client Rockin' On Inc.
Country Japan

Multiple Awards
see also Photography section, p.352

MERIT

**CONSUMER MAGAZINE,
INSERT, SERIES**
Cut Magazine, December 1998 Issue

Art Director Hideki Nakajima
Designer Hideki Nakajima
Editor-in-Chief Ken Sato
Photographers Naoki Ishizaka, Kayt Jones
Studio Nakajima Design
Client Rockin' On Inc.
Country Japan

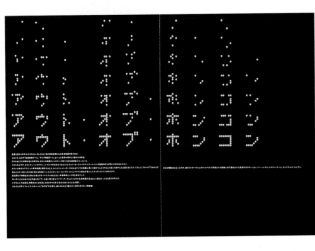

MERIT

**CONSUMER MAGAZINE,
INSERT, SERIES**
Cut Magazine, October 1998 Issue

Art Director Hideki Nakajima
Designer Hideki Nakajima
Editor-in-Chief Ken Sato
Photographers Dan Chavkin, Akira Matsuo
Studio Nakajima Design
Client Rockin' On Inc.
Country Japan

MERIT

**CONSUMER MAGAZINE,
FULL ISSUE**

2wice Magazine, Uniform

Art Director J. Abbott Miller
Designers Paul Carlos,
Scott Devendorf
Managing Editor Paul Makovsky
Studio Design Writing Research
Client 2wice Arts Foundation
Country United States

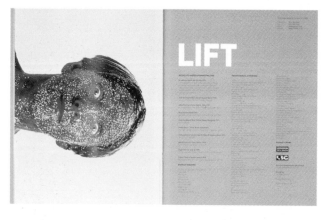

MERIT

CONSUMER MAGAZINE, FULL ISSUE

LIFT–London International Festival
of Theatre Brochure

Art Director Justina Sachis
Creative Director Frances Newell
Copywriter Anne Torreggiani (LIFT)
Photographers Various
Artwork Claire Needham
Agency Interbrand Newell
and Sorrell
Client London International
Festival of Theatre
Country England

GO! GO! PIRATES!

Multiple Awards

MERIT

**CONSUMER MAGAZINE,
FULL ISSUE, SERIES**

and MERIT

**CONSUMER MAGAZINE,
COVER, SERIES**

#19 Tribes • #20 Music + Fashion •
#21 EDC! Tokyo

Art Direction Lloyd + Co., New York,
Tycoon Graphics, Japan
Creative Direction Douglas Lloyd,
Tycoon Graphics
Editors Glenn O' Brien, Tara Sutton,
Koji Yoshida
Designer Anthony Yumul
Cover Photographers Richard
Burbridge, Alexie Hay, Higashi Ishida
Publisher Marcelo Jünemann
Director Marcelo Jünemann
Fashion Director Debbi Mason
Client Big Magazine
Country United States

287

MERIT

**CONSUMER MAGAZINE,
COVER, SERIES**

Cut Magazine, May 1998 Issue

Art Director Hideki Nakajima
Designer Hideki Nakajima
Editor-in-Chief Ken Sato
Photographers Akira Matsuo,
Naka, Jean-François Robert,
Lance Staedier, Juergen Teller,
Bruce Weber
Studio Nakajima Design
Client Rockin' On Inc.
Country Japan

Multiple Awards

MERIT

**TRADE MAGAZINE,
SPREAD, SERIES**

and MERIT

**TRADE MAGAZINE,
FULL ISSUE, SERIES**
The New Edition of
Design Exchange No.13

Art Director Wang Xu
Designer Wang Xu
Producer Wang Xu & Associates Ltd.
Studio Wang Xu & Associates Ltd.
Client China Youth Press
Country China

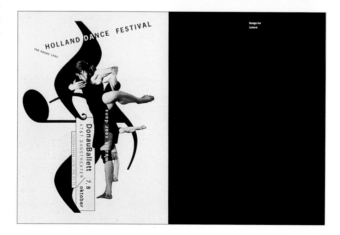

MERIT

TRADE MAGAZINE, FULL ISSUE
IT–Innovative Thinking

Art Director Mike Barton
Designer Mike Barton
Copywriters Various
Photographer Bob Carey
Agency SHR Perceptual
Management
Client Innovative Thinking
Conference
Country United States

A$2

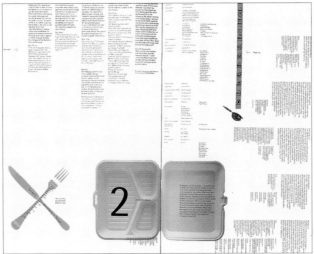

2

MERIT

TRADE MAGAZINE, FULL ISSUE
Funnel

Art Directors Graeme Smith,
Grazyna Ugarenko
Creative Director Graeme Smith
Designer Grazyna Ugarenko
Copywriters Various
Photographers Various
Illustrators Various
Editor Graeme Smith
Production Nelmes Smith
Ashton Media
Studio Nelmes Smith
Ashton Media
Country Australia

MERIT

TRADE MAGAZINE, FULL ISSUE
Menswork

Art Directors Marcos Chavez,
David Raccuglia
Designer Aimee Sealfon
Copywriters Craig Hanson,
Kurt Kueffner, Terry Lane, and others
Photographer David Raccuglia
Studio Liska + Associates, Inc.
Client American Crew
Country United States

MERIT

PROMOTIONAL
UCLA Summer Sessions 1998

Creative Director Inju Sturgeon
Designers Sean Adams,
Noreen Morioka
Agency UCLA Extension,
Marketing Department
Client UCLA Summer Sessions
Country United States

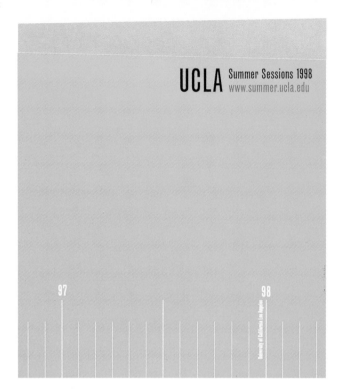

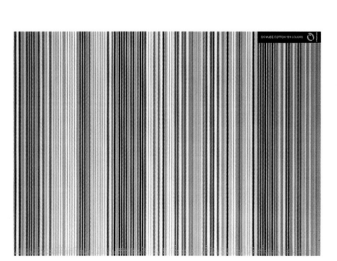

MERIT

PROMOTIONAL
OK Muse Cotton, 131 Colors

Art Director Akio Okumura
Designer Mitsuo Ueno
Studio Packaging Create Inc.
Client Oji Paper Co., Ltd.
Country Japan

Merit
PROMOTIONAL
IBM ADSM

Art Director Kenzo Izutani
Designers Aki Hirai, Kenzo Izutani
Copywriter Yoshinori Saijyo
Illustrator Tadasu Nishii
Agencies Kenzo Izutani Office
Corporation, Hakuhodo, Inc.
Client IBM Japan
Country Japan

MERIT
PROMOTIONAL
OK Muse Cotton

Art Director Akio Okumura
Designer Aki Inoue
Studio Packaging Create Inc.
Client MUSA
Country Japan

MERIT

PROMOTIONAL
Godard

Art Director Eiji Yamada
Designers Naoko-Nodera,
Eiji Yamada
Studio Ultra Graphics
Client Culture Publishers, Inc.
Country Japan

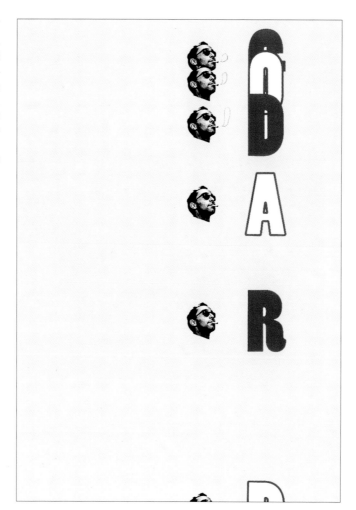

MERIT

PROMOTIONAL, SERIES
VH, OM Solar

Art Director Hiroaki Watanabe
Creative Directors Masaaki Hirose,
Satoru Miyata
Designer Ryosuke Uehara
Copywriter Asaji Kato
Studio Draft Co., Ltd.
Client OM Solar Association
Country Japan

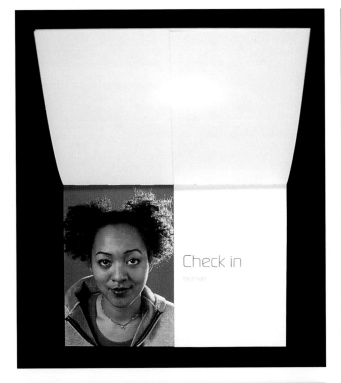

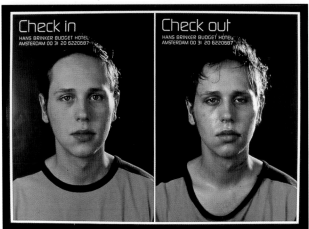

Multiple Awards
see also Advertising section, p.176

MERIT

BOOKLET/BROCHURE

and MERIT

PROMOTIONAL POSTER
Check In—Check Out

Art Director Erik Kessels
Copywriters Johan Kramer, Tyler Whisnand
Photographers Anuschka Blommers, Niels Schumm
Agency KesselsKramer
Client The Hans Brinker Budget Hotel
Country The Netherlands

MERIT

PROMOTIONAL POSTER, SERIES
MTV Brand Campaign

Art Director John Davis
Creative Director Brian Bacino
Designers Gaby Brink, Brian Collins
Copywriter Jim Di Piazza
Photographer Guzman
Agency Foote, Cone & Belding–
San Francisco
Client MTV
Country United States

MERIT

POINT-OF-PURCHASE
Girlfriend Latino

Art Director Hal Wolverton
Creative Directors Alicia Johnson,
Hal Wolverton
Designers Joe Peila, Hal Wolverton
Photographer Melody McDaniel
Illustrators Christian Clayton,
Robert Clayton
Agency Wieden & Kennedy
Studio Johnson & Wolverton
Client Miller Brewing Co.
Country United States

MERIT

POINT-OF-PURCHASE
Painted Label Holiday

Art Directors Alicia Johnson, Hal Wolverton
Creative Directors Alicia Johnson, Hal Wolverton
Designers Mary Kysar, Heath Lowe, Hal Wolverton
Agency Wieden & Kennedy
Studio Johnson & Wolverton
Client Miller Brewing Co.
Country United States

MERIT

POINT-OF-PURCHASE
Heidi

Art Directors Heath Lowe,
Hal Wolverton
Creative Directors Alicia Johnson,
Hal Wolverton
Designer Heath Lowe
Photographer Michel Haddi
Agency Wieden & Kennedy
Studio Johnson & Wolverton
Client Miller Brewing Co.
Country United States

MERIT

**ENTERTAINMENT OR
SPECIAL EVENT**
Radiohead

Art Director Ward Sutton
Designer Ward Sutton
Illustrator Ward Sutton
Client Noiseville
Country United States

MERIT

**ENTERTAINMENT OR
SPECIAL EVENT**
Best of the Flying Kids

Art Director Keiko Hirano
Designer Keiko Hirano
Photographer Takashi Homma
Hair & Make-up Kenta Miyauchi
Stylist Yasuomi Kurita
Studio Hirano Studio, Inc.
Client Victor Entertainment, Inc.
Country Japan

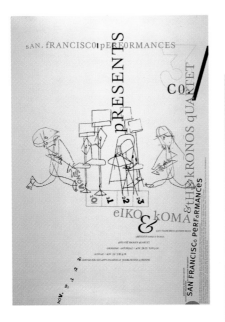

MERIT

**ENTERTAINMENT
OR SPECIAL EVENT, SERIES**
San Francisco Performances
(Anne Teresa de
Keersmaeker/Rosas)

Art Director Jennifer Sterling
Creative Director Jennifer Sterling
Designer Jennifer Sterling
Copywriter Corey Weinstern
Illustrator Jennifer Sterling
Producer/Printer Belaire Displays
Agency Jennifer Sterling Design
Client San Francisco Performances
Country United States

MERIT

**BILLBOARD, DIORAMA, OR
PAINTED SPECTACULAR, SERIES**
Whipped

Art Director John Hobbs
Designer John Hobbs
Photographer Greg Neumaier
Illustrator John Hobbs
Type Design Phil Kelly
Agency Boiler Room East
Client Hi-Rez Films NY
Country United States

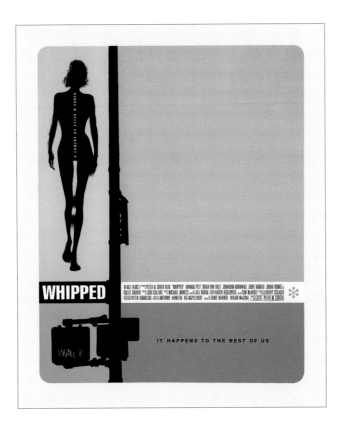

MERIT

**GENERAL TRADE BOOKS
(TEXT DRIVEN), SERIES**
Morrison, Camus, Hemingway,
Miller, Ruemkorf, Tucholsky

Art Director Walter Hellmann
Designer Walter Hellmann
Producers Joachim Duester,
Edith Lackmann, Angelika Weinert
Agency Rowohlt Verlag GmbH
Client Rowohlt Publishers
Country Germany

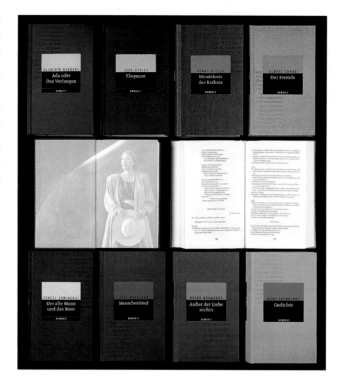

MERIT

**SPECIAL TRADE BOOKS
(IMAGE DRIVEN)**
Cream: Contemporary Art in Culture

Art Director Alan Fletcher
Designer Julia Hasting
Client Phaidon Press
Country United States

**SPECIAL TRADE BOOKS
(IMAGE DRIVEN)**
Untitled

Art Director Hideki Nakajima
Designer Hideki Nakajima
Editorial Director
Masanobu Sugatsuke
Photographer Jeff Burton
Studio Nakajima Design
Client Composite Press
Country Japan

MERIT

**SPECIAL TRADE BOOKS
(IMAGE DRIVEN)**
(noise) 3.5

Creative Directors Simon Needham,
James Sommerville
Designers The Attik
Studio The Attik
Country United States

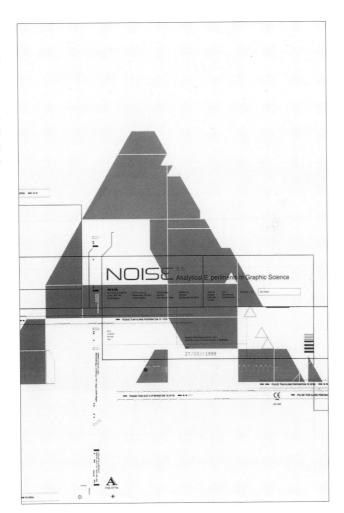

MERIT

**SPECIAL TRADE BOOKS
(IMAGE DRIVEN)**
American Photography 14

Creative Director Gary Koepke
Designers Gary Koepke,
Stacie MacKenzie
Copywriter Peggy Roalf
Cover Photograph Tom Schierlitz
Photographers Various/
Jury Selected
Director Mark Heflin
Client Amilus, Inc.
Country United States

MERIT

**SPECIAL TRADE BOOKS
(IMAGE DRIVEN)**
The Good Spell Book

Art Director Julia Sedykh
Designer Julia Sedykh
(interior and case)
Copyeditor Peggy L. Anderson
Photography Photodisk stock
images, personal archive
Editors Sarah Crichton,
Amanda Murray
Calligraphy Julia Sedykh
Publisher Little, Brown and Company
Client Little, Brown and Company
Country United States

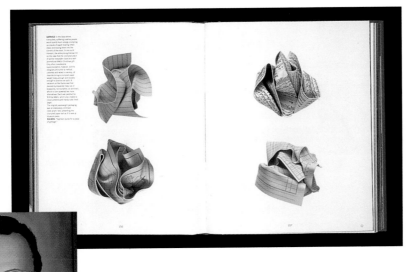

MERIT

**SPECIAL TRADE BOOKS
(IMAGE DRIVEN)**

Tibor Kalman: Perverse Optimist

Editors Michael Bierut, Peter Hall
Designers Michael Bierut,
Michael English, Tibor Kalman
Photographers Various
Studio Pentagram Design
Client Booth-Clibborn Editions
Country United States

MERIT

**SPECIAL TRADE BOOKS
(IMAGE DRIVEN)**

One Day at the Parool Newspaper

Art Director Erik Kessels
Copywriter Johan Kramer
Photographers Wubbo de Jong,
José Groot, Hans van der Meer,
Bianca Pilet
Agency KesselsKramer
Client Het Parool
Country The Netherlands

MERIT

**LIMITED EDITION, PRIVATE PRESS,
OR SPECIAL FORMAT**
Barbers Sign Project

Art Director Taku Satoh
Designer Taku Satoh
Photographer Taishi Hirokawa
Studio Taku Satoh Design Office, Inc.
Client Taku Satoh Design Office, Inc.
Country Japan

MERIT

**LIMITED EDITION, PRIVATE PRESS,
OR SPECIAL FORMAT**
Cervantes 450+1

Art Directors Oscar Heredero,
Jesús del Hoyo, Pedro López
Designers Oscar Heredero,
Jesús del Hoyo
Photographers Various
Illustrators Various
Producer Nova Era
Client Nova Era
Country Spain

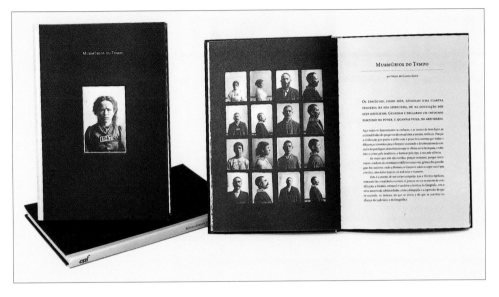

MERIT

LIMITED EDITION, PRIVATE PRESS, OR SPECIAL FORMAT

Murmúrios Do Tempo
(Whispers of Time)

Art Director Andrew Howard
Designer Andrew Howard
Printer Rocha Artes Graficas
Studio Studio Andrew Howard
Client Portuguese Centre
for Photography
Country Portugal

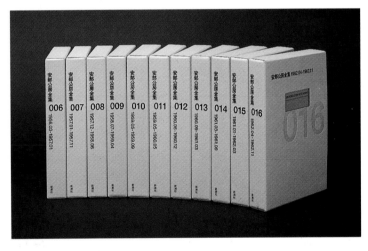

MERIT

LIMITED EDITION, PRIVATE PRESS, OR SPECIAL FORMAT, SERIES

Kobe Abe Complete Works 006

Art Director Kazuya Kondo
Designer Kazuya Kondo
Photographer Kobo Abe
Studio Kazuya Kondo Inc.
Client Shinchosya Co., Ltd.
Country Japan

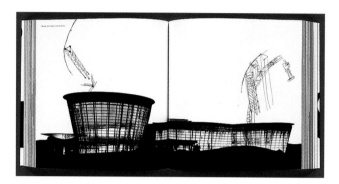

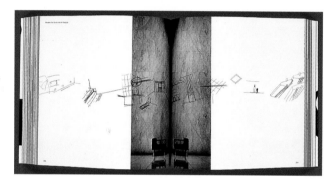

MERIT

**MUSEUM, GALLERY,
OR LIBRARY BOOKS**

Rétrospective Kurokawa Kisho–
Penser la Symbiose
(Conceiving Symbiosis)

Art Director Shin Matsunaga
Creative Director Shin Matsunaga
Designers Hidenori Ito,
Kenichi Masaki, Shin Matsunaga
Studio Shin Matsunaga Design Inc.
Client Comité Exécutif de la
Rétrospective Kurokawa Kisho
Country Japan

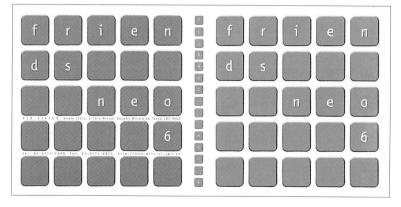

MERIT

PROMOTIONAL
NEO Vision/Photo Catalog–Friends

Art Director Atzshi Evina
Designer Atzshi Evina
Producer Mitsuharu Nakanishi
Studio Verve Inc.
Client NEO Vision Inc.
Country Japan

STYLING EDITION TEN

MERIT

PROMOTIONAL
Styling Edition Ten,
Autumn–Winter 1998

Art Director Hideki Nakajima
Creative Director Koichiro Yamamoto
Designer Hideki Nakajima
Photographer Chikashi Suzuki
Studio Nakajima Design
Client United Arrows
Country Japan

MERIT

PROMOTIONAL
Channel One Teen Fact Book

Art Director Bob Shea
Creative Director Cheri Dorr
Designer David High
Illustrator David High
Agency Lee Hunt Associates
Client Abbie Knopper
(Channel One Network)
Country United States

MERIT

BOOK JACKETS ONLY

White Lies

Art Director Susan Mitchell
Designer Rodrigo Corral
Publisher Farrar, Straus and Giroux
Client Farrar, Straus and Giroux
Country United States

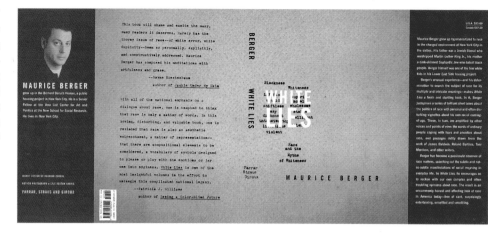

MERIT

BOOK JACKETS ONLY, SERIES

The Pocket Canons

Art Director Angus Hyland
Designer Angus Hyland
Studio Pentagram Design Ltd.
Client Canongate Books Ltd.
Country England

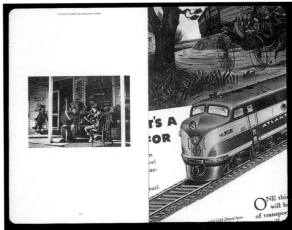

MERIT

ANNUAL REPORT
Cracker Barrel Old Country Store,
1998

Art Director Thomas Ryan
Designer Thomas Ryan
Copywriter John Baeder
Photographer McGuire
Illustrators Various
Printing Buford Lewis Company
Agency Corporate Communications,
Inc.
Client Cracker Barrel Old Country
Store, Inc.
Country United States

MERIT

ANNUAL REPORT
COR Therapeutics, 1997

Art Director Bill Cahan
Designer Michael Braley
Photographer William Mercer
McLeod
Agency Cahan & Associates
Client COR Therapeutics
Country United States

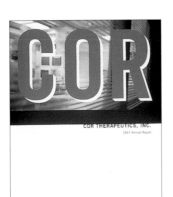

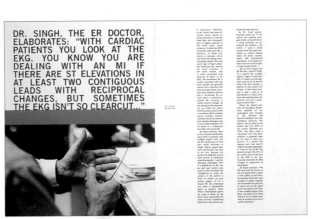

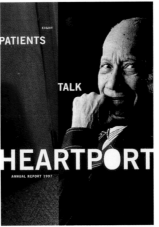

MERIT

ANNUAL REPORT
Heartport, 1997

Art Director Bill Cahan
Designer Kevin Roberson
Photographer Ken Probst
Illustrator Kevin Roberson
Agency Cahan & Associates
Client Heartport
Country United States

MERIT

ANNUAL REPORT
Swiss Army Brands, 1997

Art Director Dave Mason
Designers Pamela Lee, Dave Mason
Copywriter Steven Zousmer
Photographer Victor John Penner
Agency SamataMason
Client Swiss Army Brands, Inc.
Country United States

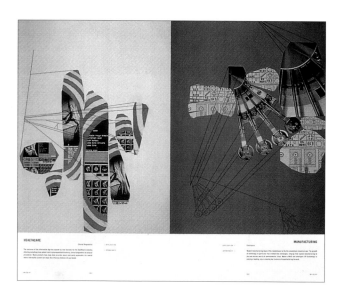

MERIT

ANNUAL REPORT
Mylex, 1997

Art Director Bill Cahan
Designer Bob Dinetz
Illustrator Bob Dinetz
Agency Cahan & Associates
Client Mylex Corporation
Country United States

MERIT

ANNUAL REPORT
Greater Alabama Council:
Strength in Numbers, 1997

Art Director Marion English
Designer Marion English
Copywriter Gary Brandon
Photographers Fredrik Broden,
Don Harbor
Illustrator David Webb
Agency Slaughter Hanson
Client Boy Scouts of America–
Greater Alabama Council
Country United States

JANUARY 13, 1998 -- GERON EXTENDS THE LIFE-SPAN OF
A HUMAN CELL USING THE TELOMERASE GENE (hTERT). THIS
ACHIEVEMENT CONFIRMS THE ROLE OF TELOMERASE AS A KEY
REGULATOR IN CELL AGING AND IDENTIFIES A POINT FOR
INTERVENTION IN A BROAD RANGE OF AGE-RELATED DISEASES.

GERON
97

MERIT

ANNUAL REPORT

Geron, 1997

Art Director Bill Cahan
Designer Bob Dinetz
Copywriter Carol Melis
Photography Family Portraits
Supplied
Illustrator Bob Dinetz
Agency Cahan & Associates
Client Geron Corporation
Country United States

MERIT

ANNUAL REPORT

Molecular Biosystems, 1998

Art Director Bill Cahan
Designer Kevin Roberson
Copywriter Bob Giargiari
Photographers Various
Agency Cahan & Associates
Client Molecular Biosystems, Inc.
Country United States

WITHOUT CONTRAST,
INTERPRETING IMAGES CAN
BE A LOT OF GUESSWORK.

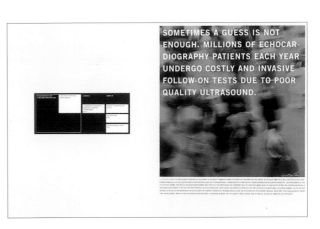

SOMETIMES A GUESS IS NOT
ENOUGH. MILLIONS OF ECHOCAR-
DIOGRAPHY PATIENTS EACH YEAR
UNDERGO COSTLY AND INVASIVE
FOLLOW-ON TESTS DUE TO POOR
QUALITY ULTRASOUND.

310

ANNUAL REPORT
Vivus, 1997

Art Director Bill Cahan
Designer Kevin Roberson
Copywriter Jennifer Schraeder
Illustrator Kevin Roberson
Agency Cahan & Associates
Client Vivus Inc.
Country United States

CAUTION:
READING THIS ANNUAL REPORT
MAY CAUSE AN ERECTION

1997 VIVUS
FACT SHEET

ANNUAL REPORT
Blue Shield of California, 1997

Art Director Jennifer Sterling
Creative Director Jennifer Sterling
Designers Amy Hayson,
Jennifer Sterling
Copywriter Lisa Citron
Photographer Marko Lavrisha
Producer H. MacDonald Printing
Printer H. MacDonald Printing
Agency Jennifer Sterling Design
Client Blue Shield of California
Country United States

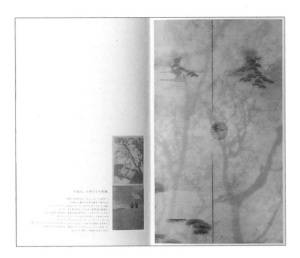

BOOKLET/BROCHURE
L' Hôtel de Hiei, un Hôtel de France

Art Director Shinya Nojima
Creative Director Shinya Nojima
Designer Shinya Nojima
Copywriter Mutsuko Tanaka
Illustrator Hiroshi Tanabe
Agency ATA Co., Ltd.
Client L' Hôtel de Hiei
Country Japan

MERIT

BOOKLET/BROCHURE
Pina Zangaro Fall Catalog

Art Director Jennifer Sterling
Creative Director Jennifer Sterling
Designer Jennifer Sterling
Copywriter Tim Mullen
Photographer Dave Magnusson
Illustrator Jennifer Sterling
Producer Logos Graphics
Printer Logos Graphics
Agency Jennifer Sterling Design
Client Pina Zangaro
Country United States

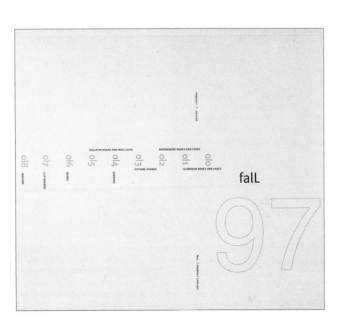

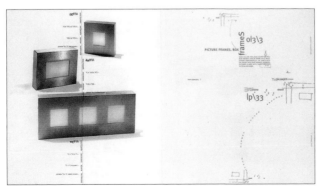

MERIT

BOOKLET/BROCHURE
Beauty in Utility

Art Directors JP Williams,
Allison Muench Williams
Copywriter Laura Silverman
Photographer Hans Gissinger
Agency Design: M/W
Client Mohawk Paper Company
Country United States

312

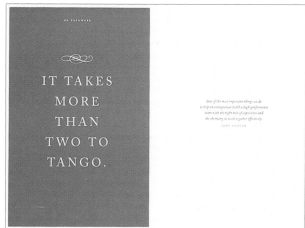

MERIT

BOOKLET/BROCHURE, SERIES
Interwest Partners

Art Director Bill Cahan
Designer Kevin Roberson
Copywriters Tim Peters,
Kevin Roberson
Illustrator Tim Bower
Agency Cahan & Associates
Client Interwest Partners
Country United States

MERIT

BOOKLET/BROCHURE
Mohawk Options Promotion

Art Director Bill Cahan
Designers Bob Dinetz,
Kevin Roberson
Copywriters Bob Dinetz,
Kevin Roberson
Photographers Bob Dinetz,
Kevin Roberson
Illustrator Riccardo Vecchio
Agency Cahan & Associates
Client Mohawk Paper Mills
Country United States

MERIT

BOOKLET/BROCHURE
Nova Mannequin Catalog

Art Director Hiroyuki Ota
Designer Daisuke Suzuki
Copywriter Koichi Sugawara
Photographer Naka
Make-up Artist Ryojl Inagaki
Producer Toru Takaoka
Stylist Kan Nakagawara
Agency ATA Co., Ltd.
Client Nova Mannequin
Country Japan

MERIT

BOOKLET/BROCHURE
Art Center College of Design
Catalog 1999–2000

Art Director Denise Gonzales Crisp
Creative Director Stuart I. Frolick
Designer Denise Gonzales Crisp
Associate Designers Carla Figueroa,
Michael French
Editor Julie Suhr
Editorial Support Karen Jacobson
Photographers Vahe Alaverdian,
Steven A. Heller
Computer Artist Audrey Krauss
Production Manager Ellie Eisner
Agency Design Office,
Art Center College of Design
Client Art Center College of Design
Country United States

MERIT

BOOKLET/BROCHURE
Alfredo BANNISTER/
Irregular '98 A/W Catalogue

Art Director Tycoon Graphics
Designer Tycoon Graphics
Creative Direction Kaz Ijima
Photographer Shoji Uchida
Styling Kaz Ijima
Hair & Make-up Takaaki Ikeshima
Props Design Tada Bijutsu
Studio Tycoon Graphics
Client Abahouse International Co., Ltd.
Country Japan

MERIT

BOOKLET/BROCHURE
Clutch Catalogue

Art Director Naomi Hirabayashi
Creative Director Sonya S. Park
Designer Naomi Hirabayashi
Copywriter Shoko Yoshida
Photographer Higashi Ishida
Agency Shiseido Co., Ltd.
Client Clutch Co., Ltd.
Country Japan

MERIT

NEWSLETTER, JOURNAL, OR HOUSE PUBLICATION, SERIES
Gallagher Bassett Advantage Newsletter

Art Director Pat Samata
Designer Kevin Krueger
Senior Editor Colleen Saurbier
Agency SamataMason
Client Gallagher Bassett Services, Inc.
Country United States

MERIT

**NEWSLETTER, JOURNAL,
OR HOUSE PUBLICATION**
Blue Shield of California
Institutional Brochure

Art Director Jennifer Sterling
Creative Director Jennifer Sterling
Designer Jennifer Sterling
Copywriter Lisa Citron
Illustrator Jennifer Sterling
Producer/Printer Active Graphics
Agency Jennifer Sterling Design
Client Blue Shield of California
Country United States

315

MERIT

**NEWSLETTER, JOURNAL,
OR HOUSE PUBLICATION**
i-jusi Brand Issue

Art Director Garth Walker
Creative Director Garth Walker
Designer Garth Walker
Copywriter Siobhan Gunning
Photography i-jusi Creative Team
Illustration i-jusi Creative Team
Studio Orange Juice Design
Client Ogilvy & Mather
Country South Africa

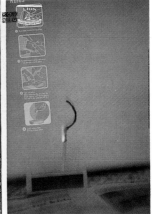

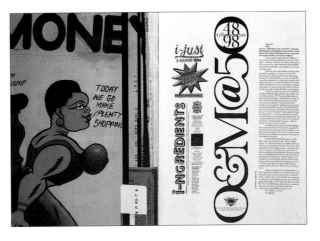

MERIT

MERIT

NEWSLETTER, JOURNAL,
OR HOUSE PUBLICATION
i-jusi #7

Art Director Garth Walker
Creative Director Garth Walker
Designer Garth Walker
Copywriter Siobhan Gunning
Photographer i-jusi Creative Team
Illustrator i-jusi Creative Team
Studio Orange Juice Design
Country South Africa

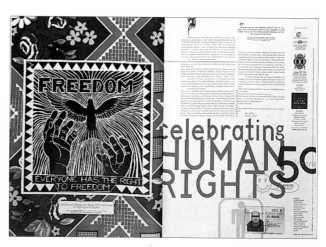

MERIT

NEWSLETTER, JOURNAL, OR HOUSE
PUBLICATION, SERIES
Ampersand

Art Director Vince Frost
Creative Director Vince Frost
Designers Andrew Collier,
Vince Frost, Melanie Mues
Managing Editor Marcelle Johnson
Editor Ruth Nicholas
Photographers James P. Cant,
Glen Erler, Paul Smith,
Jimmy Wormser
Agency Frost Design Ltd.
Client D&AD
Country England

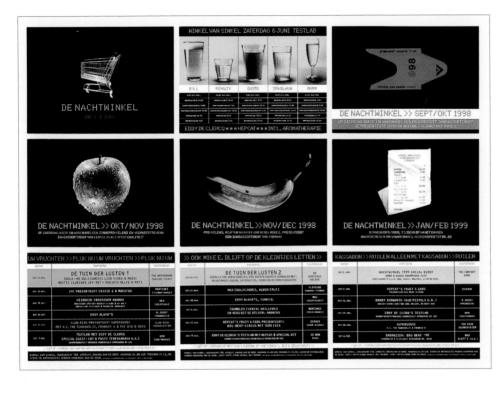

MERIT

**ENTERTAINMENT/SPECIAL
EVENTS PROGRAM, SERIES**
Nachtwinkel

Art Directors Ron Faas,
Tirso Francés
Designer Robin Uleman
Copywriters Mike E., Didier Prince
Photographer Robin Uleman
Studio Dietwee
Client Winkel van Sinkel
Country The Netherlands

317

Multiple Awards
see also Photography section,
p.373

see also Photography section,
p.373

MERIT

**ENTERTAINMENT/SPECIAL
EVENTS PROGRAM**
Life Is Sweet, MTV VMA Book

Creative Directors Tracy Boychuk,
Stacy Drummond, Jeffrey Keyton
Designers Tracy Boychuk,
Stacy Drummond, Jeffrey Keyton
Editor Soo-Hyun Chung
Photographer Micheal McLaughlin
Agency MTV Off-Air Creative
Client MTV Video Music Awards
Country United States

MERIT

**CORPORATE IDENTITY PROGRAM,
SERIES**

1837 Restaurant at Browns Hotel

Art Director John Rushworth
Designers Kerrie Powell,
John Rushworth
Studio Pentagram Design Ltd.
Client Raffles International
Country England

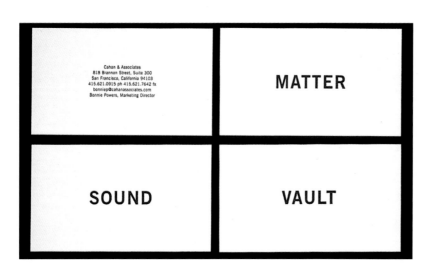

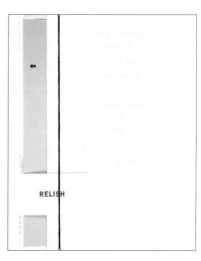

MERIT

**CORPORATE IDENTITY
PROGRAM, SERIES**

Cahan & Associates
Stationery

Art Director Bill Cahan
Designers Bob Dinetz, Kevin Roberson
Agency Cahan & Associates
Client Cahan & Associates
Country United States

MERIT

**CORPORATE IDENTITY PROGRAM,
SERIES**

Cisneros Television Group

Art Directors Carolina Bilbao (CTG),
Vanessa Eckstein (Blok Design,
Toronto)
Creative Director Monica Halpert
Designers Carolina Bilbao (CTG),
Vanessa Eckstein (Blok Design,
Toronto)
Studio Cisneros Television Group
Client Cisneros Television Group
Country United States

MERIT

**CORPORATE IDENTITY PROGRAM,
SERIES**

Lowe BCP & Partners Stationery

Art Directors Gerry Human,
Ivan Pols
Creative Directors Claire Harrison,
Gerry Human
Designers Alexa Craner,
Gerry Human, Ivan Pols
Copywriter Claire Harrison
Illustrator Ivan Pols
Producer Aldine Olivier
Contributors Alexa Cramer,
Claire Harrison
Agency Lowe BCP & Partners
Client Lowe BCP & Partners
Country South Africa

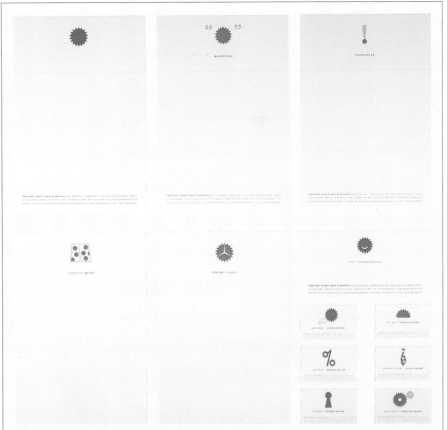

MERIT

**CORPORATE IDENTITY PROGRAM,
SERIES**
Soup Opera

Art Director Domenic Lippa
Designer Rachelle Dinnis
Photographer Nick Veasey
Agency Lippa Pearce Design
Client Soup Opera
Country England

MERIT

**STATIONERY (LETTERHEAD,
BUSINESS CARD, OR ENVELOPE)**
Richard Foster Stationery

Art Director Harry Pearce
Designers Jenny Allen, Harry Pearce
Agency Lippa Pearce Design, Ltd.
Client Richard Foster
Country England

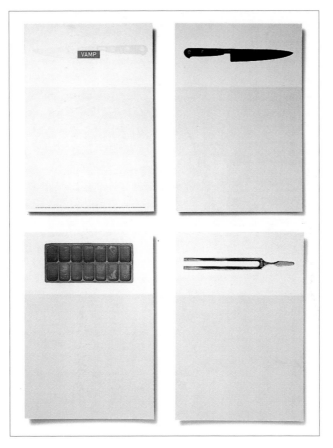

Art Director Peter Rae
Designers Roberto D'Andria, Kieron Molloy
Photographer Polly Eltes
Agency Tango Design
Client Vamp
Country England

321

Art Director Ralph Vincent Lunato
Designer Ralph Vincent Lunato
Copywriter Chris Ferguson
Producer Margaret Johnson
Agency Xon G5 Design
Client Nutrition Matters
Country United States

MERIT

LOGO/TRADEMARK
Wagamama

Art Director John Rushworth
Designers John Rushworth,
Sandy Suffield
Studio Pentagram Design Ltd.
Client Wagamama
Country England

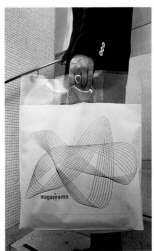

MERIT

MENU
Wagamama Restaurant Menu

Art Director John Rushworth
Designers John Rushworth,
Sandy Suffield
Studio Pentagram Design Ltd.
Client Wagamama
Country England

MERIT

PROMOTION/SELF-PROMOTION
Weyerhaeuser Cougar Opaque
Paper Promotion

Art Directors Greg Morgan,
Steve Watson
Designers Lesley Feldman,
Greg Morgan, Steve Watson
Copywriter Mark Popich
Photography Greg Morgan,
Steve Watson, Stock
Agency The Leonhardt Group
Client Weyerhaeuser
Country United States

MERIT

PROMOTION/SELF-PROMOTION
Portfolio of Works

Art Director Jennifer Sterling
Creative Director Jennifer Sterling
Designer Jennifer Sterling
Photographers John Casado,
Dave Magnusson, Tony Stromberg
Illustrator Jennifer Sterling
Producer Logos Graphics
Printer Logos Graphics
Agency Jennifer Sterling Design
Client Jennifer Sterling Design
Country United States

MERIT

PROMOTION/SELF-PROMOTION
Marko Lavrisha Photography

Art Director Jennifer Sterling
Creative Director Jennifer Sterling
Designers Amy Hayson,
Jennifer Sterling
Copywriter Eric La Brecque
Photographer Marko Lavrisha
Illustrator Jennifer Sterling
Producer/Printer
H. MacDonald Printing
Agency Jennifer Sterling Design
Client Marko Lavrisha
Country United States

MERIT

PROMOTION/SELF-PROMOTION,
SERIES
Benefit Book of Days
and Beach Towel

Art Director Stephen Doyle
Designer Lisa Yee
Studio Doyle Partners
Client Champion International
Country United States

MERIT

MIXED-MEDIA PROMOTION
Target Trends Style Guides,
Event Invitation and Teaser

Art Directors Sarah Nelson,
Sharon Werner
Creative Directors Anne Cashill,
Robyn Waters, Sharon Werner
Designers Liz McKinnell,
Sarah Nelson, Sharon Werner
Photography Darrell Eager,
Photonica
Illustrators Robert Clyde Anderson,
Monica Lind, Kathleen McNeely,
Claudia Pearson
Printer Heartland Graphics
Paper Mohawk
Agency Werner Design Werks, Inc.
Studio Werner Design Werks, Inc.
Client Target Stores
Country United States

324

MERIT

ANNOUNCEMENT/INVITATION
VH1 Fashion Awards RSVP

Art Director Dean Lubensky
Designer Dean Lubensky
Copywriter Tommy Cody
Project Manager Mary Russell
Studio VH1
Country United States

MERIT

ANNOUNCEMENT/INVITATION, SERIES

Base NYC–Studio Opening

Art Directors Thierry Brunfaut, Dimitri Jeurissen

Designer Thierry Brunfaut

Copywriter Geoffrey Cook

Photographer Dimitri Jeurissen

Producer Base Design

Agency Base Design

Client Base Design

Country United States

MERIT

CALENDAR

Black Calendar

Art Director Tadej Bratelj

Designers Tadej Bratelj, Sanja Rocco

Studio Castelvenere Design

Client Croatian Blind Union

Country Croatia

MERIT

CALENDAR

One Hundred Year

Creative Director Van So

Designer Pacey Chao

Copywriters R. V. Dougherty, Brent Heinrich

Agency JRV International

Client Yageo Corporation

Country Taiwan

MERIT

ENTERTAINMENT
Ella Fitzgerald and Duke Ellington:
Côte D'Azur Concerts on Verve

Art Director Chika Azuma
Illustrator Luba Lukova
Studio Luba Lukova Studio
Client Verve
Country United States

MERIT

ENTERTAINMENT
Miles Davis: The Complete
Bitches Brew

Art Directors Ron Jaramillo,
Arnold Levine
Artist Mati Klarwein
Studio Sony Music Creative Services
Department
Client Columbia Legacy
Country United States

MERIT

ENTERTAINMENT
Soul Bossa Trio Remixes Supernova

Art Director Manabu Koyama
Designer Manabu Koyama
Studio Tokuma Japan
Communications Co., Ltd.
Client Tokuma Japan
Communications Co., Ltd.
Country Japan

MERIT

ENTERTAINMENT
10 Speed

Art Director Jeri Heiden
Designers Jeri Heiden, Oogie Lee
Photographer Moshe Brahka
Logo Designer House Industries
Client A&M Records, Inc.
Country United States

MERIT

ENTERTAINMENT
Ken Ishii: Islands and
Continents–600 MHZ

Art Director Noriyuki Tanaka
Designers David Duval-Smith,
Kei Matushita
Photographer Shinji Hosono
Illustrator Kei Matushita
Producers Yuki Noda, Ken Ishii
Director Noriyuki Tanaka
Music Ken Ishii
Studio Noriyuki Tanaka Activity
Client Sony Music
Entertainment, Inc.
Country Japan

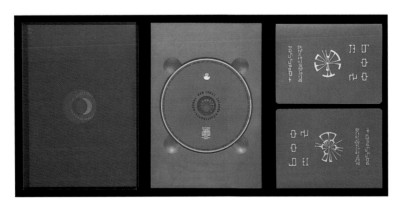

MERIT

ENTERTAINMENT, SERIES
187 Lockdown

Art Director Paul West
Creative Directors Paula Benson,
Paul West
Designers Chris Hilton, John Siddle,
Paul West
Photographer Spiros Politis
Music 187 Lockdown
Studio Form
Client Tim Coulson (East West
Records)
Country England

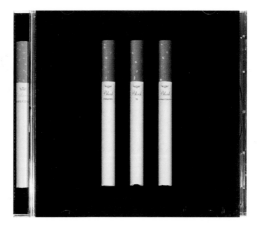

MERIT

ENTERTAINMENT
Block

Art Director Stefan Sagmeister
Designers Hjalti Karlsson,
Stefan Sagmeister
Copywriter Jamie Block
Photographers Barbara Ehrbar,
Gudmundur Ingolfson, Susan Stava
Illustrators Barbara Ehrbar,
Stefan Sagmeister
Producer Capitol Records
Agency Sagmeister, Inc.
Client Capitol Records
Country United States

MERIT

FOOD/BEVERAGE, SERIES
Target Beverage Cups–Icon Series

Art Director Laurie DeMartino
Designer Laurie DeMartino
Photographer Steve Belkowitz
Studio Studio d Design
Client Coco Connolly (Target Stores)
Country United States

329

MERIT

FOOD/BEVERAGE, SERIES
Target Beverage Cups–Crowd Series

Art Director Laurie DeMartino
Designer Laurie DeMartino
Photographer Steve Belkowitz
Illustrator Paulina Reyes
Studio Studio d Design
Client Coco Connolly (Target Stores)
Country United States

MERIT

GIFT/SPECIALTY PRODUCT, SERIES
IQ: Intelligence Cube

Creative Director Van So
Designer Van So
Copywriter Chuck Eisenstein
Photographer Lo Tung-Chiang
Agency JRV International
Client Yageo Corporation
Country Taiwan

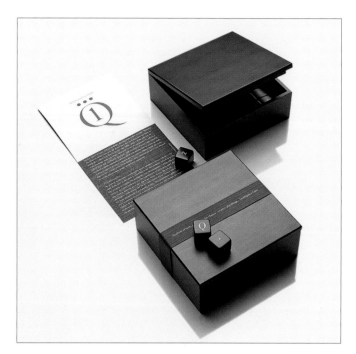

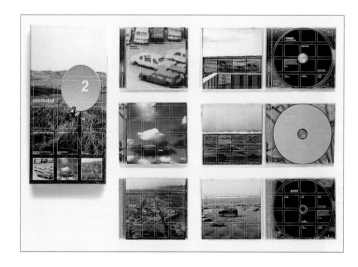

MERIT

MISCELLANEOUS PACKAGING
Connected 2

Art Directors Stefan Bogner,
A. Schildt, Boris Simon
Creative Director Stefan Bogner
Designer Stefan Bogner
Photographer Armin Smailovic
Producer Van Der Steege (BMG)
Music Electro
Agency Factor Product
Client Kosmo Records
Country Germany

MERIT

MISCELLANEOUS PACKAGING
Quickturn DAC Promotion

Art Director Jennifer Sterling
Creative Director Jennifer Sterling
Designer Jennifer Sterling
Copywriter Robert Pollie
Illustrators Jonathan Rosen, Jennifer Sterling
Producer/Printer Active Graphics
Agency Jennifer Sterling Design
Client Quickturn Design Systems
Country United States

MERIT

MISCELLANEOUS PACKAGING, SERIES
SKF F-One Inline Bearings

Art Director Ruediger Goetz
Creative Director Ruediger Goetz
Designer Ruediger Goetz
Illustrator Elke Boehm
Agency Simon & Goetz
Client SKF GMBH
Country Germany

MERIT

**WAYFINDING
SYSTEMS/SIGNAGE/DIRECTORY**

American Institute of Graphic Arts
(AIGA) Signage

Art Director Jennifer Sterling
Creative Director Jennifer Sterling
Designer Jennifer Sterling
Producer/Printer East Bay Laser Jet
Agency Jennifer Sterling Design
Client American Institute of Graphic
Arts (AIGA)
Country United States

332

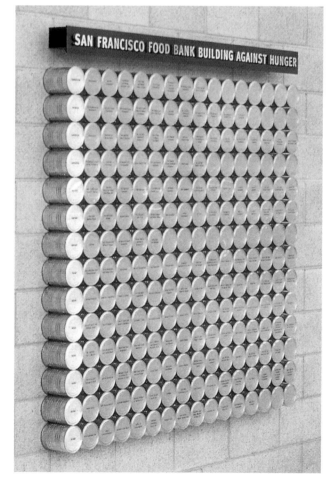

MERIT

**WAYFINDING
SYSTEMS/SIGNAGE/DIRECTORY**

San Francisco Food Bank
Dedication Sign

Designers Craig Hartman,
Lonny Israel, Jeremy Regenbogen
Studio Skidmore, Owings & Merrill
Country United States

**GALLERY MUSEUM EXHIBIT/
INSTALLATION**
Qiora, Press

Art Director Aoshi Kudo
Creative Director Shyuichi Ikeda
Designers Aoshi Kudo, Rikiya Uekusa
Video Director Hiroyuki Nakano
Music Satoru Nakada
Logo Type Designer Keiko Hirano
Lighting Harumi Fujimoto, MSG
Agency In House Creation DVS
Client Shiseido Co., Ltd.
Country Japan

MERIT

**GALLERY MUSEUM EXHIBIT/
INSTALLATION, SERIES**
Ogilvy & Mather's 50th Anniversary

Art Directors Brian Collins,
Luke Hayman
Creative Director Brian Collins
Designers Luke Hayman,
Felix Sockwell
Copywriter Rob Jacobson
Producer Tom Wagner
Agency Ogilvy & Mather
Client Ogilvy & Mather
Country United States

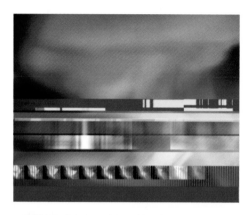

MERIT

TV IDENTITIES, OPENINGS, OR TEASERS, SERIES
SCI-FI "UHOs" Image

Art Director Graham McCallum

Designer Graham McCallum

Director of Photography
Ben Smithard

Producer Richard Churchill

Director Graham McCallum

Director of Creative Services
Michael Barry (SCI-FI)

Music Planet X

Studio Kemistry

Client SCI-FI

Country England

MERIT

TV IDENTITIES, OPENINGS, OR TEASERS
Monthly and Daily
Program Promos;
Winter Teasers

Art Directors Dmitri Lickin,
Evgeny Raitzes

Designers Dmitri Lickin,
Evgeny Raitzes, Larissa Uvarova

Producer Konstantin Ernst

Studio Lickin & Raitzes Product

Client ORT (Russian Public TV,
1st Channel)

Country Russia

MERIT

**TV IDENTITIES,
OPENINGS, OR TEASERS**
Sundance Channel:
Something New

Art Director Steve Angel

Creative Director Tom Harbeck

Designer Steve Angel

Producer Persis Reynolds

Sound Design Tom Third

Studio Head Gear Animation Inc.

Client Sundance Channel

Country Canada

MERIT

**CINEMA, OPENING
TITLE SEQUENCE**
The Avengers

Creative Director Kyle Cooper

Directors Jeremiah Chechik
(Warner Bros.), Karin Fong
(Imaginary Forces)

Art Directors Karin Fong,
Mikon van Gastel

Designers Karin Fong,
Mikon van Gastel, Scarlett Kim,
Grant Lau

Editor Fred Fouquet

Typographer Mikon van Gastel

Executive Producer Saffron Kenny

Producer Tim Thompson

2-D Animators Jennifer Chang,
Jeff Jankens, Ben Lopez

3-D Animators Emily Goodman,
Marcel Valcarce

Studio Imaginary Forces

Client Warner Bros.

Country United States

MERIT

**CINEMA, OPENING
TITLE SEQUENCE**
Artsy Fartsy Film Opening

Art Director Steve Sandstrom
Creative Director Steve Sandstrom
Designer Steve Sandstrom
Director Gary Nolton
Studio Sandstrom Design
Client Artsy Fartsy Productions
Country United States

MERIT

**CINEMA, OPENING
TITLE SEQUENCE**
Sphere

Creative Director Kyle Cooper
Directors Mikon van Gastel,
Barry Levinson (Warner Bros.),
Kurt Mattila (Imaginary Forces)
Art Directors Mikon van Gastel,
Kurt Mattila
Designers Olivia D'Albis,
Mikon van Gastel
Editors Mikon van Gastel,
Kurt Mattila
Photographer Norbert Wu
Typographer Mikon van Gastel
Executive Producer Saffron Kenny
Producer Maureen Timpa
2-D Animators Jennifer Chang,
Ben Lopez
Studio Imaginary Forces
Client Warner Bros.
Country United States

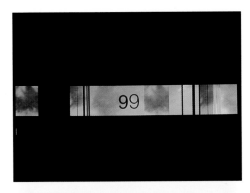

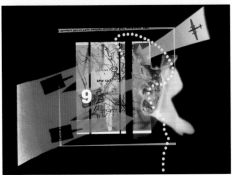

MERIT

**CINEMA, OPENING
TITLE SEQUENCE**
Slamdance

Art Director Elizabeth Rovnick
Designer Elizabeth Rovnick
Photographer Brumby Boylston
Animator Brumby Boylston
Producer Casey Steele
Executive Producer Matt Marquis
Studio Fuel
Client Fuel
Country United States

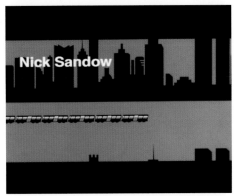

MERIT

**CINEMA, OPENING
TITLE SEQUENCE**
On the Run

Effects & On-line Facility Charlex, Inc.
Director of Visual Effects Alex Weil
Executive Producer Amy Kindred
Producer Steve Chiarello
Designer Heath Ivan Hewett
Flame/Effects Artist Marc Goldfine
Tape-to-Film Transfer Tape House Digital
Editorial Services Charlex, Inc.
Director Bruno de Almeida (Arco Films)
Director of Digital Services Alfie Schloss
Producer Steve Chiarello
Editor John Zawisha
Assistant Editor Kevin Brooks
Studio Charlex, Inc.
Client Arco Films
Country United States

338

MERIT	Art Directors Alicia Johnson,
CORPORATE/	Heath Lowe, Hal Wolverton
PROMOTIONAL VIDEO	**Creative Directors** Alicia Johnson,
MGD Solo Con Invitation	Hal Wolverton
Brand Loop	**Designers** Matt Eller, Neil Gust,
	Heath Lowe, Joe Peila,
	Tophet Sinkinson, Hal Wolverton
	Photographer Melody McDaniel
	Illustrators Christian Clayton,
	Robert Clayton
	Music Latin Playboys
	Agency Wieden & Kennedy
	Studio Johnson & Wolverton
	Client Miller Brewing Co.
	Country United States

MERIT	Art Director Doug Nichol
MUSIC VIDEO	**SFX Technicians** Francis Polve,
Pink	Philippe Pontonne (Krao)
	Producers Partizan, Midi Minuit
	Production Company Mikros Image
	Studio Mikros Image
	Client Aerosmith
	Country France

INTUITION

MERIT

**CORPORATE/
PROMOTIONAL VIDEO**
2nd Sight

Designers John Dire,
Antoine Tinguely, Jakob Trollbeck
Agency R/Greenberg Associates
Client David Carson
Country United States

Multiple Awards

see also Advertising
section, p.87

MERIT

**CORPORATE/
PROMOTIONAL VIDEO**
The Fastforward Film

Art Director Arndt Dallmann
Creative Directors Arndt Dallmann,
Guido Heffels
Copywriter Guido Heffels
Designer Oliver Bock
Producer Jassna Sroka
Director Oliver Bock
Agency Springer & Jacoby
Werbung
Client Markenfilm, Wedel
Country Germany

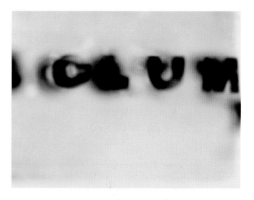

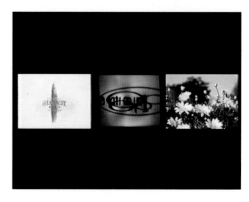

MERIT
SELF-PROMOTION VIDEO
Scott Olum/Type Reel

Designer Scott Olum
Photographer Scott Olum
Producer Dianna Turner
Studio Ride Design Studio
Client Scott Olum
Country United States

MERIT
**CORPORATE/
PROMOTIONAL VIDEO**
The Bluescreen Girl

Art Director Orazio Fantini
Designer Orazio Fantini
Photographer Jean-François Lord
Digital Artist Patrick Bergeran
Agency Behaviour
Client Discreet Logic
Country Canada

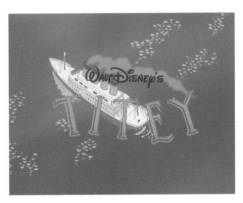

MERIT

SELF-PROMOTION VIDEO

Nest

Director Dan Salzmann

Editor Sue Moles

Director of Photography
Dan Salzmann

Costumes Marc Le Bihan

Post-Production Coordinator
Diana Giorgiutti

Music Various

Client Dan Salzmann

Country France

MERIT

ANIMATION

Titey

Copywriters Robert Smigel,
Michelle Saks Smigel,
Hal Willner

Designers Sean Lattrell,
David Wachtenheim

Voices Jason Alexander,
Whoopi Goldberg,
Gilbert Gottfried,
Molly Ringwald

Animation J.J. Sedelmaier

Agency NBC

Studio J.J. Sedelmaier
Productions, Inc.

Client Saturday Night Live

Country United States

MERIT

ANIMATION

The Masked Doctor
and the Secret Nurse

Art Directors Ron Barrett,
R. O. Blechman

Copywriter Ron Barrett

Illustrator Ron Barrett

Producers Brian O'Connell,
Richard O'Connor

Agency NBC

Studio The Ink Tank

Client Saturday Night Live

Country United States

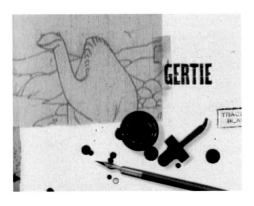

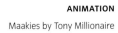

MERIT

ANIMATION

Maakies by Tony Millionaire

Director Marc Alt

Copywriter Tony Millionaire

Illustrator Tony Millionaire

Executive Producers
Alton Christensen and
Dave Tecson (Edgeworx),
Jim Signorelli (NBC)

Producer Marc Alt (Alt Digital)

Music The Human Lard Dog

Voice-over Actors Adam McKay,
Andy Richter, Sarah Thyre

Animators Marc Alt,
Michael Mattesi, Kurt Parker

Ink & Paint John Leamy

Agency Saturday Night Live
Film Unit

Studio Edgeworx/Alt Digital

Client NBC

Country United States

MERIT

ANIMATION

Cartoon Network

Designer John Dire

Director John Dire

Agency R/Greenberg Associates

Client Cartoon Network

Country United States

photo
illus

graphy
tration

thought it would be interesting this year if we gathered editorial art directors, photographers, and illustrators to judge the photography and illustration entries. The editorial art directors on the graphic design panel are responsible for some of the world's most progressive magazine design and are greatly admired for their art selection capabilities. The photographers and illustrators I chose are people that I feel are at the forefront of their respective fields. They are people I have worked with, or who have inspired me in my career.

These guys were tough, no doubt about it. But I believe the chosen entries represent the most interesting and inspired work going on right now.

As expected, the process of choosing the winners led to lively debate and a small, but tight, group of selected entries. These guys were tough, no doubt about it. But I believe the chosen entries represent the most interesting and inspired work going on right now.

Many thanks to the judges for all their hard work.

NEIL POWELL joined Joe Duffy and his group as an intern in March 1991, and seven years later is design director of Duffy NYC. Neil's work includes national and international branding, corporate identity, and Web site development for clients such as BMW, Giorgio Armani, The Lee Apparel Company, Jim Beam Brands, Tidy Cat, The Stroh Brewery Company, *Time* Magazine, The Coca-Cola Company, Hart Skis, and Faith Popcorn's BrainReserve. Neil is on the faculty of the School of Visual Arts where he is teaching a senior portfolio class.

—Neil Powell,
DUFFY DESIGN AND INTERACTIVE, NYC
DESIGN DIRECTOR

HUGH KRETCHMER graduated from Arts Center College and traveled to Southeast Asia. The portfolio that resulted from this trip earned him recognition as a finalist in the National Geographic internship program, but deciding photojournalism wasn't his forte, Kretchmer went back to the studio. His work now reflects the Russian Constructivist, Surrealist, and Dadaist movements.

PAUL VENAAS is art director of *Bikini* magazine, a division of RayGun Publishing. Previously, in Nashville, he was vice president of marketing and sales for Via records and art director for *7 Ball* magazine. Venaas also worked for Major Broadcasting Music Group as director of creative services before moving to Los Angeles where he currently resides.

WARD SUTTON designs and illustrates concert posters for bands including Pearl Jam, Beck, and Radiohead. In 1998, he created the poster artwork for the Broadway show *Freak* starring John Leguizamo. His illustrations have appeared in *Rolling Stone*, *Esquire*, and *New York Magazine*. His portrait of Prince Charles appeared on the cover of *The New York Times Magazine*. "Schlock 'n' Roll," Sutton's comic strip, runs in *The Village Voice* and many other U.S. newspapers.

JOELLE NELSON is an illustrator who first gained visibility through illustrations created for *RayGun* magazine. Current clients include Verve/Polygram Records, Old Navy, The United Way, Target, and The *Philadelphia Inquirer*. Nelson finds inspiration in synthesis, and frequently blends acrylic paint, pieces of abstract photography, and bits of textured scraps and paper. Her style often incorporates retroactive elements that integrate simple shapes and ideas with layers of meaning.

HERBERT WINKLER is art director of *Wallpaper* magazine. He has art directed many magazines including *Cash Flow*, *Gault & Millau*, *Ego* Austria and *Ego* Germany, *Ahead*, and *IQ*. In 1998, he founded a design office, section.d, in Vienna with partners Max Haupt-Stummer and Robert Jasensky. He is currently working on a redesign of *Carnet* magazine for deAgostini Rizzoli Periodici publishing house in Milan.

Multiple Awards

GOLD
**MAGAZINE ADVERTISEMENT,
CAMPAIGN**
and GOLD
POSTER OR BILLBOARD, SERIES
Arrow, Tyres, Arrest, Boxing

Art Director Tony Davidson
Creative Director John Hegarty
Copywriter Kim Papworth
Photographer Nadav Kander
Agency Bartle Bogle Hegarty
Client Levi Strauss & Co.
Country England

Multiple Awards
see also Graphic Design section, p.285

SILVER

MAGAZINE EDITORIAL, SERIES
Cut Magazine, December 1998

Art Director Hideki Nakajima
Editor-in-Chief Ken Sato
Editor Hiroshi Inada
Designer Hideki Nakajima
Photographers Naoki Ishizaka,
Kayt Jones
Client Rockin' On Inc.
Country Japan

352

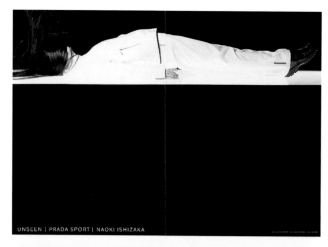

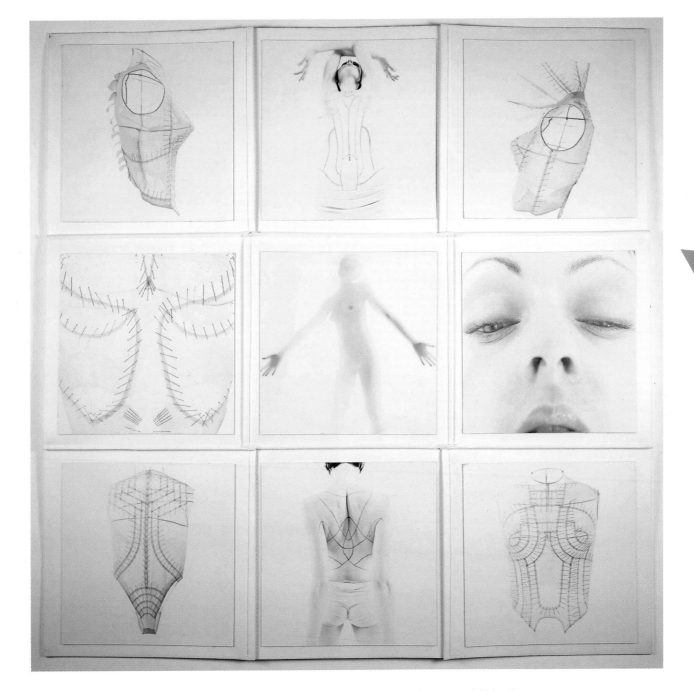

SILVER

SELF-PROMOTION, SERIES

Tracingherline Photo Quilt

Art Directors Vilma Mare, Detlef Schneider
Designer Vilma Mare
Photographer Detlef Schneider
Country United States

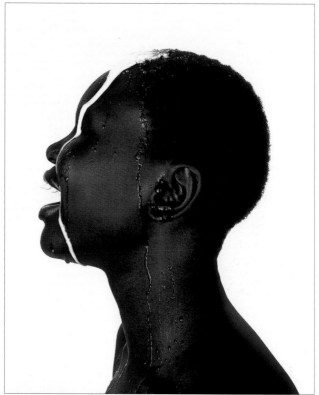

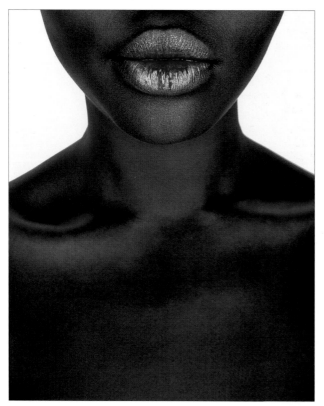

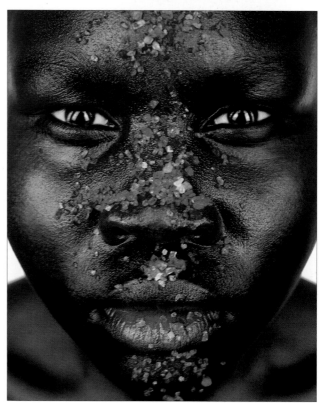

DISTINCTIVE MERIT

MAGAZINE EDITORIAL, SERIES

Black to Basics

Creative Director Linda Burns
Photographer Eva Mueller
Beauty Editor Linda Burns
Client Scene Magazine–London
Country United States

DISTINCTIVE MERIT

FASHION, SERIES
W.E.T. White Sands

Art Directors Ines Schneider,
Ivo von Renner
Photographer Ivo von Renner
Client Ines Schneider
Country Germany

Multiple Awards
see also Graphic Design section, p.281

DISTINCTIVE MERIT

PORTRAIT
Johnny Depp's Savage Journey

Art Director Fred Woodward
Designers Gail Anderson,
Fred Woodward
Photographer Dan Winters
Photo Editor Rachel Knepfer
Client Rolling Stone
Country United States

356

DISTINCTIVE MERIT

PORTRAIT
The Unsinkable Kate Winslet

Art Director Fred Woodward
Designers Gail Anderson,
Fred Woodward
Photographer Peggy Sirota
Photo Editor Rachel Knepfer
Client Rolling Stone
Country United States

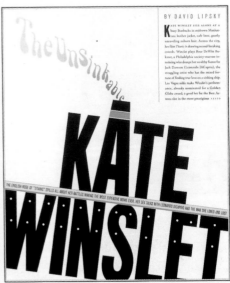

DISTINCTIVE MERIT

SELF-PROMOTION, SERIES
Wo Brands

Designer Scott Devendorf
Photographer James Wojcik
Country United States

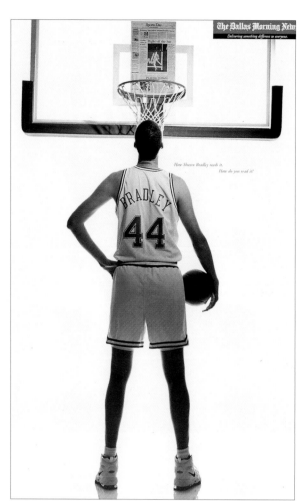

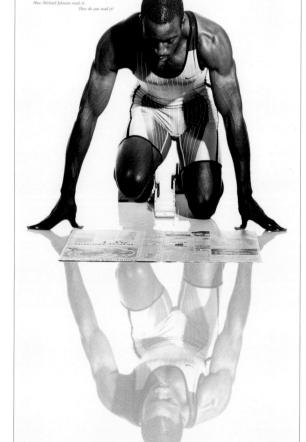

MERIT

NEWSPAPER ADVERTISEMENT, CAMPAIGN

How They Read the Dallas
Morning News: Shawn Bradley •
Stanley Marcus • Michael Johnson

Art Director Carl Warner
Creative Director Carl Warner
Copywriter Jim Hord
Photographer Lynn Sugarman
Agency DDB Needham Dallas
Client The Dallas Morning News
Country United States

MERIT

MAGAZINE EDITORIAL, SERIES
Popular Culture: Being 13

Photographer Lauren Greenfield
Client The New York Times Magazine
Country United States

MERIT

MAGAZINE EDITORIAL, SERIES
Biotech

Art Director Jackie Bacich
Creative Director Evan Schindler
Designer Zach Gold
Photographer Zach Gold
Stylist Wendy McNett
Client Black Book Magazine
Country United States

MAGAZINE EDITORIAL, SERIES
A Famine Made by Man

Art Director Rob Covey
Designer Dolores Motichka
Photographer Tom Stoddart
(IPG/Matrix)
Director of Photography
MaryAnne Golon
Photo Editor Olivier Picard
Client U.S. News &
World Report
Country United States

A Famine Made by Man

U.S. airstrikes are the least of Sudan's problems. Civil war   is causing mass starvation

Theft of life. A man steals a bag of maize from a malnourished child outside a United Nations feeding center in Ajiep, southern Sudan. This thief is well dressed and apparently rich by Sudanese standards. Government and rebel troops also steal humanitarian aid—but in a more systematic way.

WORLD REPORT

PHOTOGRAPHY BY TOM STODDART—IPG/ MATRIX

Delivering humanitarian aid is a far more dicey moral proposition than it might seem. Corruption is almost unavoidable, and armies often steal food and medicine intended for civilians. But seldom have the moral complications been so great—and yet the need for aid so stark—as they are right now in Africa's largest country, Sudan.

Last month, the United States bombed a factory in Khartoum, the capital, that was suspected of making chemical weapons as well as medicine. At the same time, America was sending—and continues to send—millions of dollars in food and medical supplies to the starving Sudanese people.

The government in Khartoum, which is strictly Islamic and predominantly Arab, is fighting a civil war against black rebels in southern Sudan who practice Christianity and traditional African religions. The war is hardly new: North has fought South for 32 of the 42 years since Sudan gained independence in 1956. Hunger is nothing new, either: Three times in the past decade, soldiers have caused famine by displacing farmers, stealing cattle, and burning villages.

This time, the effort is particularly grim. The United Nations says tens of thousands may already have died. An estimated 2.4 million people face starvation in southern Sudan. In the town of Wau, more than 70,000 famished refugees are huddled underneath trees and in market stalls.

A notice circulating among aid groups advises: Only people expected to die within 24 hours should be referred to the hospital. "There's only one other time—in Somalia—that I've seen grown men, barely skeletons, in this kind of shape," says Bob LaPrade, a veteran aid worker with CARE.

The U.N. World Food Program, mounting its largest aid effort ever, delivered nearly 15,000 tons of food last month at a cost of more than $1 million per day. The biggest donor is the United States, which has sent about $38 million of the $122 million collected by the U.N. program so far.

Villages smashed by war dot the flood plains of southern Sudan. Since rebels formed the Sudan People's Liberation

Too weak. A boy lies on a tarp (above) in Ajiep, the epicenter of the famine that threatens more than 2 million Sudanese. Many walk for days to reach the feeding center, and hundreds await each distribution of food (right).

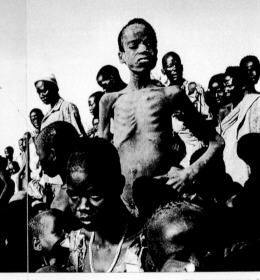

MERIT

MAGAZINE EDITORIAL, SERIES
Swing-a-Ding-Ding

Design Director Robert Newman
Designer Alden Wallace
Photographer Moshe Brakha
Photo Director Greg Pond
Fashion Director Derick Procope
Client Details Magazine
Country United States

birds in the garden

Rebuilding our fragile connection to these most delicate of all creatures

Blue-Winged Warbler

Birds bring beauty, drama, and companionship to a garden, but are best enjoyed at a distance. The birds in this story, including the Carolina chickadee (opposite) and the blue-winged warbler (this page), were all caught by licensed handlers in professional mist nets, banded for the purpose of scientific research, and quickly released. Photographer Victor Schrager has been documenting birds during mist-net captures for several years.

PHOTOGRAPHS BY VICTOR SCHRAGER TEXT BY MARGARET ROACH

Carolina Chickadee

Tufted Titmouse

House Finch

DO YOU KNOW THAT BIRDS ARE ATTRACTED TO THE SOUND OF RUNNING WATER?

Carolina Wren

Though many bird gardens are unruly, wild spaces, one of the country's oldest is decidedly formal. It is Wing Haven, in Charlotte, North Carolina, and the birds seem to like the orderliness just fine; they've been visiting it since the late Elizabeth Clarkson started her backyard garden in 1927. OPPOSITE, TOP LEFT: The garden became an official foundation in 1970, and visitors today can walk its formal brick paths, noticing neat boxwood parterres, which are juxtaposed with exuberant plantings loaded with fruit and nectar. OPPOSITE, BOTTOM RIGHT: The autumn is especially rich; on a fall afternoon, a sampling of the fruits include *Magnolia, Callicarpa, Poncirus, Euonymus, Lonicera, Rosa, Cocculus, Mahonia, Viburnum,* and *Ilex;* cover in the form of various evergreens, such as eastern hemlock, also features heavily in the design. In the forties and fifties, Clarkson, who instinctively understood the impact of chemical spraying on small creatures, would get up in the middle of the night, run out into the road in her nightgown, and block DDT spray trucks from entering the area. More than 140 kinds of birds have been sighted in the three-acre garden, and thirty or forty species may be present at one time. The birds enjoy the many nest boxes set up by the Clarkson family over the years; one has housed a pair of wood ducks almost every year since the fifties. ABOVE: Dripping or recirculating water is an additional feature. RIGHT: The garden's woodsy fringes.

PRODUCED BY MICHELE ADAMS AND AGNETHE GLATVED

MERIT

MAGAZINE EDITORIAL, SERIES
Birds in the Garden

Art Directors Agnethe Glatved, Eric A. Pike
Copywriter Margaret Roach
Designer Agnethe Glatved
Photographer Victor Schrager
Producers Michele Adams, Agnethe Glatved
Client Martha Stewart Living
Country United States

Clothes make the man. But the perfect accessories—from shiny shoes and belts to the right tie and wristwatch—can make you The Man. Photographs by James Wojcik

perfect

Newbury Street leather ankle shoes by Kenneth Cole, $170. Suede gloves by Giorgio Armani, $150.

Icon watch by Calvin Klein, $995. Ribbed tie, $95, and shirt, $200, by Donna Karan.

JANUARY 1999 • DETAILS 107

MERIT

MAGAZINE EDITORIAL, SERIES
Perfect

Design Director Robert Newman
Designer John Giordani
Photographer James Wojcik
Photo Director Greg Pond
Client Details Magazine
Country United States

PHOTOGRAPHY EDITORIAL

363

MERIT

FASHION, SERIES
Balthus Rocks

Art Director Martin R. Bourne
Creative Director Martin R. Bourne
Photographer Thom Jackson
Production Thom Jackson,
The New York Times
Fashion Editor Amy Spindler
Talent Agency LaChapelle
Stylist Martin R. Bourne
Studio Thom Jackson
Photographs, Inc.
Client The New York
Times Magazine
Country United States

364

MERIT

PORTRAIT
Born to Be Wilde

Art Director Janet Froelich
Photo Editor Kathy Ryan
Designer Paul Jean
Photographer Jake Chessum
Client The New York Times Magazine
Country United States

PORTRAIT

Elliott Smith, Waltz #2
(XO)–CD Single

Creative Director Francis Pennington
Designer Francesca Restrepro
(Design Palace)
Photographer Chris Buck
Client DreamWorks
Country United States

MERIT

PORTRAIT
Tracey Emin Close Up

Art Director Andrew McConachie
Designer Nick Thornton-Jones
Photographer Nadav Kander
Client Sunday Times Magazine
Country England

366

MERIT

PORTRAIT, SERIES
Monster Magnet "Powertrip"
Album Package

Art Directors Sandy Brummels, John Eder, Laramie Garcia, Dave Wyndorff
Creative Directors Sandy Brummels, Dave Wyndorff
Designer Laramie Garcia
Photographer John Eder
Client A&M Records
Country United States

MERIT

PHOTOGRAPHY, PORTRAIT, SERIES
Rolling Stone Sports Hall of Fame

Art Director Fred Woodward
Photographers Ruven Afanador,
Anton Corbijn, John Huet,
Sam Jones, Nadav Kander,
David LaChapelle, Matt Mahurin,
Kurt Markus, Robert Maxwell,
Mark Seliger, Peggy Sirota,
Isabel Snyder
Photo Editors Rachel Knepfer,
Fiona McDonagh
Client Rolling Stone
Country United States

PORTRAIT, SERIES
Incognito, Portraits on the
Edge of Light

Art Director Jaroslav Pecka
Creative Director Antonin Kratochvil
Copywriter Antonin Kratochvil
Designer Jan Zacharias
Photographer Antonin Kratochvil
Producer Atelier Puda
Client Galerie Pecka
Country United States

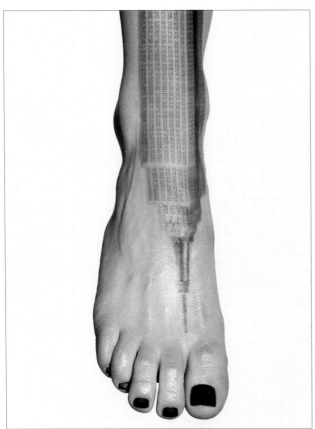

MERIT

POSTER OR BILLBOARD, SERIES

Bright Eyes Big City

Creative Director Linda Burns
Photographer Eva Mueller
Client Scene Magazine—London
Country United States

Art Director Zhang Nian Chao
Designer Zhang Nian Chao
Photographer Zhang Nian Chao
Producer Zhang Nian Chao
Country China

MERIT

SERVICE
Basketball

Designer Todd Haimann
Photographer Todd Haimann
Country United States

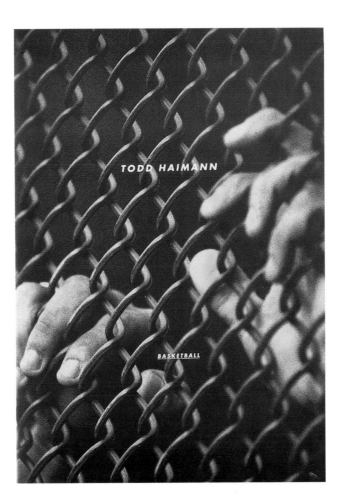

MERIT

BOOK OR BOOK JACKET
Milan Sklenar Photographs

Art Director Carmen Dunjko
Copywriters Rosemary Mahoney,
Chris Morgan
Editor Diana Shearwood
Designer Carmen Dunjko
Photographer Milan Sklenar
Client Behaviour
Country Canada

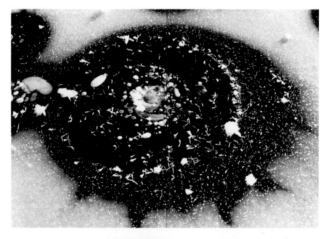

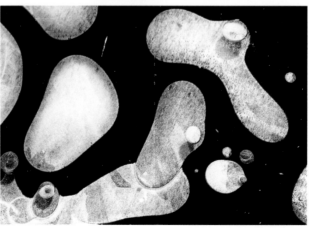

MERIT

BOOK OR BOOK JACKET
Minus Sixteen

Designer Mike Turner
Photographer Robin Broadbent
Studio Browns Design Company
Printer Westerham Press
Client Browns Publishing
Country England

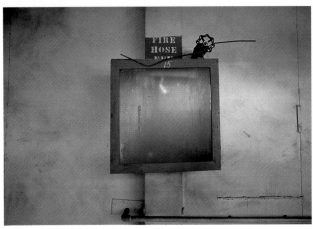

MERIT

SELF-PROMOTION, SERIES
Zone

Art Director Patrick Giasson
Photographer Diana Shearwood
Agency Behavior
Client Diana Shearwood
(Galerie Quartier Ephémère)
Country Canada

371

MERIT

SELF-PROMOTION, SERIES
e-fact

Art Director Stephan Hammes
Creative Director David Slater
Copywriters Stephan Hammes,
Anna van Ommen
Designer Stephan Hammes
Photographer Stephan Hammes
Agency e-fact. limited
Client e-fact. limited
Country England

Multiple Awards
see also Graphic Design section,
p. 317

MERIT

**CORPORATE/ INSTITUTIONAL,
SERIES**
Life Is Sweet, MTV VMA Book

Art Directors Tracy Boychuk,
Stacy Drummond, Jeffrey Keyton
Creative Directors Tracy Boychuk,
Stacy Drummond, Jeffrey Keyton
Designers Tracy Boychuk,
Stacy Drummond, Jeffrey Keyton
Photographer Micheal McLaughlin
Editor Soo-Hyun Chung
Agency MTV
Client MTV Video Music Awards
Country United States

MERIT

**CORPORATE/INSTITUTIONAL,
SERIES**
125 Jahre Müssig
(125 Years of Müssig)

Art Director Conny J. Winter
Copywriter Christa Winter
Designer Conny J. Winter
Photographer Conny J. Winter
Agency Studio Conny J. Winter
Client Wilhelm Müssig GmbH
Country Germany

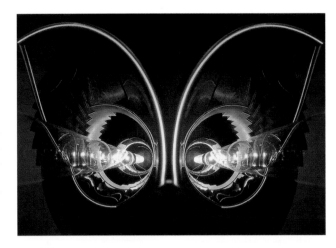

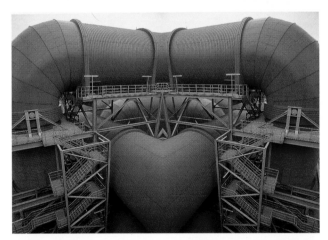

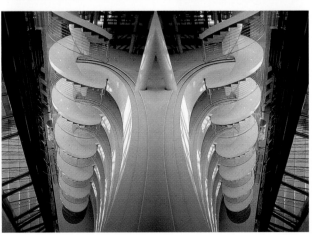

MERIT

CALENDAR, SERIES
The Mercedes-Benz
Taxi Calendar '99

Art Director Strichpunkt
Creative Director Dietmar Henneka
Director Andreas Poulionakis
Designers Jochen Raedeker,
Gernot Walter
Photographers Dietmar Henneka
and his eleven Ex-assistants
Producer Mercedes-Benz
Vertrieb Deutschland
Client Daimler-Benz AG
Country Germany

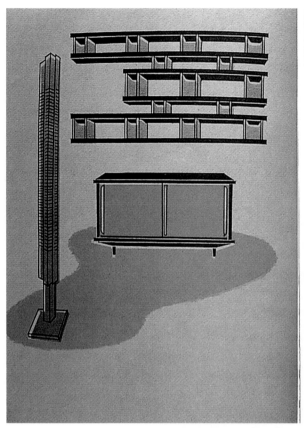

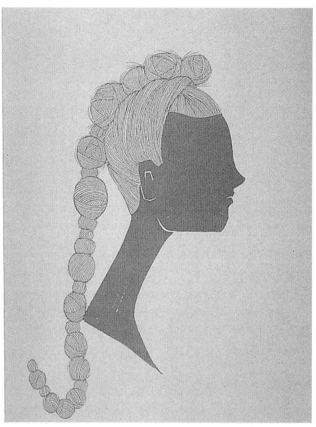

Multiple Awards
see also Graphic Design section, p.249

GOLD

BOOK OR BOOK JACKET
Blue Mode

Art Director Hideki Nakajima
Creative Director Taka Kawachi
Designer Hideki Nakajima
Illustrator Hiroshi Tanabe
Client Korinsha Press & Co., Ltd.
Country Japan

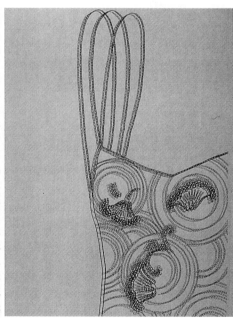

SILVER

MAGAZINE ADVERTISEMENT, CAMPAIGN

Retro Soul, Insert • Indie Pop, Awwww Yeah • Bhangra, Kizmet Rising

Art Director Jennifer Boyd
Creative Directors Peter Angelos, Lee Clow, Rob Smiley
Copywriter Scott Duchon
Illustrator Graham Rounthwaite
Agency TBWA Chiat/Day, Inc.
Client Levi Strauss & Co.
Country United States

DISTINCTIVE MERIT

MAGAZINE ADVERTISEMENT
Fusion, Orgy

Art Director Christian Cottorill
Creative Director Christen Monge
Copywriter Justin Hooper
Illustrator Jason Brookes
Agency Ogilvy & Mather
Client Elida Fabergé
Country England

MERIT

MAGAZINE ADVERTISEMENT
Fusion, Breakdancer

Art Director Christian Cottorill
Creative Director Christen Monge
Copywriter Justin Hooper
Illustrator Pete Fowler
Agency Ogilvy & Mather
Client Elida Fabergé
Country England

MERIT

MAGAZINE ADVERTISEMENT
Fusion, Wrap

Art Director Christian Cottorill
Creative Director Christen Monge
Copywriter Justin Hooper
Illustrator Graham Rounthwaite
Agency Ogilvy & Mather
Client Elida Fabergé
Country England

cool winter

We know it's cold outside. But before you zip up your parka and venture into winter's wonderland, plow through the following pages–they're packed with stylish ideas on fashion, beauty and fun. It's time to warm up to winter. Illustrations by Anja Kroencke.

Van Cleef & Arpels   FENDI   CLARINS   DAVID YURMAN   LINCOLN   Polaroid   LANCÔME

out of sight

Although it feels like the skin is on vacation, the sun still lurking, waiting to infiltrate your skin and eyes with its wicked rays. Use a sunblock every day, especially if you're out on the slopes (snow reflects light), and invest in a quality pair of sunglasses. Besides suppressing the sun's uncomfortable glare, sunglasses shield the delicate, wrinkle-prone skin around the eye. Look for frames with maximum eye coverage and lenses that feature both UVA and UVB protection. And of course, if you find a pair that make you feel like a Hollywood glamour-puss, all the better.

FENDI

FENDI
Occhiali

Special Advertising Section

just rewards

The holidays have come and gone, and the parties are over. But don't let January turn into an anticlimactic affair–pick up your mood with a precious little something. Here, the top ten reasons why January is the best month to buy jewelry:

1 You didn't get what you wanted for Christmas 2 You need an advance reward for the resolutions you're struggling to keep 3 A string of baubles keeps a girl warm at night 4 Make February easier on your valentine – let him know your new necklace comes with matching earrings 5 Gold looks gorgeous against cashmere 6 You need an incentive to lose the six pounds you've gained since Thanksgiving 7 The holiday lights have been taken down and, well, *something* has to twinkle 8 It's time to party like it's 1999 9 You'll feel better exiting the 20th century in style 10 You deserve it

Van Cleef & Arpels

The Pleasure & of Perfection

"CLOVER" Collection from $ 900

Van Cleef & Arpels

NEW YORK 744 FIFTH AVENUE

PALM BEACH, BEVERLY HILLS, HONOLULU, PARIS, CANNES, MONTE-CARLO, LONDON, GENEVE, TOKYO, HONG-KONG (800) VCA-5797

DISTINCTIVE MERIT

MAGAZINE ADVERTISEMENT, CAMPAIGN
Cool Winter

Art Director Nancy Arnold
Designer Carrie Masterman
Illustrator Anja Kroencke
Client Vogue Magazine
Country United States

Multiple Awards

DISTINCTIVE MERIT

**MAGAZINE ADVERTISEMENT,
CAMPAIGN**
Purple Low Tar

and MERIT

POSTER OR BILLBOARD, CAMPAIGN
Purple Low Tar

Art Director Carlos Silvério
Creative Directors Francesc Petit,
Carlos Silvério
Copywriter Rui Branquinho
Illustrator Al Hirschfeld
Producer Robson Ciaramicoli
Agency DPZ Propaganda S/A
Client Candelária Tobacco
Country Brazil

380

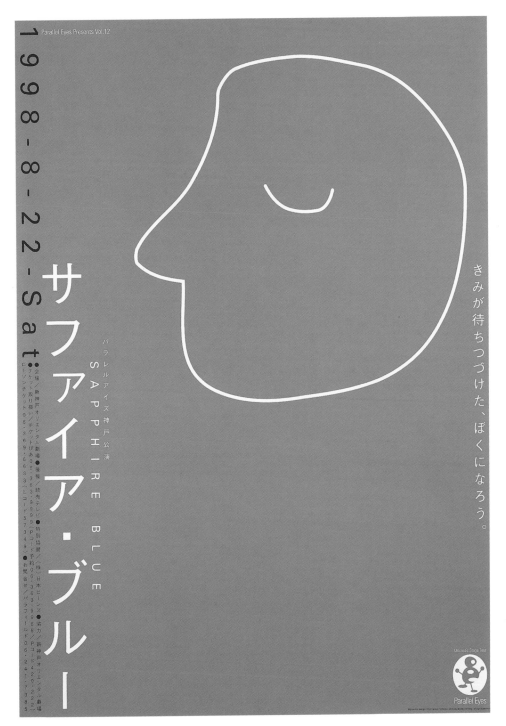

DISTINCTIVE MERIT

POSTER OR BILLBOARD
Parallel Eyes (Sapphire Blue)

Art Director Tamotsu Shimada
Copywriter Shinya Kamimura
Designer Tamotsu Shimada
Illustrator Tamotsu Shimada
Client Parafield
Country Japan

DISTINCTIVE MERIT

CORPORATE/INSTITUTIONAL

Bettina's Beauty Blitz

Art Director Naomi Winegrad-Usher
Copywriter Jill Steinbach Friedson
Designers Geneve Doherty,
Pui Kuen Wan
Illustrator Anja Kroencke
Client Allure Magazine
Country United States

STYLE OVER SUBSTANCE

Frank DeCaro

Home Is Where the Dishes Are

MERIT

NEWSPAPER ADVERTISEMENT
Home Is Where the Dishes Are

Art Director Sam Reep
Illustrator Anja Kroencke
Client The New York Times
Country United States

MERIT

MAGAZINE ADVERTISEMENT
Holiday Shopping

Art Director Christine Dunleavy
Assistant Art Director Susan Syrnick
Illustrator Anja Kroencke
Client The Philadelphia Inquirer Magazine
Country United States

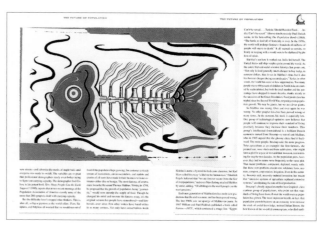

years. One researcher watched as emperor penguins tried to cope with the early breakup of ice; their chicks had to jump into the water two weeks ahead of schedule, probably guaranteeing an early death. They (like us) evolved on the old earth.

You don't have to go to exotic places to watch the process. Migrating red-winged blackbirds now arrive three weeks earlier in Michigan than they did in 1960. A symposium of scientists reported in 1996 that the Pacific Northwest was warming at four times the world rate. "That the Northwest is warming up fast is not a theory," Richard Gammon, a University of Washington oceanographer, says, "It's a known fact, based on simple temperature readings."

The effects of that warming can be found in the largest phenomena. The oceans that cover most of the planet's surface are clearly rising, both because of melting glaciers and because water expands as it warms. As a result, low-lying Pacific islands already report surges of water washing across the atolls. "It's nice weather and all of a sudden water is pouring into your living room," one Marshall Islands resident told a newspaper reporter. "It's very clear that something is happening in the Pacific, and these islands are feeling it." Global warming will be like a much more powerful version of El Niño that covers the entire globe and lasts forever, or at least until the next big asteroid strikes.

If you want to scare yourself with guesses about what might happen in the near future, there's no shortage of possibilities. Scientists have already observed large-scale shifts in the duration of the El Niño ocean warming, for instance. The Arctic tundra has warmed so much that in some places it now gives off more carbon dioxide than it absorbs—a switch that could trigger a potent feedback loop, making warming ever worse. And researchers studying glacial cores from the Greenland Ice Sheet recently concluded that local climate shifts have occurred with incredible rapidity in the past—18° in one three-year stretch. Other scientists worry that such a shift might be enough to flood the oceans with fresh water and reroute or shut off currents like the Gulf Stream and the North Atlantic, which keep Europe far warmer than it would otherwise be. (See "The Great Climate Flip-flop," by William H. Calvin, January Atlantic.) In the words of Wallace Broecker, of Columbia University, a pioneer in the field, "Climate is an angry beast, and we are poking it with sticks."

BUT we don't need worst-case scenarios; best-case scenarios make the point. The population of the earth is going to nearly double one more time. That will bring it to a level that even the reliable old earth we were born on would be hard-pressed to support. Just at the moment when we need everything to be working as smoothly as possible, we find ourselves inhabiting a new planet, whose carrying capacity we cannot conceivably estimate. We have no idea how much wheat this planet can grow. We don't know what its politics will be like; not if there are going to be heat waves like the one that killed more than 700 Chicagoans in 1995; not if rising sea levels and other effects of climate change create tens of millions of environmental refugees; not if a 1.5° jump in India's tempera-

ture could reduce the country's wheat crop by 10 percent or divert its monsoons.

The arguments put forth by cornucopians like Julian Simon—that human intelligence will get us out of any scrape, that human beings are "the ultimate resource," that Malthusian models "simply do not comprehend key elements of people"—all rest on the same premise: that human beings change the world mainly for the better.

If we live at a special time, the single most special thing about it may be that we are now apparently degrading the most basic functions of the planet. It's not that we've never altered our surroundings before. Like the beavers at work in my back yard, we have rearranged things wherever we've lived. We've leveled the spots where we built our homes, cleared forests for our fields, often fouled nearby waters with our waste. That's just life. But this is different. In the past ten or twenty or thirty years our impact has grown so much that we're changing even those places we don't inhabit—changing the way the weather works, changing the plants and animals that live at the poles or deep in the jungle. This is total. Of all the remarkable and unexpected things we've ever done as a

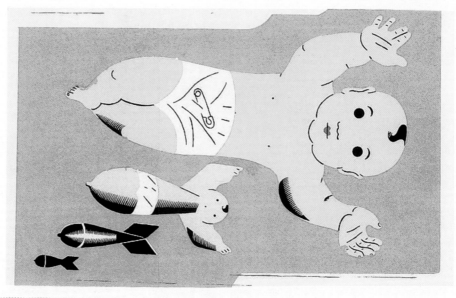

MERIT

MAGAZINE ADVERTISEMENT, CAMPAIGN
A Special Moment in History

Art Director Judy Garlan
Illustrator Brian Cronin
Client The Atlantic Monthly
Country United States

PORTRAIT

Christina Ricci

Art Director Fred Woodward
Illustrator Mark Ryden
Client Rolling Stone
Country United States

POSTER

Pearl Jam–Australia Tour

Art Director Barry Ament
Designer Ward Sutton
Illustrator Ward Sutton
Agency Amesbros
Client Pearl Jam
Country United States

Multiple Awards

MERIT

POSTER OR BILLBOARD, SERIES
Take Your Life • Self-esteem •
Proof • Join a Gang

and MERIT

POSTER OR BILLBOARD
Wilderness Survival • Use a Knife

Art Director Jay Russell
Copywriters Wade Alger,
Kevin Sutton
Photographer John Katz
Agency DDB Needham Dallas
Client Boy Scouts of America
Country United States

MERIT

BOOK OR BOOK JACKET
Mrs. Kennedy Goes Abroad

Art Director Nicholas Callaway
Designer Jennifer Wagner
Illustrator Jacqueline Duhême
Editor Antoinette White
Producer Callaway Editions
Client Artisan Books
Country United States

MERIT

BOOK OR BOOK JACKET
The Jungle ABC

Art Director Nicholas Callaway
Designer Toshiya Masuda
Illustrator Michael Roberts
Editor Edward Brash
Producer Callaway Editions
Client Hyperion Books for Children
Country United States

SELF-PROMOTION
Daily Show with Jon Stewart
Party Invitation

Art Director Vinny Sainato
Designer Naomi Mizusaki
Illustrator Jordi Labanda
Agency Comedy Central
(Off Air Creative)
Client Comedy Central
Country United States

MERIT

SELF-PROMOTION
Blue Fashion

Illustrator Anja Kroencke
Client Kate Larkworthy
Artist Rep., Ltd.
Country United States

stu

dent

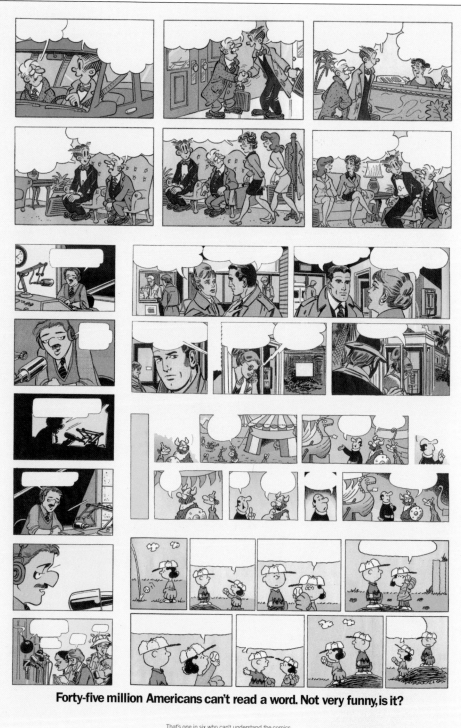

GOLD

COLLATERAL MIXED MEDIA, CAMPAIGN
MADD Guerrilla Placement, Handicap Ramp

Art Director Kohl Norville

Art Direction Department Head Norm Grey

Copywriter Cal Mc Allister

Copywriting Department Head Mike Jones-Kelley

Instructors Bart Cleveland, Cal Mc Allister, Ted Nelson

Client Mothers Against Drunk Driving

School The Creative Circus

Country United States

Where exactly are
the nuggets?

Billions and billions
of clogged arteries are
nothing to smile about.

SILVER

**POSTERS AND BILLBOARDS:
POINT-OF-PURCHASE, CAMPAIGN**
Chicken • Clown • Tuna

Art Director Thomas Hair
Creative Director Coz Cotzias
Copywriter Clay Black
Instructor Coz Cotzias
Client Subway
School VCU Adcenter
Country United States

We serve tuna.
We can't seem to find
the elusive O'Fish.

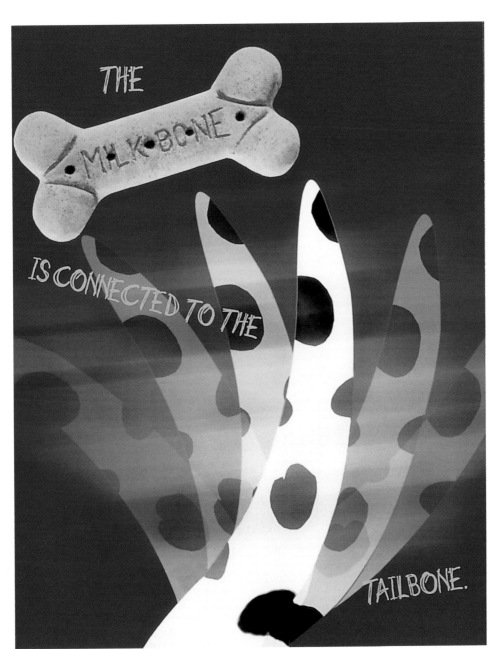

DISTINCTIVE MERIT

**PRINT ADVERTISING,
CONSUMER MAGAZINE: FULL PAGE**
Milkbone Dog Biscuit

Art Director Yara Siegelaar
Art Direction Department Head
Norm Grey
Copywriter David Laskarzewski
Copywriting Department Head
Mike Jones-Kelley
Client Milkbone
School The Creative Circus
Country United States

DISTINCTIVE MERIT

**PRINT ADVERTISING,
PUBLIC SERVICE/
NON-PROFIT NEWSPAPER:
LESS THAN A FULL PAGE,
CAMPAIGN**

Small Space—Amazon.com

Art Director Jason Stamp
Copywriter David Johnson
Client amazon.com
Instructor Tony Messano
School Portfolio Center
Country United States

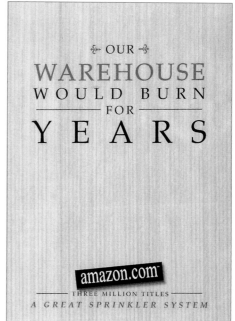

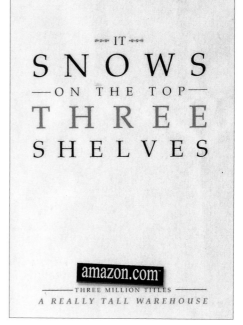

*The words "hand made" are
printed on every ball.
But you will never find the story
of whose hands made them.*

Instead of throwing balls, they stitch them. Instead of sitting in classrooms learning math, they sit on splintered factory floors 'hand crafting' merchandise for the Western world.

They are the 250 million children around the world who work full time. No play. No school. Just fourteen hour days. Many are sold to business owners for a $15 dollar bond they will never pay off. They are beaten and branded as they work for six cents an hour manufacturing soccer balls, designer clothing, rugs, surgical instruments– products Americans buy every day.

The National Labor Committee is leading the fight against bonded and child labor. We are bringing awareness to the laws governments are ignoring. And we are teaching third world nations that there are more profitable business practices than exploiting child labor. But we are a non-profit agency that needs your help. Please call 212-242-3002. Maybe someday, we can help their kids be kids again.

The National Labor Committee

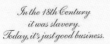

*In the 18th Century
it was slavery.
Today, it's just good business.*

"The master yells at us often," says Akbar, an eight-year-old rug maker in Pakistan. "I was beaten after I made many errors of color in a carpet. He struck me with his fist quite hard in the face."

Every year, Akbar and 250 million children like him are forced to work. No play. No school. Just fourteen hour days. Many are sold to business owners for a $15 dollar bond they will never pay off. They are beaten and branded as they work for six cents an hour manufacturing soccer balls, designer clothing, rugs, surgical instruments– products Americans buy every day.

The National Labor Committee is leading the fight against bonded and child labor. We are bringing awareness to the laws governments are ignoring. And we are teaching third world nations that there are more profitable business practices than exploiting child labor. But we are a non-profit agency that needs your help. Please call 212-242-3002, and help end slave labor forever.

The National Labor Committee

*If Nike spent less on
commercials, maybe
they could afford to pay their
employees.*

Their commercials portray children achieving on the field, on the court and, presumably, in life. Meanwhile, in Pakistan, the children who make their products are sold and re-sold like live stock.

Nike and other companies around the world indirectly employ 250 million underage children to work full time. No play. No school. Just fourteen hour days. Many are sold to business owners for a $15 dollar bond they will never pay off. They are beaten and branded as they work for six cents an hour manufacturing soccer balls, designer clothing, rugs, surgical instruments– products Americans buy every day.

The National Labor Committee is leading the fight against bonded and child labor. We are bringing awareness to the laws governments are ignoring. But we are a non-profit agency that needs your help. Please call 212-242-3002 for more information. And help us show companies like Nike that there are more profitable business practices than exploiting child labor.

The National Labor Committee

DISTINCTIVE MERIT

**PRINT ADVERTISING,
PUBLIC SERVICE/NON-PROFIT,
NEWSPAPER: SPREAD, CAMPAIGN**
Handmade • Nike • Slavery

Art Director Erik Proulx
Art Direction Department Head
Norm Grey
Copywriter Erik Proulx
Copywriting Department Head
Mike Jones-Kelley
Photography Life Magazine
Client National Labor Committee
School The Creative Circus
Country United States

DISTINCTIVE MERIT

**POSTERS AND BILLBOARDS:
TRANSIT**
Form You 3–Weightloss Centers

Art Director Yara Siegelaar
Art Direction Department Head
Norm Grey
Copywriting Department Head
Mike Jones-Kelley
Client Form You 3 Weightloss Centers
School The Creative Circus
Country United States

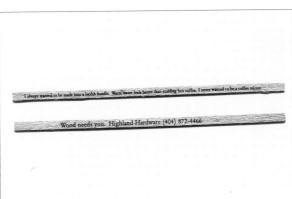

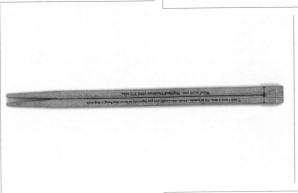

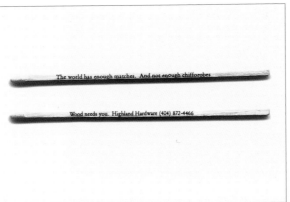

Art Director Erinne Dobson
Art Direction Department Head
Norm Grey
Copywriter Brian Ahern
Copywriting Department Head
Mike Jones-Kelley
Instructor Nick Vaggot
Client Highland Hardware
School The Creative Circus
Country United States

STUDENT ADVERTISING

399

DISTINCTIVE MERIT

**BROADCAST CRAFTS AND DESIGN:
ANIMATION**
Kid & Wolf

Art Director M. Bret Church
Illustrator M. Bret Church
Instructor Cathrin Yoder
School Art Institute of Phoenix
Country United States

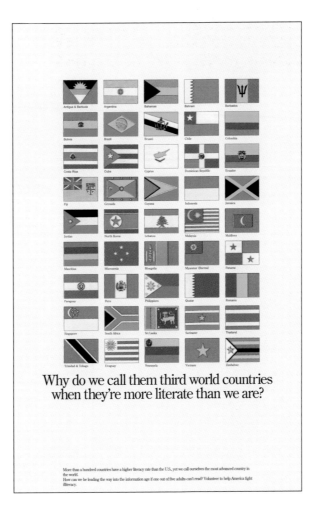

MERIT

**PRINT ADVERTISING,
CONSUMER NEWSPAPER: FULL PAGE**
Dented Steer

Art Director Sean Murray

Art Direction Department Head Norm Grey

Copywriter Dana Carvelli

Copywriting Department Head Mike Jones-Kelley

Client Brake-O

School The Creative Circus

Country United States

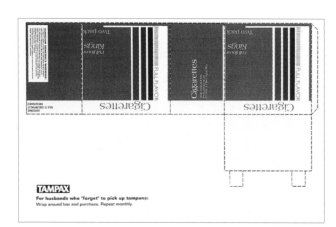

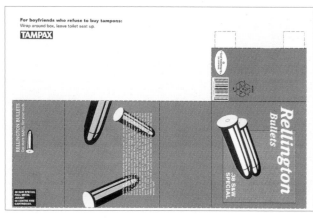

MERIT

**PRINT ADVERTISING, CONSUMER
MAGAZINE: FULL PAGE, CAMPAIGN**
Tampon Box Covers

Art Director Dino Valentini

Art Direction Department Head
Norm Grey

Copywriter Kim Nguyen

Copywriting Department Head
Mike Jones-Kelley

Instructor Norm Grey

School The Creative Circus

Country United States

Blue. A color of Tranquility
Behr Interior Paint

MERIT

**PRINT ADVERTISING,
CONSUMER MAGAZINE: FULL PAGE**
The Color of Intimacy, Tranquility, Joy

Art Director Jeff Church
Art Direction Department Head
Norm Grey
Copywriter Danielle Vieth
Copywriting Department Head
Mike Jones-Kelley
Client Behr Interior Paint
School The Creative Circus
Country United States

MERIT

**PRINT ADVERTISING,
CONSUMER MAGAZINE: SPREAD,
CAMPAIGN**
Shot • Drive Drunk • Liver Transplant

Art Director Marc Wientzek
Art Direction Department Head Norm Grey
Copywriter Dan Miranda
Copywriting Department Head Mike Jones-Kelley
Photographers Beth Klein, Marc Wientzek
Client Jägermeister
School The Creative Circus
Country United States

MERIT

**PRINT ADVERTISING,
CONSUMER MAGAZINE: SPREAD**
That's Not All Folks!

Art Director Frank Anselmo
Copywriter Frank Anselmo
Designer Frank Anselmo
Client Cartoon Network
Instructor Jack Mariucci
School School of Visual Arts
Country United States

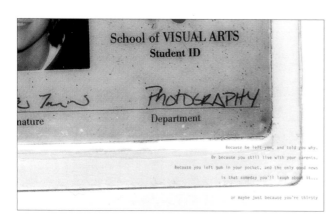

MERIT

**PRINT ADVERTISING,
CONSUMER MAGAZINE:
SPREAD, CAMPAIGN**
School ID

Art Director
Shayne-Alexis Humphrey
Copywriter
Shayne-Alexis Humphrey
Client Coors Brewing Co.
Instructor Jeffrey Metzner
School School of Visual Arts
Country United States

MERIT

PRINT ADVERTISING, TRADE MAGAZINE:
SPREAD, CAMPAIGN
Mont Blanc • Jaguar • Hennessey

Art Director Marc Wientzek
Art Direction Department Head Norm Grey
Copywriter Tom Hamling
Copywriting Department Head Mike Jones-Kelley
Photographers Beth Klein, Marc Wientzek
Client Playboy
School The Creative Circus
Country United States

MERIT

POSTER, PROMOTIONAL
Bluto's Revenge

Art Director Donald Vann
Creative Director Jerry Torchia
Copywriter Holly Thompson
Client V-8
Instructor Jerry Torchia
School VCU Adcenter
Country United States

Art Director Mike McMullen
Art Direction Department Head Norm Grey
Creative Director Rob Lawton
Copywriter Dave Laskarzewski
Copywriting Department Head Mike Jones-Kelley
School The Creative Circus
Country United States

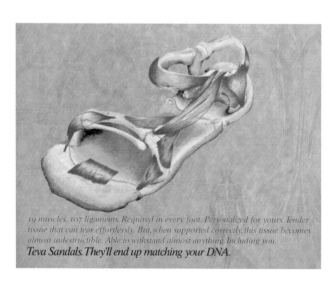

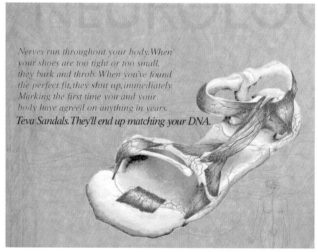

Art Director Donald Vann
Creative Director Coz Cotzias
Copywriter Shameka Brown
Illustrator Greg Cross
Client Teva
Instructor Coz Cotzias
School VCU Adcenter
Country United States

MERIT

**POSTER, POINT-OF-PURCHASE,
CAMPAIGN**
Ergonomics • Mud • Guts

Art Director Marc Wientzek
Art Direction Department Head
Norm Grey
Copywriter Dan Miranda
Copywriting Department Head
Mike Jones-Kelley
Photographer Marc Wientzek
Client KTM Sport Motorcycles
School The Creative Circus
Country United States

MERIT

**POSTER, PRODUCT OR SERVICE,
CAMPAIGN**
Change • Dryer • Washer

Art Director Amanda Berger
Creative Director Jerry Torchia
Copywriter Cindy Casares
Client Old Navy
Instructor Jerry Torchia
School VCU Adcenter
Country United States

MERIT

POSTER, PRODUCT OR SERVICE, CAMPAIGN
Butterfly

Art Director Helen Goldring
Copywriter Bridget Prophet
Designer Helen Goldring
Photographer Helen Goldring
Producer Helen Goldring
Client Tums
Instructor Bruce Turkel
School Miami Ad School
Country United States

MERIT

POSTER, PUBLIC SERVICE/ NON-PROFIT OR EDUCATIONAL
Organ Donation–Heart

Art Director Diane Magid
Creative Director David "Jelly" Helm
Copywriter Diane Magid
Designer Diane Magid
Instructor David "Jelly" Helm
School VCU Adcenter
Country United States

MERIT

POSTER, TRANSIT
Line

Art Director Jonathan Rosen
Creative Director Coz Cotzias
Copywriters Jenna Halls,
Stephen McElligott
Designer Jonathan Rosen
Client The History Channel
Instructor Coz Cotzias
School VCU Adcenter
Country United States

MERIT

**BILLBOARD, DIORAMA, OR PAINTED
SPECTACULAR, CAMPAIGN**
Papa Johns–Squirrels • Birds •
Walking • Creepy Guy • Rails

Art Director Amanda Berger
Creative Director Coz Cotzias
Copywriter Steve McElligott
Client Papa John's
Instructor Coz Cotzias
School VCU Adcenter
Country United States

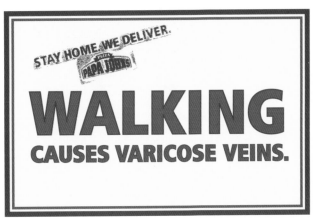

MERIT

BILLBOARD, DIORAMA, OR PAINTED SPECTACULAR
Lap

Art Director Mike McMullen
Art Direction Department Head
Norm Grey
Creative Director Norm Grey
Copywriter Peter Shamon
Copywriting Department Head
Mike Jones-Kelley
Client Power Bar
School The Creative Circus
Country United States

PowerBar sticker placed on the bottom of a lap pool

MERIT

POSTCARD, INVITATION, OR ANNOUNCEMENT
Visine–M@x Racks Postcards

Art Director Andy Minisman
Art Direction Department Head
Norm Grey
Creative Director Annie Finnegan
Copywriter Linda Gross
Copywriting Department Head
Mike Jones-Kelley
Photographer Brian Deutsch
Client Visine
School The Creative Circus
Country United States

MIXED MEDIA CAMPAIGN
Values

Art Director Rafael Antigua
Creative Director Rafael Antigua
Copywriter Rafael Antigua
Designer Rafael Antigua
Client The Partnership Against Racism
Instructor Leslie Segal
School Parsons School of Design
Country United States

Did you notice that the package is totally black outside? So, you never know what you can find behind a skin.

MERIT

BROADCAST CRAFTS AND DESIGN: ANIMATION
Jay—Final Portfolio Sequence

Art Director Nic Boudreau
Instructor Cathrin Yoder
School Art Institute of Phoenix
Country United States

SILVER

**WEBSITE/CD-ROM DESIGN,
ART/EXPERIMENTAL PROJECTS**
Brambletown
(www.brambletown.com)

Art Direction Brent Wood
Designer Brent Wood
Advisors John Blumfield, Peter Lunenfeld
School Art Center College
of Design
Country United States

Brent Wood is a recent graduate of
the Art Center College of Design's
communication and new media
graduate program.

What happens when you take the
versatile medium of comics and
recreate it on a personal computer
or on the Internet? Can you bring
the best qualities of each into a
new union? I believe comics can
make a successful transition into the
realm of the electronic if they
take advantage of being viewed
on a computer. By engaging the
computer's powerful narrative
and aesthetic possibilities with
hypertextuality, non-linearity,
and interactivity, comics can be
invigorated by their presentation
in new media.

The challenge is to initiate a rebirth
of today's comics through a fusion
of traditional media and the
capabilities of the personal
computer. The goal is to prove that
computers can deliver an engaging
narrative, and that storytelling isn't
dead on the Internet.

Brent Wood's thesis work
investigates the possibilities of
using narrative on the Internet in the
form of hypertextual digital comics.
A former film student, illustrator,
and graphic designer, Wood fuses
traditional print comics with the
multimedia capabilities of the
personal computer, thus creating
a unique hybrid form.

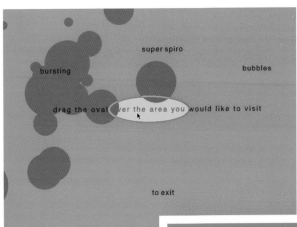

MERIT

**WEBSITE/CD-ROM DESIGN,
EDUCATIONAL**
Military Aircraft Database (CD-ROM)

Creative Director Steve Chow
Designer Steve Chow
Instructor Wells Packard
School School of Visual Arts
Country United States

Military Aircraft Database provides
a searchable database of various
characteristics of aircraft.
To enable the user to compare
aircraft, results can also be
indexed based on relevant features
and performance, such as speed
and role. The results are non-linear
and contain information including
history and specifications of the
selected aircraft.

413

MERIT

**WEBSITE/CD-ROM DESIGN,
ART/EXPERIMENTAL PROJECTS**
Test Strip (Screen Saver)

Designer Samara Umschweis
Instructor David Weisman
School School of Visual Arts
Country United States

This piece is called *Test Strip*
because it functions as a sample,
like a perfume strip in a magazine.
The title suggests something
scientific, as do some of the visual
elements and sounds used.
The inspiration for this piece was
grade school science film strips,
specifically films about atoms
and amoebas.

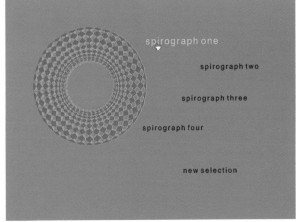

GOLD

**BROADCAST CRAFTS AND DESIGN:
ART VIDEO**
20/400

Art Director Gordon McNee
Instructors Leslie Becker,
Jennifer Morla
School California College
of Arts & Crafts
Country United States

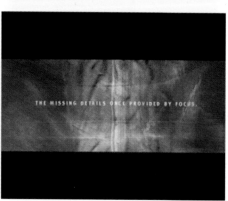

SILVER

POSTER, PROMOTIONAL
Blue Man Group—Tubes

Art Director Daisuke Endo
Designer Daisuke Endo
Photographer Daisuke Endo
Instructor Carin Goldberg
School School of Visual Arts
Country United States

SILVER

PACKAGING, ENTERTAINMENT, SERIES
Different Trains by Steve Reich

Art Director Motoko Hada
Designer Motoko Hada
Instructor William Bevington
School Parsons School of Design
Country United States

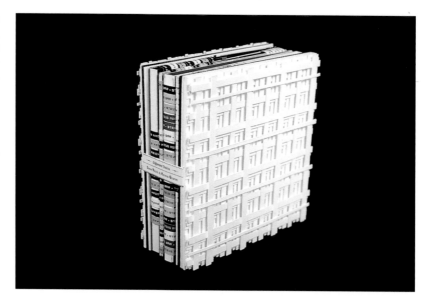

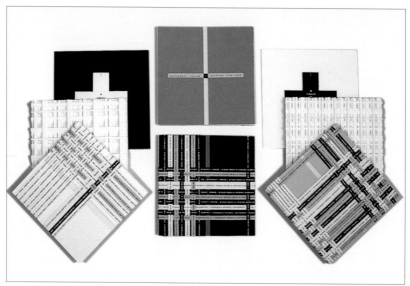

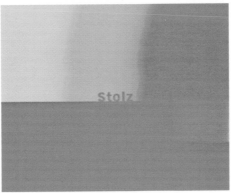

DISTINCTIVE MERIT

BROADCAST CRAFTS AND DESIGN, TV IDENTITIES, OPENINGS, OR TEASERS, CAMPAIGN
Emma

Art Directors Uta Kopp,
Alexandra Ohlenforst
Copywriters Uta Kopp,
Alexandra Ohlenforst
Designers Uta Kopp,
Alexandra Ohlenforst
Photographers Ralf Mendle,
Frank Baran
Lighting Designer Olaf Hirschberg
Directors Uta Kopp,
Alexandra Ohlenforst
Composer Axel Grube
Producer Academy of Media Arts
Client Emma
Instructors Stephan Boeder,
Michael Graham-Smith
School Academy of Media Arts
Country Germany

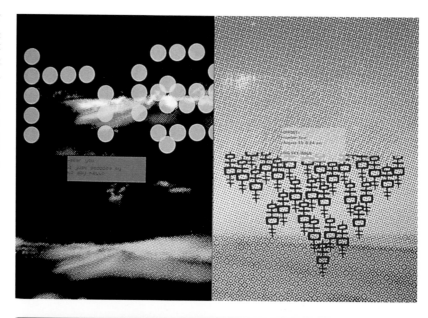

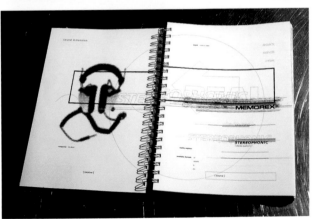

DISTINCTIVE MERIT

BOOK, PROMOTIONAL
Compound Reality Engines

Art Director Lyle Owerko
Copywriter Lyle Owerko
Designer Lyle Owerko
Photographer Lyle Owerko
Illustrator Lyle Owerko
Producer Lyle Owerko
Instructor Kevin Gatta
School Pratt Institute
Country United States

DISTINCTIVE MERIT

CORPORATE, BOOKLET
Shadows of a City

Designer Gary A. Williams II
Photographer Kort Sands
Copywriters Billy Corgan,
Richard Wright
Instructor Clane Graves
School Art Center College
of Design
Country United States

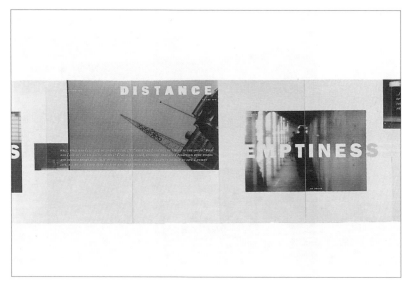

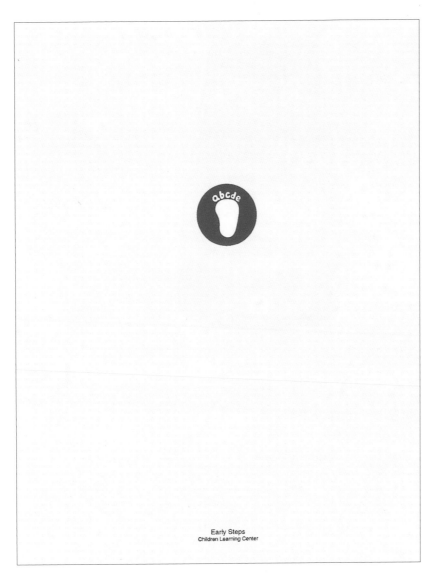

Early Steps
Children Learning Center

DISTINCTIVE MERIT

CORPORATE, LOGO
Early Steps

Designer Cecilia Karlsson
Design Department Head
Rob Lawton
Client Early Steps–Children's
Learning Center
School The Creative Circus
Country United States

DISTINCTIVE MERIT

**POSTER, ENTERTAINMENT
OR SPECIAL EVENT**
I Ain't Yo Uncle

Designer Michael Ziegenhagen
Instructor Mark Snyder
School Hartford Art School
(University of Hartford)
Country United States

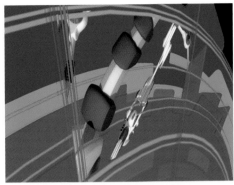

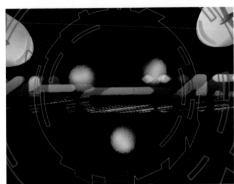

BROADCAST CRAFTS AND DESIGN, ART VIDEO
Equis

Art Director Fabian Tejada
Designer Fabian Tejada
Editor Fabian Tejada
Photographer Fabian Tejada
Illustrator Fabian Tejada
Producer Fabian Tejada
Animation Director Fabian Tejada
Storyboard Director Fabian Tejada
Chairman of Computer Art Department Bruce Wands
School School of Visual Arts
Country United States

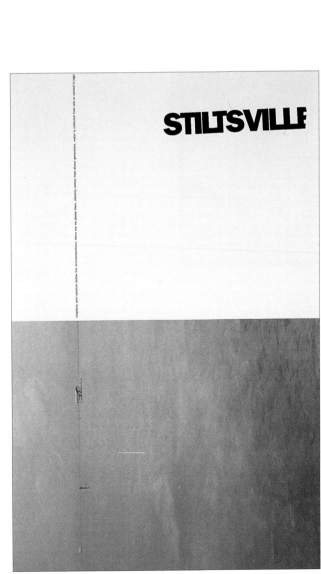

MERIT

EDITORIAL, CONSUMER NEWSPAPER, SPREAD
Stiltsville

Art Director Ken Bower
Designer Ken Bower
Instructor Paula Scher
School School of Visual Arts
Country United States

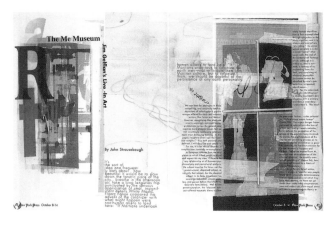

MERIT

**EDITORIAL,
CONSUMER NEWSPAPER, MULTI-PAGE**
Free Weekly Newspaper

Art Director Norikazu Nakamura

Designer Norikazu Nakamura

Instructors Barbara Dewilde, Chip Kidd

School School of Visual Arts

Country United States

MERIT

**EDITORIAL, TRADE NEWSPAPER,
FULL ISSUE**

[SIC!] Newspaper,
A Literature Supplement
of Vista Magazine

Art Director Friederike Gauss

Designer Friederike Gauss

Copywriter Thomas Girst

Illustrator Sylvia Neuner

Comic Illustrator Titus Ackermann

Instructor Hans-Georg Pospisckil

School The State Academy of
Fine Arts Stuttgart

Country Germany

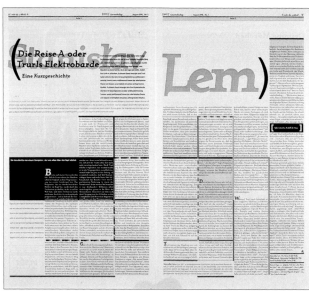

MERIT

**EDITORIAL,
CONSUMER MAGAZINE, COVER**
Emigre No. 39: The In-house Issue

Art Director Robert E. Williams
Designer Robert E. Williams
Photographer Christine Rodin
Instructor Tor Hovind
School California State University
Long Beach
Country United States

MERIT

**EDITORIAL,
CONSUMER MAGAZINE, COVER**
Quality Magazine

Art Director Daisuke Endo
Designer Daisuke Endo
Instructor Carin Goldberg
School School of Visual Arts
Country United States

MERIT

**EDITORIAL,
CONSUMER MAGAZINE, COVER**
Parabola Vol. 5, No. 2

Art Director Satoshi Takashima
Designer Satoshi Takashima
Illustrator Satoshi Takashima
Client Parabola
Instructor Yolanda Cuomo
School Parsons School of Design
Country United States

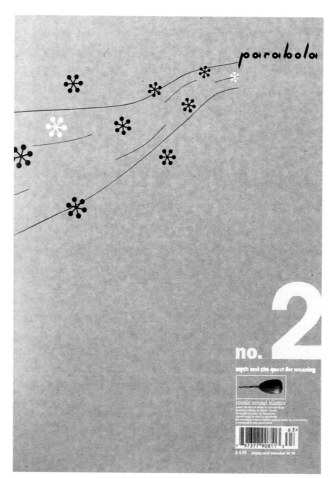

MERIT

**EDITORIAL, TRADE MAGAZINE,
COVER, SERIES**
Larger Than Life
(Re-design of Life Magazine)

Designer Donna Reiss
Instructor Paula Scher
School School of Visual Arts
Country United States

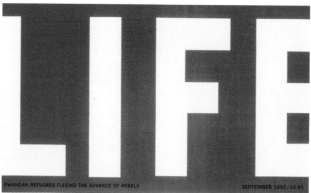

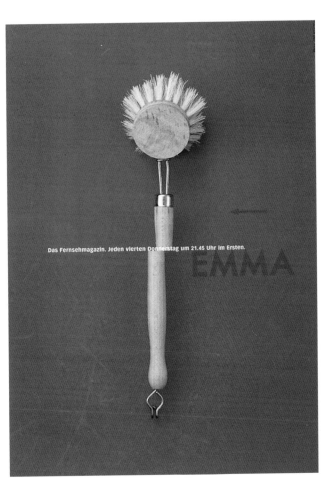

MERIT

**EDITORIAL,
TRADE MAGAZINE, COVER**
Emma

Art Directors Uta Kopp,
Alexandra Ohlenforst
Designers Uta Kopp,
Alexandra Ohlenforst
Copywriters Uta Kopp,
Alexandra Ohlenforst
Photographer Olaf Hirschberg
Producer Academy of Media Arts
Client Emma
Instructors Stephan Boeder,
Michael Graham-Smith
School Academy of Media Arts
Country Germany

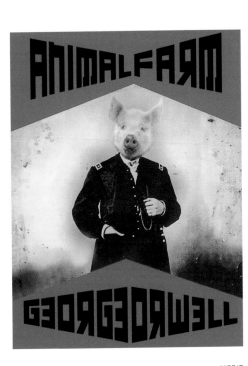

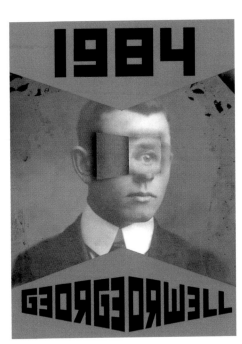

MERIT

BOOK JACKETS, SERIES
George Orwell's Animal Farm

Art Director Karen Youn Yi
Designer Karen Youn Yi
Instructor Carin Goldberg
School School of Visual Arts
Country United States

MERIT

BOOK JACKETS, SERIES
Haruki Murakami

Art Director Vanessa Chen
Designer Vanessa Chen
Instructor Carin Goldberg
School School of Visual Arts
Country United States

 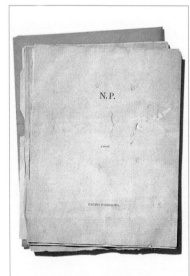 

MERIT

BOOK JACKETS, SERIES
Banana Yoshimoto

Art Director Daisuke Endo
Designer Daisuke Endo
Instructor Carin Goldberg
School School of Visual Arts
Country United States

BOOK JACKETS
Portnoy's Complaint

Art Director Frank Anselmo
Designer Frank Anselmo
Photographer Frank Anselmo
Instructor Michael Ian Kaye
School School of Visual Arts
Country United States

MERIT

CORPORATE IDENTITY PROGRAM, SERIES
The Alternative Lingerie Boutique

Art Director Korapin Thupvong
Creative Director Korapin Thupvong
Designer Korapin Thupvong
Instructor Graham Hanson
Client Urban Lingerie
School Pratt Institute
Country United States

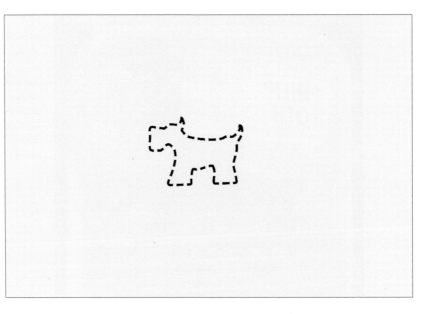

MERIT

CORPORATE LOGO/TRADEMARK
Dog Gone

Designer Benjamin Rush
Client Dog Gone Pet Retrieval System
Instructor Gary LoBue
School Texas A&M University–Commerce
Country United States

MERIT

CORPORATE LOGO/TRADEMARK
Café Opera

Designer Cecilia Karlsson
Design Department Head
Rob Lawton
Client Café Opera
School The Creative Circus
Country United States

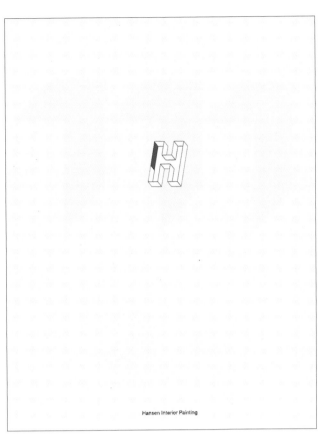

Hansen Interior Painting

Designer Cecilia Karlsson
Design Department Head
Rob Lawton
Client Hansen Interior Painting
School The Creative Circus
Country United States

STUDENT GRAPHIC DESIGN

431

MERIT

CORPORATE LOGO/TRADEMARK
Niño

Art Director Rafael Antigua
Creative Director Rafael Antigua
Designer Rafael Antigua
Illustrator Rafael Antigua
Client Childcraft
Instructor Jhon Noneman
School Parsons School of Design
Country United States

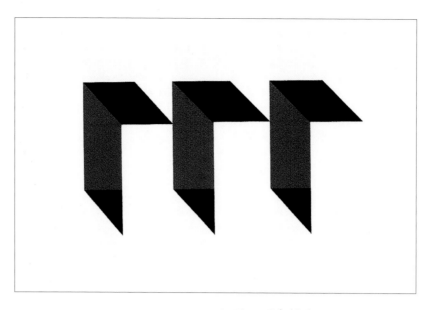

MERIT
CORPORATE LOGO/TRADEMARK
Archivos

Art Director Rafael Antigua
Creative Director Rafael Antigua
Designer Rafael Antigua
Illustrator Rafael Antigua
Client Enter
Instructor Jhon Noneman
School Parsons School of Design
Country United States

MERIT
CORPORATE MIXED-MEDIA PROMOTION, CAMPAIGN
Convergence

Art Director Stephen Van Elst
Creative Director Stephen Van Elst
Designers Third-year Graphic Design/Multimedia Students
Copywriter Andrew Fiscalini
Photographers Stacey Quick, Peter Swan
Sound Luke Chisholm
School University of Ballarat
Country Australia

**POSTER, ENTERTAINMENT OR
SPECIAL EVENT**

Propaganda: Deception, Persuasion,
and Power

Art Director Jon Jennings
Designer Jon Jennings
Photographer Jon Jennings
Illustrator Jon Jennings
Instructor Tom Kovacs
School University of Illinois
Country United States

433

**POSTER, ENTERTAINMENT OR
SPECIAL EVENT**

Swiss Chair

Designer Gary A. Williams II
Illustrator Gary A. Williams II
Instructor Jayme Odgers
School Art Center College of Design
Country United States

**POSTER, ENTERTAINMENT OR
SPECIAL EVENT**
Alvar Aalto

Art Director Ken Bower
Designer Ken Bower
Instructors Henrietta Condak,
Paula Scher
School School of Visual Arts
Country United States

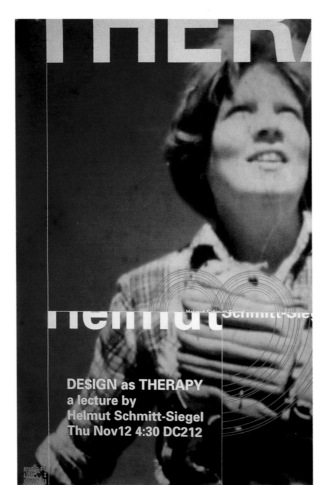

**POSTER, ENTERTAINMENT OR
SPECIAL EVENT**
Design as Therapy

Designer Erik Wysocan
Instructor Bjørn Frëshens
School Rhode Island School
of Design
Country United States

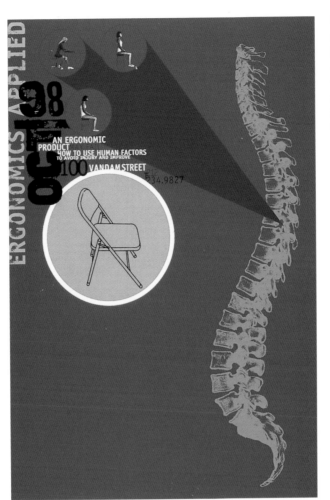

MERIT

POSTER, PRODUCT OR SERVICE
Chair Furniture Design

Designer Loan Lam
Instructor Scott Santoro
School Pratt Institute
Country United States

MERIT

PACKAGING, RETAIL: HOUSE BRAND
Vacuum

Art Director Lise S. Ellingsen
Designer Lise S. Ellingsen
Instructor Chris Gianakos
School School of Visual Arts
Country United States

MERIT

**PACKAGING,
ENTERTAINMENT, SERIES**
The Doors, Strange Days
Special CD Packaging

Art Director Motoko Hada
Designer Motoko Hada
Photographers Gary Sinick,
David Wojnarowicz,
Rosamond Wolff Purcell,
Barbara Wyeth
Illustrators John James Audubon,
Hannah Höch, Viktor Koen
Instructor William Bevington
School Parsons School of Design
Country United States

MERIT

**PACKAGING,
FOOD/BEVERAGE, SERIES**
Korea House Fast Food Restaurant

Art Director Woo Jung Chang
Designer Woo Jung Chang
Instructor Marianne Klimchuk
School Fashion Institute
of Technology
Country United States

Merit
**POSTER, ENTERTAINMENT
OR SPECIAL EVENT**
Architecture of Reassurance

Art Director Louis Terline
Designer Louis Terline
Illustrator Louis Terline
Instructor Michael McGinn
School Pratt Institute
Country United States

Art Director Lise S. Ellingsen
Designer Lise S. Ellingsen
Instructor Chris Gianakos
School School of Visual Arts
Country United States

MERIT

PACKAGING, FOOD/BEVERAGE
Pop Tootsie Roll

Art Director Howard York
Designer Hui-Ling Chen
Photographer Richard Jung
Instructor Paul Tsang
School Academy of Art College
Country United States

MERIT

**PACKAGING,
FASHION/APPAREL/WEARABLE**
Oakley Goggles

Art Director Peter Chun
Designer Peter Chun
Illustrator Peter Chun
Studio Good Design Is Here
Client Oakley
School California State University
Country United States

see 77th Annual, p.474
Multiple Awards

DISTINCTIVE MERIT

ILLUSTRATION, BOOK OR BOOK JACKET, SERIES AND SINGLE
and DISTINCTIVE MERIT

GRAPHIC DESIGN, BOOK OR BOOK JACKET
and MERIT

GRAPHIC DESIGN, BOOK DESIGN, GENERAL TRADE BOOK
American Illustration, Sweet 16

Creative Directors Tracy Boychuk, Stacy Drummond, Jeffrey Keyton
Designers Tracy Boychuk, Stacy Drummond, Jeffrey Keyton
Illustrators George Bates, Juliette Borda, Calef Brown, Steve Byram, Ed Fotheringham, Anthony Freda, Mark Gagnon, Geoffrey Grahn (cover), Jordin Isip, Ruth Marten, Filip Pagowski, Jonathon Rosen, Mark Ryden, Mark Todd, Steve Wacksman, Esther Watson
Client Amilus, Inc.
Country United States

see 77th Annual, p.339
MERIT
GRAPHIC DESIGN, CORPORATE & PROMOTIONAL DESIGN, BOOKLET/BROCHURE
The Essentials: The Potlach Annual Report Show, 1997

Art Directors Mary Moegenburg
Creative Director Dana Arnett
Copywriter Andy Blankenburg
Designer Jason Eplawy
Photographers Bill Phelps, Bart Witowski
Studio VSA Partners, Inc.
Client Potlach Corporation
Country United States

the art directors club
today

**THE COOPER UNION
SCHOOL OF ART:**
Heung Heung Chin
Agnieszka Gasparska
Petter Ringbom

**FASHION INSTITUTE OF
TECHNOLOGY:**
Jin Lee
Katrina Trninich
Erica Weisberg

**NEW YORK CITY TECHNICAL
COLLEGE:**
Violetta Karkut
Ray Ramcharitar
Ignacio Soltero

PARSONS SCHOOL OF DESIGN:
Nina Dautzenberg
Andrea Dionisio
Karin Hug

PRATT INSTITUTE:
Shilla F. Iranpour
Garrett Morlan
Billy Pennant

PRATT MANHATTAN CENTER:
Fung Mei Lee
Hitoshi Okazai
Christian Schmetzer

SCHOOL OF VISUAL ARTS:
Damon Bakun
Maya Blazejewska
Lee Kelly

**1999 JOHN PETER MEMORIAL
AWARD FOR STUDENT OF
PUBLICATION DESIGN:**
Marina Gioti, Pratt Manhattan Center

**1999 BILL TAUBIN MEMORIAL
AWARD FOR STUDENT OF
ADVERTISING DESIGN:**
Matthew Tarulli, School of Visual Arts

**1999 SHIN TORA MEMORIAL
AWARD FOR STUDENT OF
PUBLICATION DESIGN:**
Dieter Wiechmann,
Parsons School of Design

O n April 23, 1999, the Art Directors Club hosted the 22nd annual Art Directors Scholarship Foundation (ADSF) awards presentation.

That evening, I started my introduction to the proceedings by reading an excerpt from a note that we received a few years ago from one of our ADSF alumni. The note was from Parollo Matos, a Parsons School of Design Graduate and a 1996 ADSF award recipient.

It reads: "I'm deeply grateful for the Art Directors Scholarship Foundation award that helped me with my tuition. I encourage you to continue with this project that really meant a lot to us as students and future professionals."

These words underscored the fact that in the twenty-two years since members of The Art Directors Club founded the ADSF, hundreds of talented and deserving students like Parollo have benefited from the generous financial contributions of many concerned professionals. These students have felt the important recognition that comes with this prestigious award.

The ADSF is our way of giving something of value back to our community.

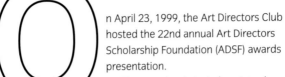

That evening, I also thanked some of the people who have helped to make the work of the ADSF, and especially the ADSF awards evening, a success: the Art Directors Club members, corporations, and friends of the Club who have given freely of their time, work, and money; Art Directors Club President Bill Oberlander and the ADC Board of Directors for continuing to support the work of the ADSF with ADC show entry contributions; Ruth Lubell, the liaison between ADSF and the ADC Board; Executive Director Myrna Davis and the ADC staff, especially Olga Grisaitis and Melissa Hirsch for their continuing support.

Special thanks were also given to all of the ADSF Board of Directors for their care and dedication, particularly Meg Crane for a long list of efforts including many previous ADSF events; and to Gladys Barton for doing such a wonderful job designing our awards presentation invitation, program, and certificate.

As art directors we receive great pleasure, satisfaction, and financial rewards as a result of our work. The ADSF is our way of giving something of value back to our community. As the Art Directors Club enters the new millennium, we look forward to the continuing effort of the members in helping to support deserving art students as they seek to become the art directors of tomorrow.

—Peter Adler,
PRESIDENT OF THE ART DIRECTORS
SCHOLARSHIP FOUNDATION, INC.

1

1   Paul Sahre
2   John Pinderhughes
3   Mirko Ilić
4   A promotion of the Saturday High School Workshop
5   Gail Anderson

2

3

4

ooper Union, Fashion Institute of Technology, Parsons School of Design, Pratt Institute, School of Visual Arts. Over the past few years, these and other art schools have continued to see a decline in qualified applicants from New York City high schools. In response to this trend—the result of cutbacks in funding for arts programs—the School Art League and the Art Directors Club have sponsored the Saturday High School Workshop at the Club for the past three years. Coordinated by Club member Susan Mayer and the League's Naomi Lonergan, programs consisting of five workshops each in the spring and the fall have exposed metropolitan-area high school juniors to viable careers in visual communications.

This year's forty-plus students joined more than 160 other high school juniors from over twenty-five New York City high schools to participate in the Saturday High School Workshop. This year's leaders, Marshall Arisman; Mirko Ilić; Manabu Inada; Diana LaGuardia; Tony Palladino; John Pinderhughes; Paul Sahre; and Pam Vassil, joined a distinguished group of volunteers including *Rolling Stone* associate art director Gail Anderson; photographers Carl Fischer and Matthew Klein; and art director Ted Pettus. Assisted by student volunteers from Parsons, these workshops have helped students develop competitive portfolios for art school applications.

Assisted by student volunteers from Parsons, these workshops have helped students develop competitive portfolios for art school applications.

5

We've also moved closer to establishing the ADC Mentoring Program, which will match alumni from the Saturday High School Workshop with club members. This year we met with our colleagues from the American Institute of Graphic Arts (AIGA) who have recently created their own mentoring program for students at the High School of Art & Design and generously shared their ideas and experience with us.

In the meantime, we're pleased to report that workshop leader Gail Anderson was awarded this year's Youth Friends Award by the School Art League. This award is presented annually to a member of the New York art community who is committed to helping students realize their potential. As you may remember, the recipient of last year's award was Marshall Arisman. We congratulate and thank them both.

We look forward to holding the fall workshops in our new quarters, and would like to invite any Club members who are interested in participating in either the workshops or the mentoring program to join us.

—Susan Mayer,
SATURDAY HIGH SCHOOL WORKSHOP COMMITTEE CHAIR

design: Duffy Design, 1998

Kellogg's Smart Start

SEPTEMBER 1998

Exhibition: BRAND AID —
A Fourteen-Year Retrospective
of Duffy Design
September 10–September 30

Started in 1984 by Joe Duffy and the partners of Fallon McElligott advertising, Duffy Design began with a small group of clients, for whom the company created groundbreaking work that was both provocative and distinctive. Duffy's mission is to enhance the brand experience through strategic thinking and exceptional design. They have created solutions for international brands including BMW, Kellogg's, Coca-Cola, and Nikon.

Speaker Series: JOE DUFFY
September 23

photo: Howard Baden

From left to right: Nigel Bogle, Joe Duffy, Neil Powell, John Hegarty

Joe Duffy understands how design affects consumer attitudes. As president of Duffy Design and Revolv, he heads the design discipline for Fallon McElligott. Have a box of Kellogg's Smart Start? A carton of Minute Maid? Then you have a carefully crafted Duffy Design work in your home.

OCTOBER 1998

Exhibition: CREATIVE OXYGEN —
Bartle Bogle Hegarty
October 8–October 30

The ADC welcomes the London advertising agency to New York by hosting an exhibition of their innovative and award-winning work for clients such as Levi's, Audi, Polaroid, and Boddingtons.

photo: Howard Baden

Creative Oxygen **installation shot, opening party**

Fall Party: RUB A DUB @ THE ART DIRECTORS CLUB — Welcome New ADC Members
October 22

A restorative tonic mixing live reggae and jazz featuring musicians from Sting's band, The Mingus Big Band, and Steel Pulse. Refreshments and Jamaican treats are served.

photo: Howard Baden

One Drop singing reggae at Rub A Dub party

NOVEMBER 1998

Black-Tie Dinner, Presentation, and Exhibition Opening:
HALL OF FAME 1998
November 5

photo: Howard Baden

Hall of Fame Laureates from left to right: Alex Steinweiss, Red Burns, Paula Scher, Myrna Davis, Tom Geismar

Induction of 1998 Laureates: Tom Geismar, Chuck Jones, Paula Scher, and Alex Steinweiss. Hall of Fame Educator's Award to Red Burns.

ADC New Media Committee Presents: ROGER BLACK —
From Print to the Web
November 12

Roger Black (Interactive Bureau, Font Bureau, and Roger Black Incorporated) talks about the danger of getting caught in the Net.

Roger Black

photo: Jeff Newelt

Richard Saul Wurman

photo: Jeff Newelt

Speaker Series:
RICHARD SAUL WURMAN
November 18

Founder and Chairman of the TED Conferences, Wurman is the author of over sixty-four books including *Information Anxiety* and *Follow the Yellow Brick Road*.

DECEMBER 1998

Exhibition: YOUNG GUNS NYC II
December 3–December 28

Reception: December 3

A biennial exhibition first presented here in 1996, Young Guns NYC showcases the next generation of talented visual communicators whose work may not yet have received the recognition it deserves. The artists, all thirty-five and under, include art directors, designers, multi-media artists, photographers, illustrators, product and environmental designers, and Web designers, as well as advertising, film, video, and 3-D display artists.

photo: Howard Baden

Young Guns NYC II **window installation by Rudy Speerschneider**

Holiday Party: A collaboration between ADC, Type Directors Club, and Society of Publication Designers
December 14

Unwrapped new toys and children's books donated to Bellevue and New York Hospitals.

JANUARY 1999

Exhibition: F.I.T. Toy Design—
10 Years of Imagination, Inspiration & Innovation
January 19–February 5

Invitation to F.I.T. *Toy Design* **exhibition**

design: Harold Burch Design, illustration: Scott Menchin

FIT

YO

TOY

An exhibition of over 500 classic toys, new toys, and prototypes celebrates the FIT Toy Design Department's 10th anniversary as the world's first accredited baccalaureate program in toy design.

Among the popular products designed by F.I.T. alumni on display are such favorites as Tickle Me Elmo, Street Sharks, Blues Clues, Don't Spill the Beans, and Hot Wheels. Gallery browsers also listen to a talking Babe, test drive a new generation of turbo-powered remote-controlled cars, and even sample high-tech candies that double as playthings.

Panel Discussion:
LOOKING FOR WORK
January 27

design: Lois Pyanowski, illustration: J. Scott Klossner

Invitation card to *Looking for Work*

Find out, from those who hire and those who get people hired, what you should be doing to get a better job, or perhaps a killer job doing what you love to do most. Panelists include Richard Wilde (SVA–Dean of Advertising/Graphic Design), Alexander Isley (Alex Isley Design), Jill Schroeder (McCann Erikson), Roz Goldfarb (Roz Goldfarb Associates), and Maria Reveley (Paladin).

design: Christiane Gude

Invitation card to *Creative Differences: Revenge of the Nerds*

FEBRUARY 1999

Panel Discussion: CREATIVE DIFFERENCES 2–CHIC GEEKS IN NEW MEDIA: ADVERTISING AND THE INTERNET
February 2

Moderated by Anthony Vagnoni of *Advertising Age*. Are the New Media people the pinheads or prophets of advertising? Are these Internet gurus ahead of the curve and laughing all the way to the bank? Panelists include Kyle Shannon (AGENCY.COM), Rich Lefurgy (Interactive Advertising Bureau), John Carlin (Funny Garbage), Jason Chervokas (@NY), Will Metzger (Ogilvy Interactive), and Howard Fishman (Real Media).

MARCH 1999

Exhibition: THE NEW YORK TIMES MAGAZINE: The Way We Are Now

March 5–March 30

Events. Personalities. Argument. Photography. Style. Celebrating the award-winning collaboration of journalism and design. Showcasing the current magazine design, photography, and illustration, and a sampling of the past.

Speaker Series: JANET FROELICH
March 10

Janet Froelich, art director of *The New York Times Magazine*, is a designer with an addiction to news. Topics include her collaboration with editors, artists, and photographers for a magazine format; the conceptual cover and why it's great not to be on newsstands; creating and maintaining a "brand."

APRIL 1999

Speaker Series: TODD and ERIC TILFORD
April 21

Todd and Eric Tilford's philosophy: normal=average=mediocre=suicide. Since beginning their careers, the Tilfords have relentlessly crusaded to revolutionize advertising. Todd is creative director/partner at PYRO in Dallas. Clients include Dr. Martens, AMG Hummer, and DreamWorks Interactive. Eric is creative director/partner at CORE in St. Louis. Clients include Monsanto, Zebco Quantum Rods & Reels, and Urban Decay Cosmetics.

Premiere Screening: NEGATIVE FORCES–Witchcraft and Idolatry by The Attik
April 22

The Attik has been in the subway in pursuit of their latest creative project, a visual diary based on twenty-four hours spent traveling the New York City subway system. This is part of a move to take their hard-edged, uncompromising vision of design off the page and into film and television. *Negative Forces, Witchcraft and Idolatry* was screened on April 22nd at the ADC along with a one night-only exhibition. It then went on to be screened in London, San Francisco, Hollywood, Santa Monica, and other locations.

Awards Presentation: 1999 ART DIRECTORS SCHOLARSHIP FOUNDATION WINNERS
April 23

The works of this year's ADSF scholarship recipients from seven New York area art schools was presented as a slide show. The winners and their deans were in attendance to receive this year's awards and scholarships.

Invitation card to *Creative Differences: The Latest vs. the Greatest*

Panel Discussion: CREATIVE DIFFERENCES 3— ADVERTISING: THE LATEST VS. THE GREATEST
April 27

Old school rabble-rousers versus new school snot-noses. What do advertising's creative incendiaries from the good ole days think of today's Gen-X ad leaders, and vice versa? We staged an intergenerational mosh pit to find out. Panelists included Jerry Della Femina, Ed McCabe, Allan Beaver, Jeff Weiss, Marty Cooke, and Steven Grasse.

MAY 1999

Exhibitions: ORGANIC INFORMATION–Work from the Aesthetics & Computation Program at the MIT Media Laboratory
May 6–May 21

Over 100 applets and experimental interactive graphic work on ten iMac computers representing three years of educating hybrid designer/technologists. Curated and featuring work by John Maeda, Interval Assistant Professor of Design and Computation at M.I.T. Media Lab, and principal of Maedastudio.

SPRING PAPER EXPO with Guest Speaker Alexander Gelman of Design Machine
May 12

Invitation card to *Paper Expo*

Review the latest offerings from twenty of the best paper manufacturers including: Canson-Talens, Champion, Consolidated Papers, Inc., Crown Vantage, Donside, Domtar/EB Eddy Specialty Papers, Fox River Paper Company, Gilbert Paper, Mead Coated Papers, Potlatch, Sappi Fine Papers, Unifoil, Wausau Papers, Yupo Corporation, and more.

Abitare Party
May 14

During the ICFF 1999 (International Contemporary Furniture Fair), Italian design and architecture magazine *Abitare* launched their special issue featuring New York arts and

John Maeda installation shot, Abitare party

architecture with a private party at ADC New York which was well attended by the international design community. This special issue on a metropole is part of their annual one-city issue published since the 1970s.

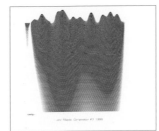

John Maeda *Composition # 3*, 1999

Speaker Series: JOHN MAEDA
May 19

Bridging the gap between past and future, computer scientist and graphic designer, John Maeda is Interval Assistant Professor of Design and Computation at M.I.T Media Lab and principal of Maedastudio.

Maeda develops advanced print and digital projects, including the recent *Tap, Type, Write*, the fourth in the Reactive Book series of CD-ROMS and booklets by Digitalogue in Tokyo. According to *Print Magazine*, "At the heart [of his work] is a childlike playfulness born out of a love of structure."

JUNE 1999

Word has it that the creative community needs a little stimulation....

The Art Directors Club 78th Annual Awards GALA and EXHIBITION PREVIEW

Celebrating Gold and Silver Medalists and Distinctive Merit Winners
June 3

Silver Medalist from Poland, during the 78th Awards Gala Party

Faustworks performance during the 78th Awards Gala Party

Winners dressed up for an evening that entertained, inspired, and paid homage to the year's most provocative work. Included a multi-media smorgasbord and sporadic/sonic bursts.

Elegant edibles and bubbly beverages were served.

Exhibition: The ADC 78th Annual Awards
June 4–July 30

The ADC Gallery presented the works of medalists and distinctive merit winners in national and international print and television advertising, graphic design, broadcast, packaging, publication design, photography, illustration, and new media.

JULY 1999

Panel Discussion/Party: Behind the Scenes of the ADC 78th Annual Awards
July 29

The last great event of the season and the last look at the 78th Annual Awards Exhibition until the book is released.

Panel discussion with the 78th judging chairs John Hegarty (BBH), Advertising; Neil Powell (Duffy Design), Graphic Design, Photography/Illustration; Charles Altschul, New Media; and winners Arthur Bijur (Cliff Freeman & Partners, twenty-three awards); Jon Kamen (@radical media, thirteen awards); and moderator Eleftheria Parpis, Creative Editor of *Ad Week*.

Party with an encore performance by Clark Gayton and the Ska-Swing All-Stars, including musicians from Sting's band, Steel Pulse, Queen Latifah's band, and Mingus Big Band.

AUGUST 1999

NOTE: The ADC is moving to an exciting new space in the Fall: 104 West 29th Street, New York, New York 10001

ADC—PUMPING VISUAL FUEL WORLDWIDE

Check www.adcny.org for event updates and date changes. Please call to confirm all reservations and for gallery hours on closing dates of exhibitions.

Gallery hours: Monday-Friday, 10am-6pm.

THE ART DIRECTORS
SCHOLARSHIP FOUNDATION,
INC. (ADSF)

**1999/2000
BOARD OF DIRECTORS**

Peter Adler
President

Meg Crane
First Vice President

Lee Epstein
Second Vice President

David Davidian
Treasurer

Diane Moore Behrens
Assistant Treasurer

Dorothy Wachtenheim
Secretary

Gladys Barton
Assistant Secretary

Walter Kaprielian
Director

Robert Pliskin
Director

Nancy Stamatopoulos
Director

SPECIAL THANKS

78TH CALL FOR ENTRIES

**Stacy Drummond
Tracy Boychuk**
Art Directors and Designers
Jordan Nogee
Illustrator
(MTV Off-Air Creative Office)

Yupo®78# text
Paper

W.E. Andrews of Connecticut
Printer

78TH AWARDS INVITATION

**Kirshenbaum Bond & Partners,
New York**
Design

Finch Paper and Reich Paper
Paper

MG Prints
Printer

CORPORATE MEMBERS
APPLICATION FORMS

Mohawk Paper Mills, Inc.

ADC PUBLICATIONS, INC.

Jackie Merri Meyer
President

Joseph Montebello
Vice President

Nicholas Callaway
Secretary

Myrna Davis
Treasurer

Stefan Sagmeister
Director

ADC PAST PRESIDENTS

Richard J. Walsh, 1920–21
Joseph Chapin, 1921–22
Heyworth Campbell, 1922–23
Fred Suhr, 1923–24
Nathaniel Pousette–Dart, 1924–25
Walter Whitehead, 1925–26
Peirce Johnson, 1926–27
Arthur Munn, 1927–28
Stuart Campbell, 1929–30
Guy Gayler Clark, 1930–31
Edward F. Molyneux, 1931–33
Gordon C. Aymar, 1933–34
Mehemed Fehmy Agha, 1934–35
Joseph Platt, 1935–36
Deane Uptegrove, 1936–38
Walter B. Geoghegan, 1938–40
Lester Jay Loh, 1940–41
Loren B. Stone, 1941–42
William A. Adriance, 1942–43
William A. Irwin, 1943–45
Arthur Hawkins Jr., 1945–46
Paul Smith, 1946–48
Lester Rondell, 1948–50
Harry O'Brien, 1950–51
Roy W. Tillotson, 1951–53
John Jamison, 1953–54
Julian Archer, 1954–55
Frank Baker, 1955–56
William H. Buckley, 1956–57
Walter R. Grotz, 1957–58
Garrett P. Orr, 1958–60
Robert H. Blattner, 1960–61
Edward B. Graham, 1961–62
Bert W. Littmann, 1962–64
Robert Sherrich Smith, 1964–65
John A. Skidmore, 1965–67
John Peter, 1967–69
William P. Brockmeier, 1969–71
George Lois, 1971–73
Herbert Lubalin, 1973–74
Louis Dorfsman, 1974–75
Eileen Hedy Schultz, 1975–77
David Davidian, 1977–79
William Taubin, 1979–81
Walter Kaprielian, 1981–83
Andrew Kner, 1983–85
Edward Brodsky, 1985–87
Karl Steinbrenner, 1987–89
Henry Wolf, 1989–91
Kurt Haiman, 1991–93
Allan Beaver, 1993–95
Carl Fischer, 1995–97

CORPORATE MEMBERS

Adobe Systems
AGFA
ArtByte
Children's Television Workshop
GoCard
Hound Dog LLC
Interport Communications
Lowe & Partners/SMS
Madison Direct Marketing
McCall's Magazine
McCann-Erickson
Nickelodeon
React Magazine
Rolling Stone Magazine
Scheufelen North America, Inc.
Shiseido Co., LTD
Tetra Design
The Black Book
Tony Stone Images
Union Camp Corp., BBA Division
Winslow Press

UNITED STATES

Abu-Nimah, Ruba
Acanfora, Massimo
Adamek, Tina
Adams, Cornelia
Adams, Gaylord
Adams, Lauren
Adams, Phil
Adelman, Jim
Adler, Peter
Adorney, Charles
Allen, Heidi Flynn
Altenpohl, Peggy
Altschul, Charles
Alvey, Patricia
Anderson, Jack
Anderson, Roy
Andreozzi, Gennaro
Andrews, Lynn
Angotti, Adriana Amanda
Ansari, Kimia
Arias-Perez, Luise E.
Auman, Cynthia
Babitz, Jeff
Bach, Robert
Bacich, Jaqueline Anne
Bacsa, Ronald
Badger, Madonna
Baer, Charles
Baer, Priscilla
Baker, Eric
Ballance, Georgette
Ballister, Ronald
Bank, Adam
Baron, Richard
Barron, Don
Barrow, John
Barthelmes, Robert
Barton, Gladys
Baumann, Mary K.
Bazarkaya, Toygar
Beane, Maryann

Beaver, Allan
Bender, Lois
Bennett, Edward
Benshoff, Kirk
Berg, John
Bernard, Walter
Bertulis, Frank
Best, Robert
Bevington, William
Beylerian, George
Binzen, Barbara
Blanc, Jonathan
Blank, Peter
Blechman, R.O.
Blend, Robert
Bogart, Jeff
Bonavita, Donna
Bond, Mindy
Bossio, Peter
Boucher, Lorna
Bourges, Jean
Bowman, Harold
Boyd, Doug
Braguin, Simeon
Brauer, Fred
Braunstein, Douglas
Braverman, Al
Brazell, Karen
Brenner, Jay
Breslin, Lynn D.
Briggs, Kelley
Brodsky, Ed
Brody, Ruth
Brown, Beth Ann
Brown, Beverly
Brown, George
Bruce, Robert
Brugnatelli, Bruno
Bucher, Stefan
Buckley, William H.
Burris, Sara
Cabangon, Charlton
Cadge, Bill
Cafritz, Jodi
Calderwood Pratt, Chalkley
Callaway, Nicholas
Canniff, Bryan
Cardillo, James
Carey, Peter
Carnase, Thomas
Casado, Ralph
Casarona, Chris
Castagnetti, Michael
Castellano, Tony
Catherines, Diana
Cecere, Tina Marie
Ceradini, David
Chant, Michelle
Chaplinsky, Jr, Anthony
Chavira, Daniel
Chen, Jack
Cheng, Chris
Chermayeff, Ivan
Chernik, Lazarus
Chester, Laurie
Cheung, Julietta
Chiang, Peiken
Choi, HeesunLisa

Christie, Allen
Chung, Shelly
Church, Stanley
Churchill, Traci
Churchward, Charles
Chwast, Seymour
Cirlin, Scott
Clemente, Thomas
Cline, Mahlon
Coale, Howard
Cohen, Peter
Cohen, Sally Ann
Cohn, Barrie
Cohn, Karen
Coll, Michael
Compton, Jeff
Conner, Elaine
Contarino, Vince
Cook-Tench, Diane
Coron, Fabienne
Cory, Jeffrey
Cotler, Sheldon
Cotler-Block, Susan
Cowles, Bette
Cox, Phyllis Richmond
Cox, Robert
Coxwell, Chris
Craig, James Edward
Crane, Meg
Crane, Susan
Crossley, Gregory
Crozier, Bob
Crumlish, Arthur
Curry, Alison Davis
Curry, Christine
Cusick, Lori
Cutler, Ethel
D'Andria, Matthew
D'Elia, Michelle
Darula, Kathryn
Davidian, David
Davis, Barbara Vaughn
Davis, Herman
Davis, J.Hamilton
Davis, Paul
Davis, Randi
DeCardona Reed, Maria
Deegan, Faith
DeHaan, Stuart
DelSorbo, Joe
Delmundo, Tom
Demoney, Jerry
Despart, Susan
Deutsch, David
Diecks, W.Brian
Dignam, John
Dorfsman, Louis
Dorian, Marc
Dorr, Cheri
Doss, Davis
Douglas, Kay E.
Doyle, Stephen
Druiz, Fae
Drummond, Stacy
Dubiel, Ann
Dubois, Ken
Dudley, Francis
Duffy, Donald

Eckman Silverstein, Heidi
Eckstein, Bernard
Edgar, Peter
Egner, Amy
Einarsson, Einar Gunner
Eisenman, Nina
Eisenman, Stanley
Eisner, Robert
Elder, Karen
Ellis, Judith
Endewelt, Jack
Epstein, David
Epstein, Lee
Ericson, Shirley
Ermoyan, Suren
Erschfeld, Elke
Evans, Janet
Fable, Kathleen
Fajardo, Camilo
Fales, Gordon
Fedele, Gene
Federico, Gene
Fencenko-Lyon, Karen
Fenga, Michael
Ferrell, John
Ferrell, Megan
Finzi, Sylvia
Fiore, Louise
Fiorenza, Blanche
Fischer, Carl
Fisher, Ann
Fitzpatrick, Bernadette
Fitzpatrick, Wayne
Flock, Donald
Flynn, Tracy
Fowler, Nichole
Fraioli, John
Frankfurt, Stephen
Fredy, Sherry
Freeland, Bill
Friedland, Kenneth
Friedland, Ruby Miye
Frith, Michael
Fritz, Stephen
Fu, Heidy
Fujita, Neil
Fury, Leonard
Gage, Robert
Gallentine, Todd
Gallo, Danielle
Galore Kaminsky, Missy
Ganton, Jr., Brian
Garlanda, Gino
Gavasci, Alberto Paolo
Geismar, Tom
Geissbuhler, Steff
Gelman, Alexander
George, Jeffrey
Geranmayeh, Vida
Germakian, Michael
Gibson, Kurt
Ginsberg, Frank
Giovanitti, Sara
Giraldi, Bob
Glaser, Milton
Gleason, Maureen
Glicksman, Jon
Gliserman, Tom

Gobe, Marc
Goettel, Manfred
Gold, Bill
Goldfarb, Roz
Gonzales, Marie
Goodfellow, Joanne
Gorkin, Baruch
Gottlieb, Michael
Govoni, Jean
Grace, Roy
Green, Michael
Greenberg, Karen
Greiss, Abe
Grey, Judith
Griffin, Jack
Groglio, Glen
Grossman, Michael
Growick, Phillip
Grubshteyn, Raisa
Gruppo, Nelson
Guild, S. Rollins
Haber, Meredith
Hack, Robert
Hagel, Bob
Haiman, Kurt
Hall, Crystal
Halter, Lisa
Halvorsen, Everett
Hama, Sho
Haney, David
Harris, Cabell
Hassel, Jennifer
Heit, Amy
Heller, Steven
Henderson, Jim
Hensley, Randall
Hill, Chris
Hill, Scott
Hillsman, William
Hirsch, Peter
Ho, Charles
Hodges, J. Drew
Hoerchler, Kari
Hoffenberg, Harvey
Hoffmann, Nancy
Hoffner, Marilyn
Holden, Robert
Holguin, Rafael
Holland, Barry
Horn, Steve
Hortens, Michael
Houser, William David
Howard, Paul
Howlett, Brett
Hutter, Brian
Igarashi, Takenobu
Ilic, Mirko
Inada, Manabu
Iocca-Fritzlo, Susanne
Jacobs, Harry
Jaffee, Lee Ann
Jamilkowski, John
Jamison, John
Janerka, Andrzej
Jenkins, Jennifer
Jerina, Patricia
Jervis, Paul
Jeurissen, Dimitri

Jones, John
Jones, Karen
Joyner, Holly Paige
Joyner, Polly-F
Jubert, Joanne
Kalayjian, Vasken
Kalish, Nicki
Kamen, Jonathan
Kaprielian, Walter
Katchmar, Ted
Kay, Leslie
Kay, Woody
Kaye, Michael Ian
Kelly, Brendan
Kenny, Alice
Kent, Nancy
Kenzer, Myron
Keyton, Jeffrey
Kim, Anne Hyun
Kim, Cheolan
Kinch, Greg
Kindred, Amy
Kirshenbaum, Susan
Klein, Alexander
Klein, Judith
Klueger, Peter
Klyde, Hilda Stanger
Kner, Andrew
Knoepfler, Henry
Koepke, Gary
Kokinos, Christopher
Komai, Ray
Kopeck, Jeanne
Korpijaakko, Kati
Krauss, Agnes
Kriegner, Herta
Kurtz, Mara
Kushman, Naomi
Kwik, Sharon
Kyer, Kelly
LaBarge, Robert
LaPetri, Anthony
LaBounty, Sean
Lacava, Vincent
LaFleur, Stephanie
Lai, WaiChing
Lamarque, Abril
Lanotte, Michael
LaRocca, Mark
LaRochelle, Lisa
Lazzarotti, Sal
Lee, David
Lee, Mark
Leeds, Gregory
Leimer, Kerry
Lemkova, Anya
Leon, Maru
Leu, Kristin
LeVesque, Shawn
Levin, Jennifer
Levine, Peter
Levine, Rick
Lewi, Jennifer
Lewis, Abbi
Liberman, Alexander
Liska, Steven
Lloyd, Douglas
Locke Monda, Robin

Loftus, Scott
Lois, George
Lott, George
Loughran, PJ
Lubell, Ruth
Lucci, John
Lucci, Ralph
Lurin, Larry
Lyon, Jr., Robert
Lyons, Michael
Macagba, Jonathan
MacFarlane, Richard
Machauf, Eva
MacInnes, David
Mack, Gary
Macrini, Carol Dietrich
Magdoff, Samuel
Magnani, Lou
Maisel, Jay
Malatesta, James
Mangan, Kate
Marcellino, Jean
Marcus, Helen
Margolis, David
Marino, III, Leo
Mariucci, Jack
Mariutto, Pam
Marmet, Roger
Marquez, Andrea
Martinez, Zoa
Mason, Joel
Matson, Robert
Mayer, Susan
Mayhew, Marce
McCaffery, William
McCantey, Amanda
McDonald, Roy
McIntyre, David
McLaughlin, Maureen
Mednick, Scott
Meher, Nancy
Melendez, Frances
Meltzer, Rachel
Merkley, Parry
Merritt, Suzan
Messier, Nadine
Metzdorf, Lyle
Metzner, Jeffrey
Meyer, Jackie Merri
Mifsud, Carin
Mihaltse, Elizabeth
Milbauer, Eugene
Miller, Christopher
Miller, Joshua
Miller, Lauren
Milligan, John
Minor, Wendell
Miranda, Michael
Mitchell, Susan
Modu, Chi
Mok, Clement
Mongkolkasetarin, Sakol
Montebello, Joseph
Montone, Ken
Moore, Diane
Moore, Tina
Moran, Paul
Moriconi, Lou

Morita, Minoru
Morrison, William
Morton, Amy
Moses, Louie
Moss, Tobias
Muench, Allison
Munoz, Antonio
Munoz, Roberto
Murphy, Colleen Sargent
Musmanno, Anthony
Nash, Jennifer
Nash, Wylie
Nessim, Barbara
Newman, Robert
Newman, Susan
Ng, William
Nicholas, Maria
Nichols, MaryAnn
Nicosia, Davide
Nissen, Joseph
Noether, Evelyn
Norman, Barbara
Norris, Stephen
Norton, Thomas
Noszagh, George
November, David
O'Connor, Sandra
Oberlander, Bill
Ogilvie, Andrew
Okladek, John
Okudaira, Yukako
Oldenburg, Miguel
Olson, Stephen Scott
Omin, Paul
Orange, Lisa
Orht, Darryl
Ortiz, Jose Luis
Osius, Gary
Ovryn, Nina
Owett, Bernard
Paccione, Onofrio
Paganucci, Robert
Pallas, Brad
Pascoe Fischbein, Kathleen
Pastorelli, Suzanne
Paz, Janet
Pedersen, B. Martin
Peeri, Ariel
Perine, Shawn
Perry, Harold
Peslak, Victoria
Petrocelli, Robert
Petrucelli, Daniel
Pettus, Theodore
Pfeifer, Robert
Philiba, Allan
Phipps, Alma
Pinar, Ebru
Pioppo, Ernest
Pliskin, Robert
Pomierski, Diane
Powell, Neil
Quackenbush, Michael
Quattlebaum, Lisa
Queener, Charles
Quesada, Mary
Ragusa, Maria
Rambo, Michael

Ramirez, Adela
Ratchik, Mitchell
Raznick, Ronald
Reed, Samuel
Reinke, Herbert
Reitzfeld, Robert
Remington, Dorothy
Renaud, Joseph Leslie
Rhodes, David
Rich, Tony
Richards, Stan
Richardson, Hank
Rigelhaupt, Gail
Rinko, Kate
Ritter, Arthur
Roberts, Joseph
Roberts, Renee
Robinson, Bennett
Robinson, William
Robison, Charles
Rockwell, Harlow
Rodin, Yana
Rogers, Brian
Romano, Andy
Romano, Dianne
Romero, Javier
Rosenthal, Bobbi
Rosenthal, Slade
Rosner, Charlie
Ross, Andrew
Ross, Richard
Rowe, Alan
Rubenstein, Mort
Rubin, Randee
Rubinsky, Shelley
Ruis, Thomas
Russell, Henry
Russo, Deborah
Ruther, Don
Ruzicka, Thomas
Sabins, Rahul
Sacklow, Stewart
Sagmeister, Stefan
Saido, Tatsuhiro
Saks, Robert
Salkaln, Don
Salpeter, Robert
Salser, James
Salzano, James
Salzburg, Diana
Samerjan, George
Sample, Scott
Sayles, John
Saylor, David
Scali, Sam
Scarfone, Ernest
Schaefer, Peter
Schenk, Roland
Scher, Paula
Scher, Sandra
Scherrer, Randall
Scheuer, Glenn
Schick, Jennifer
Schmalz, Paul
Schmidt, Klaus
Schneider, Doug
Schoeller, Geraldine
Schrager-Laise, Beverly

Schroeder, Jill
Schultz, Eileen Hedy
Seabrook, Alexis
Seabrook, III, William
Seabrook, IV, William
Seagram, Blair
Sedelmaier, J.J.
Segal, Ilene
Segal, Leslie
Seidler, Sheldon
Sellers, John
Sergison, Peter
Shachnow, Audrey
Shadoan, Jesse
Shaw, Dwayne
Shova, Martin
Silver, Ilene
Silverstein, Louis
Simmons, Rosemary
Simon Johnson, Andrew
Simpson, Milton
Singer, Leslie
Sirowitz, Leonard
Skoll, Steve
Sloan, Cliff
Smith, Carol Lynn
Smith, Robert
Smith, Virginia
Snyder, Douglas
Sobel, Edward
Soffel, Deborah
Solomon, Martin
Solomon, Russell
Sommese, Lanny
Sosnow, Harold
Souder, Kirk
Spears, Harvey
Spruell, Jim
Stamatopoulos, Nancy
Stansfield, Shelly Laroche
Stanton, Mindy Phelps
Steele, Cecilia
Stefanides, Dean
Steigelman, Robert
Steinbrenner, Karl
Steiner, Vera
Stern, Barrie
Sternbach, Ilene
Stessel, Francine
Stevenson, Monica
Stewart, Daniel
Stewart, Gerald
Stith, Steve
Stone, Bernard
Stoohs, Kevin
Storch, Otto
Storrs, Lizabeth
Stout, D.J.
Strongwater, Peter
Strosahl, William
Stroud, Steve
Su, Yung-Nien
Sullivan, Pamela
Sutton, Ward
Tang, Khiem
Tansman, JoAnn
Tashian, Melcon
Tauss, Jack

Teixeira, Daniela
Tekushan, Mark
Tharp, Louis
Thayer, Alden
Thompson, Andrew
Thorton, Jamie
Toland, Toni
Torres, Martin
Trasoff, Victor
Trombley, Michele
Truppe, Doug
Tsiavos, Staz
Tsukerman, Roman
Tully, Joseph
Twomey, John
Udell, Rochelle
Vasquez, James
Vipper, Johan
Vischio, Amy
Vitale, Frank
Vogler, David
Wachtenheim, Dorothy
Wajdowicz, Jurek
Wallace, Joseph
Walsh, Brendan
Warlick, Mary
Waxberg, Larry
Weber, Jessica
Weeeng, Joy
Weinstein, Roy
Weiss, Jeff
Weiss, Marty
Weitenauer, Janine
Weithas, Art
Welsh, Michael
West, Robert Shaw
Wilde, Richard
Williams, Nicholas
Windecker, Dora
Wittenberg, Ross
Wolf, Henry
Wolf, Jay Michael
Wong, Nelson
Woods, Laura
Woodson, Elizabeth
Yates, Peter
Yonkovig, Zen
Young, Frank
Young, Shawn
Yu, Laurene
Zaidi, Nadime
Zheng, Ron
Zhukov, Maxim
Zielinski, Jeffrey
Zielinski, Mikael
Ziff, Lloyd
Zlotnick, Bernie
Zwiebel, Alan

ARGENTINA

Berro Garcia, Gonzalo
Stein, Guillermo
Vidal, Jorge

AUSTRALIA

Dilanchian, Kathryn
Musson, Alexander James

AUSTRIA

Demner, Mariusz Jan
Klein, Helmut
Kulovits, Oskar
Lammerhuber, Lois
Lammerhuber, Silvia
Merlicek, Franz
Moucka, Silvia
Reidinger, Roland

BELGIUM

Nandi, Alok

BRAZIL

Cipullo, Sergio
De Barros, Lenora
Gamboa, Claudia
Govea, Claudio
Martinelli, Fernanda
Petit, Francesc
Stefhan, Elaine Margarete
Tsumori, Elza

CANADA

Carter, Rob
Lacroix, Jean-Pierre
Power, Stephanie

CHILE

Cavia, Manuel Segura

CHINA

Chuen, Tommy Li Wing (Hong Kong)
Freyss, Christina (Hong Kong)
Fu, Lixia
Liao, Zhang
Tin-yau, Martin

FINLAND

Bergqvist, Harald
Manty, Kirsikka
Virta, Marjaana

FRANCE

Douvrey, Oliver
Leconte, Michel

GERMANY

Bagios, Jaques
Bayram, Bulent Eten
Becker, Manfred
Ernsting, Thomas
Falkenburg, Rene Von
Haas, Harald
Hebe, Reiner
Koch, Claus
Kohl, Chris
Leu, Olaf
Meier, Erwin
Mojen, Friederike
Mojen, Ingo
Nebl, Lothar
Pham-Phu, Oanh
Prommer, Helga
Ramm, H. Diddo
Schneider, Frank
Spiekerman, Erik
Van Meel, Johannes

INDIA

Pereira, Brendan

IRELAND

Helme, Donald

ISRAEL

Reisinger, Dan

ITALY

Anelli, Luigi Montaini
Barbella, Pasquale
Diaferia, Pasquale
Fabiani, Titti
Guidone, Silvano
Moretti, Gianfranco
Sala, Maurizio
Stoppini, Luca

JAPAN

Akiyama, Takashi
Aoba, Matuteru
Inoue, Kogo
Iwata, Toshio
Izutani, Kenzo
Kaneko, Hideyuki
Kashimoto, Satoji
Katsui, Mitsuo
Kida, Yasuhiko
Kinoshita, Katsuhiro
Kiyomura, Kunio
Kobayashi, Pete
Kojima, Ryohei
Maeda, Kazuki
Matsui, Keizo
Matsumoto, Arata
Matsumoto, Takao
Matsunaga, Shin
Matsuura, Iwao
Mizutani, Koji
Nakajima, Hideki
Nakazawa, Jun
Nishimura, Yoshimari
Nomura, Sadanori
Ohsugi, Manabu
Oseko, Nobumitsu
Shinmura, Norito
Suzuki, Zempaku
Takeo, Shigeru
Tanaka, Ikko
Tanaka, Soji George
Tomoeda, Yusaku
Watanabe, Yoshiko
Yamamoto, Akihiro
Yamamoto, Yoji

KOREA

Chung, Bernard
Chung, Joon
Kim, Kwang Kyu

MALAYSIA

Lee, Yee Ser Angie
Wong, Peter

MALTA

Ward, Edwin

MEXICO

Beltran, Felix
Flores, Luis Efren Ramirez

THE NETHERLANDS

Brattinga, Pieter
Dovianus, Joep

PHILIPPINES

Abrera, Emily
Pe, Roger

POLAND

Piechura, Tadeusz

PORTUGAL

Aires, Eduardo
Aurelio, Mario

ROMANIA

Musteata, Silviu

SINGAPORE

Eng, Chiet-Hsuen

SPAIN

Bermejo Ros, Ricardo

SWEDEN

Palmquist, Kari

SWITZERLAND

Bundi, Stephan
Dallenbach, Bilal
Gaberthuel, Martin
Jacobs, Marie-Christi
Jaggi, Moritz
Mauner, Claudia
Netthoevel, Andreas
Oebel, Manfred
Schuetz, Dominique Anne
Syz, Hans
Welti, Philipp

UNITED KINGDOM

Birdsall RDI, Derek
Blamire, Richard
Ray, Shubhankar
Stothard, Celia

in

dex

Ad space
available here.

The Art Directors Club Annual Awards Exhibit. Coming soon to a gallery near you.

AGFA is proud to bring you some of the year's best advertising, design and new media creative at The 78th Art Directors Annual Traveling Exhibition. For more information, times or locations near you, visit www.adcny.org. The Art Directors Club Annual Awards Exhibit. It's where you'll see the work the way the creatives intended it to be. Framed and admired.

The complete picture.

sappi IS YOUR BEST IDEAS

The strongest pieces in your book. The magazines you most admire. The annual report you designed. (And the ones you wish you had.) The papers that make you proud to work in print. From a company that gives you as much support as we do paper. We know how to lift a mental block, find a source of inspiration, provide an exchange of information and technical solutions. Contact the Idea Exchange to see what others have done, and let them see what you have done. Call 1-800-882-IDEA or visit our Web site at www.warren-idea-exchange.com.

sappi

The word for fine paper

Sappi Fine Paper North America S.D. Warren Services Company
225 Franklin Street Boston, MA 02110 Telephone 1.800.882.IDEA
www.warren-idea-exchange.com ©1999 S.D. Warren Services Company

beyond

seein

www.gkdesign.com

Glazer and Kalaylian, Inc. Communications Design Group 301 East 45th Street, New York, NY 10017 Telephone: 212.687.3099 Facsimile: 212.983.3473

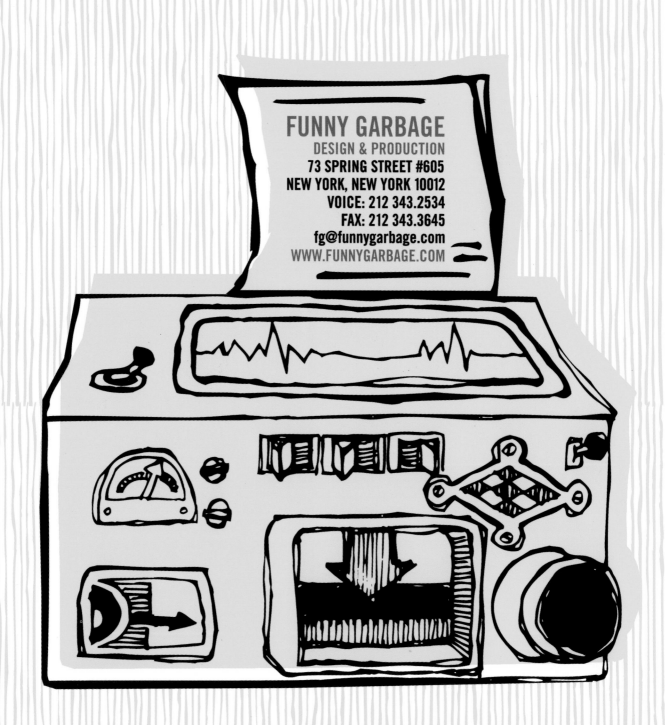

FUNNY GARBAGE
DESIGN & PRODUCTION
73 SPRING STREET #605
NEW YORK, NEW YORK 10012
VOICE: 212 343.2534
FAX: 212 343.3645
fg@funnygarbage.com
WWW.FUNNYGARBAGE.COM

IF IT'S NOT UPDATED

IT'S OUTDATED

New images every week. Online research. Free comps.
Virtual lightbox tools. Full e-commerce. Updated, not outdated.

TONY STONE IMAGES | www.tonystone.com

Darren Robb. #BC8872-001

"Trading cards for the tragically hip."

CRAIN'S

WWW.GOCARD.COM
IN THE U.S. 212.925.2420

Corbis Images

celebrity fine art contemporary historical

TRADITIONAL LICENSING | ROYALTY-FREE

After nine weeks of intensive research, your agency's
focus groups conclude that the ad
should feature a healthy, bouncing, baby boy of indeterminate ethnicity.

Deliver.

See, it's not so hard to make everybody happy. Corbis Images offers an unmatched spectrum of high-resolution stock photography. We have everything from celebrity and historical shots to fine art and contemporary work. Over 25 million images in all. And we have nice, friendly people who will help you find whatever you want, fast. Whether you're in the market for traditional licensing or royalty-free. Best of all, you won't have to go through a lot of layers to get what you want. Imagine that. Why not visit our Web site to search our collection of 1.4 million images. Or give us a call at 1-800-260-0444.

www.corbisimages.com

Corbis

WILL YOU HELP ME?

Like thousands of other art director comps, Fluffy dreamed of being a beautiful camera ready artwork. But, alas, she fell into the wrong hands.

Use Black Book talent and make other rough sketches' dreams come true. We have over 800 top photographers and illustrators waiting to hear from you.

THE BLACK BOOK
GET IT RIGHT. www.blackbook.com

beyond

www.gkdesign.com

Glazer and Kalayjian, Inc. Communications Design Group 301 East 45th Street, New York, NY 10017 Telephone: 212.687.3099 Facsimile: 212.983.3473

FINE ART OFFSET PRINTER
150 VARICK STREET, 3RD FLOOR, TELEPHONE [212] 337-3400
www.mgprints.com

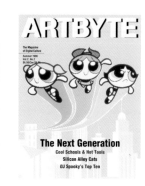

>>Whirling through these pages…sheets of orange, flipping cubes

Revolving past icons of past and future fame, rhythmed by vivid solid planes that divide words…

You'll remember them.

for more exhilarating design
dive into Vertigo

Moving pop images halted, overlapping frames of frozen digital reality

Open your eyes

Winners are color engraved

Look at this book

Running down through columns, black lines along the white parchment…

vertigo design, inc
900 broadway new york, ny 10003 212-529-4550